Honey, Honey, Miss Thang

LEON E. PETTIWAY

Honey, Honey, Miss Thang

Being Black, Gay, and on the Streets

TEMPLE UNIVERSITY PRESS
PHILADELPHIA

Temple University Press, Philadelphia 19122
Copyright © 1996 by Temple University

Published 1996

Printed in the United States of America

♾ The paper used in this publication meets the requirements of the American National Standard for Information Sciences—Permanence of Paper for Printed Library Materials, ANSI Z39.48–1984

Text design by Judith Martin Waterman

LIBRARY OF CONGRESS CATALOGING-IN-PUBLICATION DATA
Pettiway, Leon E., 1946–
    Honey, Honey, Miss Thang : being black, gay and on the streets /
Leon E. Pettiway.
        p.   cm.
        ISBN 1-56639-497-X (CLOTH). — ISBN 1-56639-498-8 (PBK.)
        1. Transvestites—United States—
Interviews.   2. Transvestism—United States.   3. Male
prostitutes—United States—Interviews.   4. Male prostitution—
United States.   5. Afro-American gays—Interviews.   6. Narcotic
addicts—United States—Interviews.   I. Title.
HQ77.P44   1996
305.3—dc20   69-20077
                                                        CIP

In Memory of My Mother
Blonnie J. Pettiway
December 17, 1910 – July 20, 1994

Contents

Acknowledgments

The accounts presented here originated in a research project funded by the National Institute on Drug Abuse (NIDA) of the Department of Human Services under Grant Number ROI DA 05672 while I was a faculty member in the Department of Sociology and Criminal Justice at the University of Delaware. I would like to extend my appreciation to Mario De La Rosa, my project officer at NIDA, for his support and assistance. As a first-time grantee, I found his help to be critically important, and I thank him for his technical assistance, moral support, and professionalism.

At the University of Delaware I would like to offer my appreciation to James A. Inciardi. Jim was the first person to suggest that I submit a grant proposal to NIDA. Mary Richards, Dean of the College of Arts and Sciences, and Frank Scarpitti, Chair of the Department of Sociology and Criminal Justice, provided me with the resources necessary to complete the research project. Margaret Andersen, Ruth Horowitz, Cynthia Robbins, Steve Martin, and Ann Pottieger provided intellectual stimulation. I thank them for being true scholars and colleagues.

When I left Delaware in the fall of 1994 and joined the faculty of the Department of Criminal Justice at Indiana University in Bloomington, I found another group of warm and compassionate scholars. Dean Morton Lowengrub of the College of Arts and Sciences provided research incentive funds that enabled me to transcribe the remaining taped interviews. I would also like to thank Robert Orsi, Professor of Religious Studies, whose enthusiasm for this book has been unceasing. Since my arrival in Bloomington, he has attempted to help me make the transition to the Midwest and to a smaller community and has become a good friend and colleague. I would also like to thank William Oliver, Kip Schlegel, Hal Pepinsky, Jill Bystydzienski, and Stephanie Kane for their suggestions and encouragement. Most of all I would like to thank Coramae Richey Mann, who hounded, cajoled, and encouraged me to apply for a position at Indiana. She is a scholar of the first order, and I am proud to call her a colleague and even prouder to call her friend. She is the mother I miss.

My field staff and I spent eighteen months in 1990–1991 collecting data from 431 individuals who were both drug- and non-drug-using criminals. Life history interviews were conducted with forty-eight individuals, some of whom were a part of the larger sample of 431 people. Of these forty-eight people, sixteen were gay men and women.

My deepest thanks go to my staff members. The field staff consisted of Althea Heggs, Karen D'Arcy, Kevin McCann, Thurston Collier, and Bernard Bryant. While they were not responsible for conducting any of the interviews contained in this book, they conducted thousands of quantitative interviews and were responsible for suggesting and recruiting some of the individuals who are presented here. At the Project Office at the University of Delaware, I would like to thank Tracey Dixon, Kimberly Bell, Linda Granger, Teresa Robeson, Linda Keen, and Eloise Barczak for transcribing many of these life history interviews, interviews that ranged from five to ten hours in length.

I extend heartfelt thanks to the staff of Temple University Press. In particular, I would like to thank David Bartlett, Director of the Press, for his enthusiasm for this project and Doris Braendel, my editor, for her professionalism and good cheer. Many thanks to Janet Francendese for all of our initial discussions about what makes a good book and what I should do with these materials.

During the time I conducted this research, my priest, Father Tim Lyons, was my spiritual counselor and assisted me in ways I could never express. We have become friends, and even now out here in the Midwest he is my touchstone and reminds me of what my life is meant to be. Over the years he and other members of the St. Vincent's Catholic community have given my life new meaning. I thank Father Greg, Brother Al, Sister Ruth, Bernadette, Lynn Horoschak, Valerie Lee Jeter, Laura, Brian Fagan and Fred Brown, Sharon Browning and Jim Lafferty, and Mary Ann Buckez for being part of my religious community and my brothers and sisters in faith. And to all of my friends back east—John and Elaine Devanny, Mary Ann and George Fong, Larry Friedman, Phil and Ellen Harris, Jim and Ann Finn, Irene Boyle, William Bradley, Robert McGinley, Alex Morisey, and others who supported me during this project—I miss you terribly.

Bloomington, Indiana

Introduction

Voices from the Shadows

Crumbling brick and mortar, stifling automobile exhaust, gunshot victims lying in the street, the smelly, unwashed flesh of homeless, faceless crowds—these are prominent images of the inner city. For the most part, the social science discourse has emphasized these "darker" and more sinister subcultures of urban life. Researchers have entered the nether world of subcultures to understand the shadows of the city.

The shadows protect long-legged women with dresses to the middle of their thighs, hair beyond their shoulders, and high-heels that seem to be spikes. These women look the part of "hookers." Other women stand and pose with only subtle suggestions of their trade. There are men there too. They stand with their hands in suggestive places while they wait for the next car to circle the block and the next piece of money to exchange hands.

Street corners are shadowy places where addicts drive to or line up to cop a fix. Street corners are the gathering places for men who are members of families in which no one has been legally employed in generations. Out there on the sidewalks of these streets, winos, the homeless, and the "crazies" lie on steam grates while the rest of humanity stride by.

The social science interest in these images of urban life and the impact of urbanism on the human condition descend in large part from Georg Simmel (1950) and Louis Wirth (1938), who commented on the qualitative value of human experiences and who believed that urbanism transformed individual consciousness. For Simmel the city freed the individual from the restrictions of traditional society; modernity meant the possibility of immense individual freedom and the formation of subcultures.

It is from these subcultural shadows that this book derives its central characters—five African-American, drug-using, street-walking hustlers who are gay men but dress and view themselves as women. Many Americans would see these people and their lifestyles as pathological or dysfunctional. Most Americans would never embrace them as neighbors, as co-workers, or as friends. However, this book is intended to celebrate the lives of these individuals—Shontae, China, Keisha, Detra, and Monique. These are C. Wright Mills's (1959) trapped people; their stories are the stories of everyday people attempting to make sense of what is changing from moment to moment in their lives. Their accounts enable us to enter imaginatively into their struggles to survive and to maintain lives of dignity and value in the face of their drug use and their crime participation. All five vary in terms of their background, the manner in which they entered a transgendered world, and their initiation into the drug subculture. They vary in their attitudes toward their experiences and in their plans for the future. But their stories reveal a common struggle to remain a part of the human family, and their lives are a profound expression of the human experience and spirit.

In part these stories describe tremendous hardships. But they also show that one can find dignity, compassion, strength, resilience, and love in unexpected places and in unexpected lives. They demonstrate that lived experiences are complex and move between and include times of triumph and defeat, humiliation and pride. They reveal what we always knew—that life is filled with ambivalence and ambiguity. It is never neatly situated along the axes of hope or despair, pleasure or pain, dignity or defeat, good or bad. Therefore, this volume maintains not only that deviant people live lives of value but that denying this premise does violence to our ability to conceptualize the lives of those we consider deviant.

This book is meant to be shared and is intended to evoke questions, discussion, and a re-evaluation of our positions on a variety of social issues. It is a book derived from my interests in the social science enterprise but resonates with my concern for humanity, for the poor and the rejected among us. It asks if there are other ways to give expression to the lives of those labeled as deviant. Are there other truths about their character, dreams, and aspirations that speak beyond the visible signs of their poverty and perceived wretchedness and antisocial behavior? What do the hustler, the "queer," the addict, and those who have fallen outside the mainstream of American life reveal and teach us?

The presentation of these voices is unusual in criminology. Criminology, like all disciplines, has its own discourse and apparatuses of knowledge. Criminologists have, for the most part, presented deviant frames of action as monolithic, singular in character and purpose. The criminological discourse tends to emphasize negativity, hopelessness, or some other singular drive or failure as characterizing the lives of deviant people. Disciplinary power is exercised through "the production of effective instruments for the formation and accumulation of knowledge—methods of observation, techniques of registration, procedures for investigation and research, apparatuses of control" (Foucault, 1986: 102). As such, these apparatuses of knowledge are ideological constructs and seats of power. But Foucault reminds us that the researcher's concern should not be with the contents, methods, or concepts of a science, but rather with the "centralising powers which are linked to the institution and functioning of an organised scientific discourse" (Foucault, 1986: 84). Criminology in general, and deviance studies in particular, stand in need of this warning. We have managed to bury some historical content through our need for functionalist coherence or formal systemization. The result has been the creation of subjugated knowledges. These subjugated knowledges are "a whole set of knowledges that have been disqualified as inadequate to their task or insufficiently elaborated: naive knowledges, located low down on the hierarchy, beneath the required level of cognition or scientificity" (Foucault, 1986: 82).

Some voices have been disqualified from the hierarchy of knowledges and sciences; some have been distorted by being interpreted and analyzed according to the historical dictates of the discipline. Some of those whose insights have been bypassed—who possess subjugated knowledges—have been excluded or have had their voices distorted because they fail to fit into "a unitary body of theory which would filter, hierarchise and order them in the name of some true knowledge and some arbitrary idea of what constitutes a science and its objects" (Foucault, 1986: 83). But who confers upon these voices the power to speak, or prohibits them from speaking, and who determines the manner of that speech and the form in which that speech will appear? Can the disqualified and illegitimate knowledges of Shontae, China, Keisha, Detra, and Monique withstand the functionalist or systematizing theory that has tended to mask their historical experiences and the representation of those experiences? What we—as sociologists and criminologists—know about them and their sisters exists primarily in the texts that are written about them (e.g., Clifford and Marcus, 1986; Marcus and Fischer, 1986). Their voices are filtered by their interpreters.

Within sociology, Norman Denzin (1990) has called for a new set of voices, proclaiming that even Mills was trapped in the rhetoric of the theories he valued—by such terms as "alienation," "anomie," "class," "status," "power," and "occupation."[1] According to Denzin, Mills "kept the wrong company" and created the wrong version of the sociological imagination. He failed to listen to the little people. He chose to view ordinary people as the "other" and felt that he could objectively explain and describe their lives through the use of classical theory.

Other sociologists have followed his lead, filling their life histories about sex workers and drug addicts with concepts such as anomie and alienation in post-industrial societies. In the pursuit of theory, Denzin suggests, sociologists have forsaken minimalism and have abandoned the social in the name of sociology. Advocating a return to story-telling, he asserts that the social comes alive in the telling of stories and that stories result from cultural and group production. Sociological theories about ordinary people and their troubles are also cultural and textual creations. For Denzin, only two categories of storytellers exist in any culture: "the ordinary people who talk and tell stories to one another; and the self- and society-appointed experts . . . who write and tell stories about others' stories" (Denzin, 1990: 7). Therefore, sociologists who possess a sociological imagination, empowered by a minimalist theoretical preconception, can grasp the historical and biographical intersections of society.

In this book I wanted Shontae, China, Keisha, Detra, and Monique to speak without explicit interpretation by a self- or society-appointed expert. They conceptualize their own personhood. In the ethnographic research situation, insiders and outsiders meet, interact, and reciprocate. Because I am present as interviewer, editor, and moderator, I have arranged the textual space of this book so that Shontae, China, Keisha, Detra, and Monique can challenge my power by claiming their own voices. In doing so, I invite the reader to enter the dialogue of interpretation and meaning and to look beyond the models of pathology and dysfunction. Thus, I believe a certain rhetorical power is derived from my explicit absence and that that power makes room for the active reader to be drawn into the process of inquiry and discovery. This is a radical departure from Denzin's suggestion of a "minimalist theoretical preconception," and it also breaks with the traditional life-history frame to attempt an experiment in modernist ethnographic techniques (for examples see Marcus and Fischer, 1986).

This book demonstrates that there are aspects of the lives of deviant people that not only attest to their humanness but that may demonstrate positive adaptations and responses to poverty, drug use, and crime—responses that are not invariable signposts of pathology, but rather the necessary and sufficient responses to adverse situations. The imperative to survive in the face of disappointment, violence, disease, discrimination, and poverty can produce strength and creativity. This imperative constructs a social frame that provides meanings based upon the patterns of life that adjust to the ebb and flow of living.

Because their profession trains them as students of social "problems," criminologists have developed a plethora of theoretical constructs that center on either dysfunction or the dysfunctional adaptations of those who find themselves outside the dominant, "mainstream," culture. Here, the individual is dissected and inevitably compared to those individuals who do not possess the social problem being studied. In this mode, the positivist tradition assaults social problems by using the scientific method and an array of statistical techniques to test hypotheses derived from theoretical constructs that are largely based on aggregate data. In many cases, these studies are carried on by people who have never conducted field research and who have never talked with the very people they are studying.

Virtually every "scientific" article submitted to any refereed journal *must* be grounded in one of the prevailing theoretical criminological traditions. It must proclaim its niche in order to achieve its relevance. At the university level, members of some academic departments across the country penalize, disrespect, and minimize the work of those colleagues who do not subscribe to a model of science that theorizes, conceptualizes, operationalizes, and observes. In the name of "science," criminologists have utilized the scientific method and its precision to yield the most parsimonious explanatory factors. The supposed objectivity of the method renders the individuals being studied and those conducting the research equally invisible. What emerges are supposedly value-free observations obtained by observers who have distanced themselves from the individuals of inquiry. While our research has become more rigorous and "scientific," we are in danger of losing the texture, the fabric, and the complex nuances of the human experience if we rely *solely* on this form of production.

That other kinds of inquiry can produce valuable results is indisputable. Qualitative research designs have provided us with some startling accounts of the human experience. David Snow and Leon Anderson's *Down on Their Luck* (1993) and Elliot Liebow's *Tell Them Who I Am* (1993) provides a vivid discussion of homelessness. Elijah Anderson's *Streetwise* (1990) and Elliot Liebow's *Tally's Corner* (1967) speak to the richness and complexity of urban life. These works supplement our theoretical constructs and methods with strategies and techniques that provide texture, give us knowledge of the human experience, and enrich our understanding of the social world. If we remember to focus on the *quality* of people's lives, we will be less likely to misrepresent the social reality of deviant persons by imposing contrived notions of reality on their human experiences. Otherwise, our thick theory, in the absence of thick description, may have very little to do with the social world of deviant people, but merely provide the fodder for our own existence in the academic community.

When viewed from the standpoint of dysfunction, deviant people are said to experience personal disorganization. For example, we say that where there is a breakdown in the normative controls in a community, there is also an increased likelihood that there will be a breakdown in the moral constraints of the individuals who live in those communities. Social disorganization disrupts socialization, the process by which traditional beliefs, values, and norms are passed from one generation to another. Failed socialization weakens internal normative constraints. In this world view, inner containment consists of such factors as self-control, good self-concept, ego strength, well-developed superego, high frustration tolerance, high sense of responsibility, and goal orientation. According to the control theory perspective of Walter Reckless (Reckless, Dinitz, and Murray, 1956; Reckless, Dinitz, and Kay, 1957; Reckless and Dinitz, 1967; Reckless, 1973), these inner constraints isolate an individual from the gravitational forces of a deviant lifestyle. Similarly, Travis Hirschi (1969) sees socialization into society's conventional belief system as central to bonding and social control, the internal constraints that protect the individual from deviance. Similarly, attachment to those individuals who conform to society's normative standards, commitment to conventional ways of behaving by virtue of social rewards, and involvement in the pursuit of conventionality are seen as external factors preventing deviance.

Those researchers who present the individual as having failed on some important social-psychological dimension construct one manner of "truth" and they represent one mode of disciplinary construction. However, we must go beyond what appears on the disciplinary envelope of tradition in order to discover other facets of the hearts and minds of those who have been labeled "deviants." Criminology's theoretical frameworks must be viewed as partial elements in the struggle for power and knowledge. Criminology requires a more reflexive self-critique and experimental sociological analysis. Where are the stories of courage, faith, devotion, fear, and creativity that must come with survival during periods of adversity and strife? This book hopes to spark the recognition that the sum total of the deviant person's life and world view is more than his or her failure to socialize according to some prescribed set of norms. Insofar as it is successful, it challenges the discipline's myopic view of who the deviant person really is and asks us to evaluate the principle of dysfunction and its meaning as a causal nexus in light of courage, faith, devotion, fear, survival, and creativity.

While we may be horrified by acts that offend both our individual and collective senses of humanness, we must not fail to recognize the intrinsic value of each person whether serial killer, child molester, or sex worker. While they maybe separated from their own humanity by acts of "deviance," the core of their humanity, the self, linkers and waits for conversion while the ego lives in history. The self, the core of being and humanness united with a spiritual universe that is beyond comprehension, exists whether the person has access to it or not.

There is a very different criminological perspective that is not concerned with the causes of crime. From this perspective, the individual actor is inconsequential. The classical perspective,[2] while a departure from the demonic or supernaturalistic explanations that preceded it, emphasizes the calculative rationality of human reason. It sees human actions as a free and rationally calculated choice between pleasure and pain. Consequently, it stresses individual responsibility and hedonistic pleasures. In the classical tradition, humans are rational hedonists who can only be controlled by the administration of punishment that is more painful than what they can gain from the pleasures of nonconformity. Retribution derived from rationally sanctioned punishment becomes an important means of social control and the means to deter future acts of deviance (Pfolh, 1994).

To balance these constructions of reality, however, there is a tremendous need for accounts that focus squarely on the individual, accounts that chronicle not only the individual's life but also the circumstances and contextual nature of living lives filled with adversity. All too often the construction of the deviant person as a hedonist who has failed in some fundamental fashion perpetuates and enlivens one of the most punitive criminal justice systems in the world. As faith in rehabilitative treatment dies, the tenets of classical thought and dysfunction find their way into the hearts and minds of modern criminologists. Consequently, punishment, its severity and swiftness, becomes the top priority of the criminal justice system, and our research questions become rooted in strategies that warn offenders that there are no exceptions to punishment. We are left with such arbitrary and unworkable tenets as the elimination of disparities in sentencing, the imposition of fixed and mandatory sentences, the elimination of indeterminate minimum and maximum sentences, the elimination of the insanity defense, the abolition of parole, the adjudication of juvenile offenders in adult courts, and the eradication of early release programs. James Q. Wilson and his "new realism" provide fodder for today's political conservatives and their thundering appeal for the punishment to fit the crime and to hell with the individual. The success of such a viewpoint is possible because deviant people have no face or voice in the formulation of the "new realism."

At one level the question is why those who are the most rejected in our society have been portrayed as outsiders. Why does there appear to be a tendency to separate the rejected members of American society from those in the mainstream? I believe the answer is that we have been unable to look beyond human weakness or "sin" to discover the beauty and the presence of those qualities that can transform and "redeem" the human spirit. All human beings possess these qualities. Saints have been able to achieve this level of insight and oneness; the rest of us come close when we are intimate, when we are friends, when we experience and share the traumas, the sadness, and the joys of life with each other. When there is a failure to build or recognize the connections between us and to serve as stewards to one another, the disconnectedness of insiders and outsiders emerges.

There are countless examples of this dichotomy and its effect. For example, the lives of Shontae, China, Detra, Keisha, and Monique have not been very different from my own. I am an Afro-American male born at a time when there were basic questions as to the humanity of black folks. I grew up in Durham, North Carolina, and I recall at the age of five my mother dragging me to the back of the bus because even little black boys and girls could not sit in the front. I remember separate rest rooms and water fountains. I heard of the those awful deeds committed further South, in Alabama, Georgia, Mississippi, and Louisiana where sojourners of justice fell victims at the hands of klansmen and ignorance. I was bused from one side of the county to the other side because that was where black students had to attend high school. I remember how some black men dropped their heads as a sign of deference to whites regardless of who they were. It was "yes, sir" and "no, sir" for whites and "Helen," "Mary," "John," or just simply "nigger" for us. To the wider culture, we were irresponsible and inept children. But within our own communities, to each other, we were infinitely complex, interesting and full of potential and possiblity.

Another example of the dichotomy is the treatment of AIDS victims. When AIDS surfaced, two types of victims emerged—the innocent and the guilty. The guilty were of two kinds: intravenous drug users and male homosexuals, the primary victims. The sexual promiscuity associated with male homosexuals and their participation in anal and oral sex were seen as an affront to God's divine covenant. Intravenous drug users acquired the infection by their own irresponsibility—by sharing needles they used to push "dope" into the bodies. These two groups, therefore, acquired the infection because of their own lack of responsibility or self-control, and homosexuals and intravenous drug users became, for many, the guilty and faceless victims punished by God for their sins. For others, however, the victims were not faceless. When you see your brother, your friend, your partner suffering, you only wish for their agony to end. When death comes, your grief reveals your connection to them and is a profound affirmation of their humanness. It was in this spirit that the first panels were quietly fashioned of what was to become the AIDS Memorial Quilt.

A third example is our attitude toward "the poor." The poor have always been with us. They can be found in the Appalachian foothills, in the bayous of Louisiana, under a weeping fig tree in Santa Barbara, in Cabrini-Green in Chicago, and on cardboard beds on the sidewalks of New York City. They are welfare recipients and they are single females with "too many" children. They are mentally challenged and homeless. They are young and old, and they are as colorful as the rainbow. From a conservative position, they are at their very core lazy and individually irresponsible. From the more liberal perspective, their plight is one born out of powerlessness or out of exploitation by those who are governed by self-interest.

In all of these cases, the humanity of African Americans, of those suffering from AIDS, and of those surviving lives of poverty is recognized and celebrated when we are most connected with them and when we are able to bear witness to their lives. In doing so, we recognize how much we do share together. When researchers reach this insight, our research subjects cease to be "outsiders," but are presented more nearly as they experience themselves rather than as representations of our perceptions, interpretations, and eventual construction of who they are. They are human beings who lead complex and difficult lives.

Social policies are all too often a reflection of the perceptions that policy makers have of their target groups. At the very least, policy makers derive their solutions for social change from a set of shared cultural values. Those individuals whom they view as "belonging"—as sharing their cultural world, as having a stake in the system—are seen as having understandable, if unfortunate, "problems" and are given the benefit of the doubt in policy decisions. "Outsiders" lack their understanding and are treated more negatively.

The differential sentencing practices associated with cocaine powder users and crack users are a case in point: cocaine powder users generally receive lighter sentences than their crack-using counterparts. Certainly inner-city crack users are not understood by policy makers, who are removed, in terms of their experiences, from the plight of the poor in the inner city. Crack use evokes images of minority and lower-class status. Crack users have been vilified in the media, which have all too often highlighted the systemic violence that surrounds the use of crack. Cocaine powder use, on the other hand, evokes images of affluence and recreation, as being the drug of choice among middle-class white Americans—that is, the social world of most policy makers. Therefore, cocaine powder use is more "understandable" and its users enjoy lighter prison sentences.

The United States is one of the richest industrial nations in the world, but of all the industrial nations it also has the highest crime rates and the largest prison population (Mann, 1993; Rothenberg, 1992). It is not surprising that African Americans and Hispanic Americans—as "outsiders"—constitute the bulk of the prison population. Social policy makers who are intimately familiar with their target populations are more compassionate and devise more humane policies. It is through "intimate familiarity" that our images and perceptions of others are challenged. When their knowledges are no longer subjugated, their opacity dissolves.

This book allows the voices of some of these "outsiders" to speak. It results from the face-to-face interactions that occurred in a field setting, amid a research process that promoted involvement and enmeshment rather than distance. In the final analysis, the book is a testament to the participants' trust and generosity, which allowed me to enter their world as a "friend." It was in this "friendship" that a space was created for them to share not only the darker sides of their lives but also the humor, the daily pleasures, indeed the ethos of their existence. Understanding the world of Shontae, China, Keisha, Detra, and Monique exposes their normalness. The more we manage to uncover what they do and how they feel, the more logical and accessible they become. By positioning them within their own frame we dissolve their opacity (Geertz, 1973).

It must be understood that there is no clear window to the inner life of any human being. My construction of my own reality is just as much a social construction as my construction of the world of the deviant person. Gender, race and ethnicity, social class, and language cloud our view. No observation is objective but is situated in the social world of the observer and the observed. Shontae, China, Detra, Keisha, and Monique, like any other individuals, are seldom able to give full explanations for their actions. What they provide are accounts of what has happened in their lives and why they think they did what they did.

The methods employed in field research are necessarily imperfect. One question is the generalizability of this research. There are many transgendered individuals who do not use drugs and who do not subscribe to the fast life. All I claim is that these five individuals represent the gay, drug-using, transgendered respondents who participated in the research project. When one considers issues such as relationships, fear, creativity, self-awareness, reflectiveness, hope, dignity, courage, and resilience, these participants are no different from either the other gay (n=11) respondents or the straight (n=32) respondents who were interviewed but who are not presented in this book. They all expressed similar emotions and experiences. Can these observations be replicated by another independent researcher given the rather personal nature of the observations? If these observations depend solely on me and my interactions with the respondents, then the accounts are more valuable as a source of particular insight than as general truth. We can only know their generalizability if we continue to explore and to affirm the more positive attributes associated with those who have been labeled "deviant."

This is deliberately a non-interpretive work. My voice is implicitly present: after all, I framed the questions, focused the interviews, and created the narratives that are included in this book. But I want to refrain from speaking with the authority of a researcher and a university professor about the meaning of their lives.

I recognize that what is presented here is the product of a reflexive process and portrays only part of the participants' existential reality. Moreover, these accounts are the edited versions of the raw transcription of the taped interviews. Care was taken so as not to break the original chains of thought and the original conception of the chronology. In some accounts, substantial amounts of the original material were deleted in order to reduce the overall length of the manuscript and to reduce unnecessary repetition within and between accounts. Some materials were also rearranged for readability since some themes were constantly revisited at different points in the interview process. However, in removing and rearranging materials, care was taken not to diminish the essential narrative expression of the individual. In all instances editing was done to retain the uniqueness of the speaker and the essential flavor and texture of the interview.

To the reader, the first challenge of this book is to learn to approach the language of the stories. The language takes some time to get used to. It can be extremely succinct, terse, and allusive. Sometimes a single sentence may contain passing references to several stories within the stories. I recommend that you read slowly. Your learning curve may improve significantly if you begin by reading passages aloud so as to become familiar with each narrator's cadence and style. The language of each woman creates a world of meaning that is interpersonal and referential; they constantly refer to other people and situations, sometimes very concisely and without names or elaboration. But being attentive to the language will pay off in the insights you will gain into the way of life revealed by the language.

Some readers will try to find some kind of chronology in these stories. But these women do not present their lives in a linear fashion. The distinctive orientation is one where time is measured in terms of relationships, and what emerges is a chronology of intimacy. Detra, for example, remembers when her father returned home from prison:

My father came back home to live with us during my preschool age. Like I say, we lived in the projects then. And it was a knock on—I'll never forget this one—it was a knock on the door, and I answered the door. And he said, "Is your mother home?" So I said, "Yeah." But I knew who he was, you know. I don't know how, but I knew who he was. And I jumped up in him arms.

Similarly, she remembers her relationship with Curt this way:

I met a fellow and moved over Somerset County with him, right over in Bedford. This took me away the family-hood, you know, the family and stuff. . . . I was around twenty, twenty-one when I met Curt.

This chronology of intimacy marks time in terms of the profound connections these women have with other people. Time exists in relation to experiences. It is not marked by fleeting hours of the days and months but rather by the "feel" of being black, gay, and a transvestite as well as the experiences of courage, resilience, resistance. These are stories woven around the fabric of these individuals' relationships to their family, to their peers, to their drugs, and to their work. One understands them, not through the order of the events in their lives, but through their interactions with the various elements of their lives.

Remember that these are men who seek to live their lives as women. These are men whose sexuality found expression when they were still children and at their most vulnerable. These are black men whose culture strongly opposes homosexuality, but they have had the courage to give expression to their sexuality by becoming "drag queens." These are men, brought up in families, who sought the fast life and who make their living in the secrecy of dark alleys, in cars, and in hotel rooms not too far from their stroll. These are men who experimented with drugs because that behavior conformed to the subcultural norms of the fast life. Now they are addicted to drugs and commit sex work.

These are men who provide us a glimpse into their social construction of gender and identity. They are stigmatized but they have endured the affronts made to their character by both significant and insignificant members of their social world. More importantly they manage not one stigmatized identity, but multiple stigmatized identities and countless acts of prior abuse and neglect. Consequently, they bear multiple pressures, yet they survive and they reveal a sense of self-realization that many non-stigmatized members of our society wish they could emulate. They speak openly about the things they have done, and they demonstrate that they have to some extent learned to live with themselves and to forgive themselves. Most of all, their lives unfold in terms of their relationships and interactions with others.

With these realizations in mind, we can see more clearly that crime reform policies, urban policies, and drug prevention and reduction policies must recognize the positive values of those labeled as "deviants" rather than persisting in the almost exclusive reliance on those values that emphasize negativity and hopelessness. It is through a greater appreciation of these positive attributes that policy makers may affect change.

As I have already suggested, these stories reflect the dynamics of the interview situation as well as the existential realities of Shontae, China, Keisha, Detra, and Monique. The accounts come from a research project conducted from a field site in a large urban center. Initially, collecting data on homosexuals was never my intent, but because many of the individuals who came to the field site were gay and because I found their descriptions of their lives to be so profound, I felt their stories needed to be told.

Besides filling out questionnaires, many of the participants in the research study took part in weekly interviews that surveyed their crime and drug participation as well as their travel arrangements. For each of the life history interviews participants received twenty dollars. Legal protection for respondents was assured by anonymity and a Grant of Confidentiality from the National Institute on Drug Abuse, which guaranteed that project employees could not be compelled by any court or law enforcement agency to reveal information sources or questionnaire data. In the accounts presented in this book, all information that might readily identify the participants has been deleted. In addition, I have changed personal identifiers such as the individual's code name, the city in which the research was conducted, place names and the names of establishments, the neighborhood and street names where their activities were conducted, as well as the names of other individuals mentioned.

The interview participants sat with me, one at a time, in a small room with a tape recorder, and the interviews were conducted over a two-day period. The length of the interviews varied and depended primarily upon the individual's attentiveness. In conducting these life history interviews, I began with a qualitative guideline; however, it became clear that that method was sometimes restrictive. Some people's lives just did not fit the guideline, and in those cases I crafted questions based upon the unique attributes of the person's experiences. For example, I had interviewed a number of participants before I encountered anyone who defined themselves as gay, and I was surprised to learn that I had no questions that addressed the issues he was facing.

Overall, my role was to coax and direct the conversation as if we were old friends, but always maintaining my position as "Doc," which I was respectfully called. The participants knew nothing of my background other than that I was a university professor. However, as a black gay man, I offer a perspective and a population that are relatively absent from the criminal justice discourse. To some extent the depth and quality of these interviews are tied to who I am. When I listened to the accounts of the participants, I found in their lives a hundred points of intersection with my own. I have stood where they have stood, seen much of what they have seen, felt the degradation and insults they have felt, and struggled just as they have struggled for self determination and wholeness. My biography and history allowed me to conceptualize questions, to anticipate responses, to challenge responses in light of my own experiences and the experiences of other gay men and lesbians I have known, to provide a non-judgemental space where they could feel safe, to show empathy and compassion when their accounts touched the core of my own humanity, and to recognize their humanity and treat them with respect. These situational issues created an interview setting that allowed them to speak so openly.

In these interviews, my goal was to create an environment in which the participants felt that their stories were important, that their stories were worth telling, and that others would benefit by knowing them. I allowed them to carry the discussion, and I revisited themes and situations when I felt there were pieces that had been left unfinished or in need of further clarification. When I felt they were not being honest or forthcoming, I would say so. On almost all occasions I emerged from these interviews emotionally and physically drained, partly because of their length but also because of their power, their sadness, and their hope. There was something magical about these interviews, and I believe my life was immensely enriched by having met the participants and having shared their stories. They seemed genuinely willing to share their stories, because they wanted others to know what living had meant for them. So, they lifted their voices.

I marveled at their candor and honesty. As I have told many of my friends, I am not sure that I would have been so forthcoming if I had been in their place. I am a very private person, but the experience of conducting these interviews and writing this book has been enlightening. These people approach life with courage and with a faith that in the end the most important and powerful position in life is simply being who you are. This is the manner in which they live their lives. At this point in my life, I can do no less. I will never forget this simple but powerful lesson that they reinforced in me.

The participants come from different communities, and while they may not be representative of the city's historic and colorful past, they are perhaps representative of those who have not escaped the ravages of urban decline, crime, drugs, and poverty so often associated with the inner city. They live in a city that prides itself on its diversity of neighborhoods. There are areas like Andover Heights, where lawyers from prestigious law firms can glimpse, through the rhododendron hedges, the homes of doctors, educators, and former politicians. Few residents of "the Heights" follow the cobblestones of Georgetown Avenue to its other end, but if they did, they would find the slums of South Jefferson, full of ramshackle buildings with windows left empty, roofs that sag, and porches that seem to lean a little more with each passing day. Here one finds decent people, many struggling to make a living for their families, but there are few doctors, lawyers, or educators living here. In fact, there are few children living here. The children became adults long ago. It is in South Jefferson, or in neighborhoods like it, that the five individuals who tell their stories here grew up or spent significant portions of their lives.

So from somewhat different places in our lives we sat together and talked about living life, and I listened and asked questions. There were extremely funny moments when we laughed till we cried, but there were also extremely poignant moments when the tears were reminders of trauma and sadness. The women varied in terms of their articulateness and in their story-telling abilities. Keisha, for example, is the least articulate, but she is a great story teller. She tends not to be very reflective or to talk about the nuances of the decisions associated with her life, but she brings to life in vivid detail the experiences that fill it. Shontae is probably the most articulate in her use of language. Keisha, Detra, and Monique best capture the street lives of gay hustlers, while China speaks eloquently about the deception and false security engendered by drugs and drug use. They are at their very best when they become reflective about the choices they have made and when they talk about the challenges of their lives.

They all—but particularly Monique and Shontae—have the ability to use language in creative ways. Monique admits that she lives in an "abandominium"—an abandoned house where she took up residence when she became homeless. Detra speaks of being away from the "family-hood"—that collection of friends and associates who form her gay family, as distinct from her biological family. They refer to another gay man as a "flippy" or as not being "a Bisquick Man"—one who is both active and passive in sexual encounters. You will marvel at expressions like "That one was a pain in my chewy" and "I was an L7, a square," as well as the expressive play they use with their friends: "Oh, Miss Thang. Child, please. Bitch, it ain't all about you." You will marvel at their use of imagery and the power of their voices. Monique, for example, characterizes living on the streets as living in a "world of chances," and she talks about "going out into a flock of wolves when I am only one lonely sheep."

These accounts also reveal the many facets of the "deviant's" life. Certainly, much of each individual's existence is taken up with the struggle to survive. But that struggle itself is extremely complex. Can the deviant person's survival strategies be explained simply in terms of Hirschian[3] sociology when she lives in what Monique describes as a world of chances?

It's called the world of chances. You . . . you . . . you take a chance on living and dying. You take a chance on being hurt and not being hurt. You take a chance on finding a friend and finding an enemy. You see, the world of chances.

In this world of chances these women have survived. They are survivors of abuse and tragedy. Detra tells the story of being raped as a child by a young man in her neighborhood and how this incident led to her despair and attempted suicide. Keisha tells of being raped in her late teens by a potential customer and left in an abandoned house naked and beaten. Monique has been pistol whipped, and has been left on the street to die after a potential client slit her throat and slashed her face. And then there are those stories of other wounds. Detra misses a vein and shoots the heroin and cocaine into her leg instead, producing an abscess and leaving her with a slight limp. Monique carries the HIV virus, and seemed to be getting weaker with each passing day.

The women also talk about the turning points in their life courses and the consequences these experiences had for their personal development. They describe being seduced for the first time. They describe the joy of finding other gay children and learning that they were not unique. They talk about being introduced to the fast life. Some, like China, turn to drugs and sex work out of grief. Others, like Detra, are enticed by new friends and new experiences. Their turning points include the traumatic and the joyful, but they all agree that they entered the fast life because of the seductive nature of the streets. The streets afforded them the opportunity to give expression to their creativity.

These are stories that mark the hard-won confidence and self-acceptance of being gay, of learning, as Detra asserts, God made her gay. Like the rest of us, these women see themselves and their life choices as complex and evolving; they are realistic and matter-of-fact about their lives. They recognize that they have had to do some depraved things in order to endure hard times. But they also feel that they have strong codes of decency and that they know the difference between what is right and wrong.

They talk of honesty and being authentic in the face of all manner of ridicule. That is a subject about which they can talk with assurance. They came to the interviews dressed as women, but to varying degrees they still appeared masculine. Some had thick hands, wide shoulders, and large feet, and no matter how they attempted to disguise their voices, their big adam's apples vibrated to produce sounds that hinted at a masculine voice. After several hours of listening, however, it became apparent that one was not talking to a man at all. They were women. In their hearts and minds they were truly women, and it became natural to refer to them as women.

Keisha speaks for all of them when she describes her earliest longing to rid herself of her male form and be the person who lurked beneath the surface and who she most admired, a woman:

> Well, when I was growing up, only person I looked up to . . . was women. I was going to be a woman, right. I looked in the mirror, in East Jefferson, and I said, "Ooh, I wanna be a woman." And I don't know if it's foolish or what, I just said, "I wanna be woman. I know God didn't make me no woman, but I wanna look like a woman." And bam! I start throwing makeup. Start looking like a woman. Arch my eyes. Hair started growing like a woman. Perm. My nails. Then I started taking female hormones. Taking pills. I started just taking them. Then I started getting more effeminate. Then people start mistaking me as a real woman in the world. See, I went in the world to test it, see. Just like I was walk into a store and they was like, "Excuse me, miss. You can go ahead." A gentleman would say that. Then I knew, right then and there, I'm on the right track, you know. Not acting. See, you gotta be yourself in order to be a woman also. You can't just act out "I'm gonna be a woman" and get and be all flaming. Yeah. You can't be all like this. 'Cause a woman is not like this. She's natural. She's unique. That's her, you know.

To have learned to recognize their sexuality and to celebrate it has demanded of them a great deal of courage, courage simply to live their lives according to their creative energies. Certainly, we should not overlook their acts of inhumanity, the violence and selfishness they have heaped upon others. However, their lives also inform us of their courage and their will to survive. Shontae says it best:

> Courage! You have to have it from the jump street. The courage to come out, you know, to deal with. If you don't have the courage, first thing somebody says to you, you'll run back in and do what they want you to and still be unhappy. You know what I mean? You've got to have it, and you've got to want it, you know, to be yourself when you come out here. You got to start with yourself first. You have to got to like you, first. You have to look at it from the standpoint that there has to be some realization of self-love. You ain't gonna last but so long out there without it. That just like trying to be a ballplayer and you know damn well you can't swing, you can't hit this motherfucking ball coming at you this fucking fast. But you're gonna go out there and fake that you're a ballplayer, and you're gonna have your little feelings hurt when they tell you you're a wimp and get off the field. You know what I mean? You really thought these guys were your friends. You know what I mean?

Their struggle to be authentic is continual. Sometimes they get tired; sometimes they allow the taunts to rest in their hearts; and sometimes they believe in themselves with confidence and courage. They are resilient.

Being gay and owning one's sexual identity comes with great personal costs. Even in their own families, they were sometimes devalued. Monique describes her father's treatment of her this way:

> "That boy's gonna be a faggot." He used to always say it and used to point at me. So I knew he was talking about me. So I mean, I mean, that's logic right there. He's pointing and apparently he was talking about me. "That boy's gonna be a faggot." The first time I heard him say that I think I was about six and I used to ask my mother, "Why did he ever say that to me?" It was a big strain on me because I used to go to school and

people used to say "faggot" and . . . I didn't understand what it
meant. I thought it was a nice word, that I was a nice person,
and all the time was telling me in a sense that I was gay. Since
I hear my father say it, I thought it was a nice word, so I used to
hear that and say "thank you" to people.

"Faggot," "sissy," "punk," "fruit cake," "queer"—all five women talk
about learning to deal with the desolation of knowing they were different. They describe the ceremonies of degradation and humiliation carried out by children in their neighborhoods and schools. They also
describe the hypocrisy that sometimes underlay these behaviors. Many
of the boys who perpetrated these acts of degradation would have
clandestine sexual encounters with them, forced or agreed upon. In
most cases, these liaisons did not involve a display of mutual intimacy,
but were acts that merely relieved the sexual tensions associated with
adolescence. In some cases, however, the boy would insist that they lie
naked together and make love as he would with his girlfriend.

Involvements with boys and men who define themselves as "straight,"
but who engage in homosexual activities, are recurring events in the
lives of these women. They describe boys and men who participated in
homosexual encounters without apparently feeling any overt or sus-
tained threat to their presentation of the male image. This is particularly
true if these encounters were surreptitious or if their penises were
serviced and they never became the receivers of anal penetration. But
even men in long-term relationships with other men are defined as
"straight" if they never play a passive role.

These women also speak of the more painful aspects of living a gay
lifestyle. They talk about the difficulty of dealing with the taunts from
strangers. Each has her own strategy, but they are unanimous in their
belief that they are human beings who deserve respect. Monique's
strategy is to have those words pass right by her; she keeps reminding
herself, "It's not who you are, it's what you are. I am a person." China
maintains that the way you are treated on the streets depends on "how
you carry yourself." She does not let people get away with insults in her
presence. Shontae insists on never being disrespectful in those situations

and says she deals with rejection politely and as "fantastically sweet as I possibly can." And throughout their stories they echo Monique's plea: "Let me be."

In their early years these women encountered a significant amount of humiliation and degradation, but created effective strategies to cope and construct their own reality. So in the face of opposition from their families, peers, strangers, and every other social institution imaginable, they learned not only to accept their homosexuality but to express their sexuality in a most provocative manner. They became drag queens. For the most part, they had few friends during their pre-teenage years or at least they do not identify many significant friendships. During their early teens, however, they met classmates or neighborhood peers who validated something that prior to their meeting was indefinable. Meeting people like themselves proved, in part, that they were not alone in the world and confirmed that they were not an isolated blunder, a freak of nature. It is out of these friendships that they emerge from what China refers to as their darkness. They do not see themselves as emerging into deviance but as taking possession of a fuller expression of their being.

They speak of their metamorphosis from being a "sissy" to being fully female. The manner by which each finds herself in the streets and in drag is unique; however, for all five their friendship formations play a significant role in their creation of a sexual image. It is through these associations that they fine-tune the witticisms associated with the subculture and it is through these associations that they create and interpret all things female. The timbre of the female voice, the enhancement of their bodies to conform to the female silhouette, the use of makeup to create a new face, and the art of walking with a suggestive swagger find their origins in the cooperative play of friends and acquaintances as well as in their inherent creativity.

Imitation is an important part of that cluster of transvestites who take care of each other, who bond by their desire to emulate each other, and who display a fascination with glamour and illusion. They craft their own identities by closely observing, learning, and giving expression to the imagined styles they encounter. In this way they become improvisors of gender, and their metamorphosis emerges, in part, through their relationships. They excite the fantasies of others through illusion, and they undermine the distinction between male and female reflected in the dominant cultural discourse. So if there is presumed solidarity in meaning in such notions as being "gay," "straight," "man," and "woman," this certainty in meaning begins to unravel and becomes incredibly blurred after one encounters these women.

Observing becomes central to their identity, and their world is the world of the eye. These women do not see themselves as the victims of the gaze. Instead, there is power in observing and being observed. Shontae is always the looker. For Detra there is power in the play of illusion, in creating the object of another's gaze, controlling the illusion, and incarnating the desires of others. She says:

> To me it's more like acting, acting, and illusion. You know, the fact that I'm a male and I can . . . . I guess that's the power play in it. I'm a male and I can make another male fantasies come true. Things that he always fantasized, I can bring them to life. When I'm high, I feel like, what's that "Fantasy Island," I can say and do things to make men lust for me like Cleopatra. I gets into a fantasy world like that, you know.

Central to illusion is performance. As Monique remarks, "So what you do is act like the man on the stage. Perform. Only thing's different, I'm not getting that Emmy Award for it." Transvestism, she says, "amazes the eye."

They feel a fascination for all things feminine. They portray their mothers as matriarchs like those who have been so often depicted ruling their nests in sitcoms as well as in the academic press. Moreover, they do not present their mothers as a source of dysfunction. Though most of them come from female-headed households, they do not speak of the social disorganization of the Afro-American family with its higher rates of family dissolution that supposedly disrupts the organization of lower-class families. They do not see their mothers as household heads who contribute to the lack of normative controls that foster deviance. Instead mothers are resourceful providers who are strong and determined, and who are the first lines of defense from both internal and external threats to their children's emotional and physical well-being. Therefore, in comparison to men, women are good. As Shontae remarks:

> The majority of the guys, they wanted to have some kind of fierce gang war, standing on the corners drinking out of wine bottles. These little things totally disassociated me with those boys. I didn't see males as nothing positive. For real, coming along during then, I already figured that you will be dead sooner or later, you know, you just a no-good person.

The mother may have used drugs, as Detra's did, or she may have slept with other men to support her family, as Monique's mother did, but all five women show a sense of deep and unswerving loyalty to their mothers, a sense of devotion that pardons any blemish of character. In the end, mothers simply do the best they can in the face of overwhelming odds. They communicate their hopes and dreams to their children, and they instill their sense of humanity and values in their children. So the stories of their mothers are not simply stories about older women who are strong; they are stories of women who are valued not only for their virtue but also for the order and discipline they instil, for their rule setting, and, most of all, for their love. Shontae, for example, recalls a time, as an adult, when she was lying on the couch in the dining room and her mother stood over her just messing with her covers, just playing with her. For her, this simple act recalls and proclaims how deeply her mother loved her.

Besides the family, there is the family-hood, those bonds formed with other members of the gay and transvestite subculture. Mentoring by older queens like Kathleen, Detra's play mother, helps Detra to traverse the subcultural world. Detra's family-hood consists of Kathleen, who is thirteen or fourteen years older than Detra, and Kathleen's three "sisters," Detra's "aunts." In addition, it "came to a point where you have a grandmother . . . the real older queens like Miss Flossie . . . . They were like your grandmother and stuff."

Similarly, Keisha uses the language of family when she speaks of her roommates:

> And we be for real with one another. When we got a problem we can come to one another and talk about it, you know. Not

all that bullshit and everything. Put that on the side and we sit
down and have a really serious talk, you know. Just like a
family. See, that's our family outside our real family.

Thus, these women live their lives in community, not in isolation.
While they may be invisible to and denied by the dominant culture, they
have a circle of like-minded friends and companions with whom they
can share the simple pleasures of jumping rope or forming a singing
group. Shontae speaks of her relief to find a circle of like-minded individuals
in jail:

Jail was absolutely horrible! Well, what was good about it was
as soon as I got in . . . they ask you all about yourself. When
they found out that you're a homosexual and before you know
they put you on the block with all the rest of the girls. Well, I
was never so relieved to see a bunch of faggots in my life.

The family-hood provides support, advice, imitation, and friendship;
it connotes far more intimacy than "neighborhood." It implies a more
porous boundary between one's home and others' homes as well as
between one's family space and the spaces of the streets. It is a rich term,
and it indicates the geography of connection through which the women
move and live.

But Shontae, China, Keisha, Detra, and Monique also reflect on the
ugly aspects of their lives. They consider the consequences of their drug
use, their crime participation, and other aspects of their lives. They
admit that when they began to work as sex workers, they never realized
what was down that road, that it would take them into a whole different
world. When reflecting on working in the streets, Monique and Keisha
describe themselves as playing Russian roulette. Being on the streets
hardens your heart, making you conniving and distrustful of others.
They find many of the things they are called to do repulsive and degrad-
ing. Some learn to avoid these acts by being more cunning than their
clients; they define their real object as getting the money with the least
effort possible. So Keisha learns to make a man think he is having sex
with a woman when he only has his penis between her legs. From
others in her clique Detra learns to spot where her client keeps his

money or credit cards and how to skillfully "dip" into his pockets while she performs fellatio. And while she steals his wallet from pant pockets that are now below his knees, she make grunting noises to conceal the sounds of rustling money. The women learn that hormones soften their bodies and their voices and produce breasts that serve to entice men and earn more money. By imitating their mothers, their sisters, and other queens on the street, they learn to dress so they can walk that walk and talk that talk.

All of this occurs on the streets while they protect themselves from the unwanted invader, the police, who interrupt their hustling. So a night of hustling may be interrupted by being hauled off to spend the night in jail. Then they are released and the hustling begins anew when evening comes. And there are always drugs to soothe the pain.

China sounds the heartache and despair associated with crack use:

> Crack cocaine is not for anybody, at all. It's not even for rich
> white man to do, and got all the money he can possibly want
> to spend on this bullshit. It's not even good for him. 'Cause it
> will bring him rock bottom. I miss all my material things I had.
> All of them. That I gave up for that bullshit.

The others have not reached this point, and they continue to chase the glass pipe or continue to bang in order to see their blood mix with heroin to produce that nod. They continue to use drugs in spite of witnessing people being stabbed or robbed in crack houses and shooting galleries while all they want to do is finish their "shit, and get the hell out of there. . . . The high told me not to leave. The high just told me not to." Their addiction makes holding a legal job impossible; their lack of education would keep them from all but the most menial work anyway. So they spend their nights hopping in and out of cars or being chased by the police from one corner to another. Sometimes they find themselves in altercations where they respond with violence or they seek money in ways that cause them to be sentenced to jail for more serious crimes than walking the stroll. There, a man claims you as his wife and provides you with gifts and protection as long as you act right. So what began as something thrilling becomes a necessity because it supports their addiction and enables them to survive.

Despite the sordidness of some aspects of their lives, these women are powerful actors in control of their destiny. They take responsibility for their actions. They blame no one for their position in life. They acknowledge that their lives are of their own creation and choice. Keisha says, "I can't blame nobody but myself. Me being hard-headed, not listening, thinking I'm knowing it all, you know." China also recognizes the choices she made in using drugs when she says, "They didn't hold a gun to my head to use this shit. The only person I blame is myself." Elsewhere she insists, "I chose this life. I was given the tools. I just didn't use them."

They long for friendship and intimacy. Notwithstanding the traumas they have experienced in their lives, they have developed deep and lasting friendships. They have shared laughter, money, and clothes with friends and roommates. They have consoled and watched friends die of AIDS, mourned friends who have been murdered, held a lover who died in her arms, and comforted friends who were violently attacked on the streets. In their intimate relationships with men they epitomize women of the 1950s. They see themselves as cooking and cleaning, catering to their lovers, and being passive in bed, while their male partners are loving, caring, supportive, and completely masculine. Their ideal man is sexually active and dominant in terms of his performance and cannot define himself as gay. He must be straight. Any other definition and sex role would result in gender confusion. Therefore, all sexual encounters must have clearly defined sexual roles. They all dream of having intimate relationships that seem reminiscent of June and Ward Cleaver.

For them, being gay is associated not only with their sexual image but also with whether the individual is sexually active or passive. A gay person is always passive and is never the dominant sexual character in the relationship. Since they perceive themselves as women, it is inconceivable that they would enter a relationship with anyone other than a "straight" man. Most of them would be insulted if their partner asked them to play the dominant sexual role. At the same time, they recognize the power inherent in their position as women in their relationships. They see themselves not only as the controllers of money and the real decision makers in the relationship but also as the person who defines when and how much sexual intimacy occurs. In most cases, the men

with whom they have been intimate were not their ideal. In many cases
they became the victims of domestic abuse. Their partners were flawed
by their use of drugs or alcohol, and their relationships disintegrated
from the constant arguments and physical abuse centered on their mutual use of drugs.

God is also present in these accounts. These women refuse to be
religiously alienated. They insist that even His eyes can be amazed by
them, amazed by what they have done with what He gave them when
He created them. China depends on her "higher power" in order to
recover from cocaine addiction: "I'm grateful to God today that I have a
higher power that I can recover from drugs. . . . And pray to my higher
power that He will keep me off that bullshit." In memory of her dead
partner, China says she "pray[s] for him every day . . . I pray to God that
he's up there. I pray for him every night." And China wants to be
reconciled with God when she says, "It is a good God. I'm strongly
trying to find my way back to Him. Not back to Him but into Him
again. Like I was." Keisha speaks of her efforts to resist being alienated
from God when she says:

> I mean the Lord made everybody. So something He doing,
> you know, for . . . they may say . . . well, some people say,
> "You going to hell" and "Change your life over and every-
> thing." But I don't believe that. 'Cause nobody don't know
> where they going at. I can't say right now if I die where I'm
> going at. I was raised up on one person, the Lord.

They refuse to be alienated from God.

Through their stories, these women confront not only the world of
the dominant culture but also the culture of the professional diagnostic
and therapeutic social service world composed of judges, social workers, therapists, and others. Their stories challenge the social service
world to confront those strategies that alienate the individuals they are
supposed to serve. They refer to bitter encounters in which the social
service world seems to them to violate their created image. Monique
describes an encounter in a rehabilitation center where she is told to
wear a baby's bib:

> The day that they found out that I was using drugs, they said,
> "You think you know so much." Then I rolled my eyes. "Oh,
> you're a big spoiled brat." Then they gave me a baby's bib and
> a diaper to put on and told me to sit in the window. And I was
> like this, "Well, tell your mother to go and sit in the window
> 'cause I'm not sitting there."

There are many reasons why some people will have difficulty with this volume. Some will be appalled by who Shontae, China, Keisah, Detra, and Monique are and what they represent—gay, transvestites who are drug addicted and who commit sex work. Some will be offended by the assertion that Shontae, China, Keisah, Detra, and Monique have constructed self-realized lives. Some will be offended by the fact that their struggles for self-realization parallel the struggles that we all face. At some deeper level, some will be offended because these women do not live lives of misery. Other will be offended by the fact they are referred to as women. Those who have deep convictions concerning the orthodoxy of dysfunction and failed socialization will take issue with the possibility that there are redeeming attributes associated with the lives of those defined as deviant. Those who believe in the legitimacy of retribution will recoil at the suggestion that some of the positive attributes displayed by these women may suggest the efficacy of criminal justice policies that do not center on retribution. Within the academic community, some of my colleagues would prefer a more quantitative book, or a more theoretical one. They will be concerned that the Shontae, China, Keisha, Detra, and Monique are the dominant voices, and my voice appears on the surface to be muted. They will ask: Where is the voice of the social scientist? Where are the theoretical notions and policy issues that give a book meaning, viability, and substance. Where is the analysis? What is the utility of these stories? The private troubles of being black, poor, gay, transvestite, and drug using should be transformed into the public issues of homosexuality, drug addiction, sexual identity, poverty, crime control, and race relations. To be sure, these are important issues, but I believe the dominant question is not why and how these women live lives that offend the sensibilities of "normal" folks but rather how they are able to construct a social reality of dignity

regardless of their private troubles. It is not their dysfunction that is the key to social reform. Rather it is the recognition of the similarities in the normative rules and values that exist between all individuals that will solve both private as well as public troubles.

Whether these are issues raised inside or outside the academic community, they reflect deeply felt concerns driven by both ideological and philosophical convictions. I can only offer my apologies for not meeting everyone's expectations, and I offer my sincere desire that we enter into a dialogue where we begin to discuss the issues raised by the lives of these individuals in relation to current theory and popular discourse. I believe this book rests at the very heart of the sociological imagination in that it centers on the importance of the lived experiences, through the use of biographies, played out in relation to the social structure at particular points in history.

Regardless of all they have done in their lives that may offend the sensibility of many who read this book, and regardless of what I have done in this book that may offend others, we can learn from the courage of these women, from their resilience, from their determination to live and to survive, and perhaps we can learn from their mistakes. Their stories add a dimension to the social science enterprise that is absent and provide an intimate view of individuals living life in the context of the city. As such, they are not viewed in the aggregate and lost in percentages and regression equations. From these stories we develop a sense of intimacy, and a sense of gratitude for this brief glimpse into their lives. So it is my hope that this book allows us to see these women as human beings struggling to make sense of their reality. Such an approach is essential if we are to achieve sane policies and programs for individuals whose experiences and backgrounds may be radically different from our own. In the end we can feel fortunate that our lives are by comparison ordinary and mundane. We can pray that our society will respond with greater compassion for all those who are the rejected among us and that their knowledge will no longer be subjugated.

Before we listen to these women's stories, I have another story to tell. It concerns an incident that took place a number of years ago at the Catholic church I attended when I lived back East. There is a point in the liturgy just prior to the readings from the Bible when the priest stands with his hands outstretched, and says, "Let us pray." Ordinarily, after a brief pause, the priest would proceed to read the appropriate prayers from the prayer book being held for him by his altar person. On this particular Sunday, however, there was a homeless person in attendance who was apparently not familiar with the liturgy. Consequently, when the priest said, "Let us pray," he obediently stood and began, loudly, to pray the "Our Father." His voice reverberated through the assembly and throughout the congregation you could hear faint gasps or see embarrassed smiles. The priest, however, simply waited until the man had finished praying. Then he said, "Amen," adding, "I'm not the only person who knows how to pray."

Notes

1. Terms that were embodied in the work of classic social analysts such as Emile Durkheim (see Durkheim 1952, 1964, 1965), Karl Marx (1932, 1936), Auguste Comte (1957), Herbert Spencer (1967), Thorstein Veblen (1919), and Max Weber (1946).

2. For example, see Beccaria (1963); Gibbons (1979); Gibbs (1968); Glasser (1965); von Hirsch (1976); Wilson (1975).

3. Hirschi examines factors associated with the production of social conformity. Control theory as presented by Hirschi is concerned with processes that lessen the likelihood that people will be normally constrained, and focuses on the social bonds which tie people to the normative web of conventional society. Accordingly, delinquency results when the bonds to society are weaken or broken. See Hirschi (1969).

References

Anderson, Elijah. 1990. *Streetwise: Race, Class, and Change in an Urban Community*. Chicago: University of Chicago Press.

Beccaria, Cesare. 1963. *An Essay on Crimes and Punishments*. Trans. Henry Paolucci. Indianapolis: Bobbs Merrill.

Clifford, James and George E. Marcus. 1986. *Writing Culture: The Poetics and Politics of Ethnography*. Berkeley: University of California Press.

Comte, Auguste. 1957. *A General View Of Positivism*. J. H. Bridges (Trans.) New York: R. Speller.

Denzin, Norman K. 1990. "Presidential Address on the Sociological Imagination Revisited." *Sociological Quarterly* 31: 1–22.

Denzin, Norman K., and Yvonna S. Lincoln. 1994. *Handbook of Qualitative Research*. Thousand Oaks, CA: Sage Publications.

Foucault, Michel. 1986. *Power/Knowledge: Selected Interviews and Other Writings, 1972–1977*. Ed. Colin Gordon. Trans. Colin Gordon, Leo Marshall, John Mepham, and Kate Sopher. New York: Pantheon Books.

Geertz, Clifford. 1973. *The Interpretation of Cultures: Selected Essays*. New York: Basic Books.

Gibbons, Don. 1979. *The Criminological Enterprise: Theories and Perspectives*. Englewood Cliffs, NJ: Prentice-Hall.

Gibbs, Jack. 1968. "Crime, Punishment, and Deterrence." *Social Science Quarterly* 48 (Spring): 515–530.

Glasser, William. 1965. *Reality Therapy: A New Approach to Psychiatry*. New York: Harper and Row.

Hirschi, Travis. 1969. *Causes of Delinquency*. Berkeley: University of California Press.

Liebow, Elliot. 1967. *Tally's Corner: A Study of Negro Streetcorner Men*. Boston: Little Brown.

———. 1993. *Tell Them Who I Am: The Lives of Homeless Women*. New York: Free Press.

Mann, Coramae R. 1993. *Unequal Justice: A Question of Color*. Bloomington: Indiana University Press.

Marcus, George E., and Michael M. J. Fischer. 1986. *Anthropology as Cultural Critique: An Experimental Moment in the Human Sciences*. Chicago: University of Chicago Press.

Marx, Karl. 1932. *Capital: The Communist Manifesto and Other Writings*. New York: The Modern Library.

———. 1936. *Capital: A Critique of Political Economy*. Samuel Moore and Edward Aveling (Trans.). New York: The Modern Library.

Mills, C. Wright. 1959. *The Sociological Imagination*. London: Oxford University Press.

Pfohl, Stephen. 1994. *Images of Deviance and Social Control: A Sociological History*. New York: McGraw Hill.

Reckless, Walter C. 1973. *The Crime Problem.* 5th ed. Englewood Cliffs, NJ: Prentice-Hall.

Reckless, Walter C., and Simon Dinitz. 1967. "Pioneering with Self-Concept as Vulnerability Factor in Delinquency." *Journal of Criminal Law, Criminology, and Police Science* 58: 515–523.

Reckless, Walter C., Simon Dinitz, and Barbara Kay. 1957. "The Self-Component in Potential Delinquency and Potential Non-Delinquency." *American Sociological Review* 22 (Oct.): 566–570.

Reckless, Walter C., Simon Dinitz, and Ellen Murray. 1956. "Self-Concept as an Insulator against Delinquency." *American Sociological Review* 21: 744–746.

Rothenberg, Paula S. 1992. *Race, Class, and Gender in the United States.* New York: St. Martin's Press.

Simmel, Georg. 1950. *The Sociology of Georg Simmel.* Trans. Kurt H. Wolff. Glencoe, IL: Free Press.

Snow, David A., and Leon Anderson. 1993. *Down on Their Luck: A Study of Homeless Street People.* Berkeley: University of California Press.

Spencer, Herbert. 1967. *The Evolution of Society: Selections from Herbert Spencer's Principles of Sociology.* Chicago: University of Chicago Press.

Veblen, Thorstein. 1919. *The Place of Science in Modern Civilization and Other Essays.* New York: B. W. Huesbsch.

von Hirsch, Andrew. 1976. *Doing Justice: The Choice of Punishment.* New York: Hill and Wang.

Weber, Max. 1946. *From Max Weber: Essays in Sociology.* Translated, edited and introduction by H. H. Gerth and C. Wright Mills. New York: Oxford University Press.

Wilson, James Q. 1975. *Thinking about Crime.* New York: Vintage.

Wirth, Louis. 1938. "Urbanism as a Way of Life." *American Journal of Sociology* 44: 1–24.

Honey, Honey, Miss Thang

*"I'm standing there stuck with
twenty dollars and a promise
that you'll be back."*

Shontae

I was an active, creative child who knew what I wanted and grew up to be a drag queen and I worked at it. I have always desired men, so I went for them. Other than that, I learned the rest along the way. Every now and then there are regrets. Yeah, there's a few, but my regrets don't come until after my early years. My early years, those are the ones I wish I could go back to. You know, those were the safe years. Especially if I could go back to before my sister Melody died, you know. Those were the real secure days, totally.

I know my parents loved me even during the hard times. Most definitely. Mommy always wanted us to learn to try to accept things as they are and not try to change them, be at peace with yourself. You know, that's what Mommy used to say all the time. Start with you, you know . . . start with yourself and . . .

I think my parents wanted me to be happy when I grew up. As for a profession, they wanted whatever I wanted. Mommy would even get in arguments with other people. Like, "You don't live . . . you just raise your children and do the best you can. You let them live their lives. All you can try to do is to be happy. Because the rest of this world is gonna try to sock it to you." That's what Mommy used to always try to tell us, "Just try to be happy, as long as it's not hurting nobody." But for my mother it was always about love. Mommy was one of the best women

1

in the world. I wish I had a chance to be a little better. I wish I hadn't said and did some of the things I put her through.

I would like being like my father too. He never minded nobody else's business. I would stay to myself like he does. I wouldn't involve myself in nothing that didn't concern me. And he always tried to say the best thing he possibly could about anybody. If he ain't have nothing nice to say about you at all, he ain't gonna talk about you. I'm just like that because I ain't gonna sit around and talk about nobody that I can't stand.

My parents got along beautifully. They were supportive of each other and very affectionate. They were never afraid to show their love for each other. The more people around, the more they showed off. Mommy was always pulling at Daddy. She would always be grabbing him and then they would start. Or there might be something on television or something or we might be playing records or something and they would start maybe like showing us an old dance or something. And you know as soon as one of them would try something everybody would fall out laughing. They had a happy marriage. Mommy was more quick-tempered than Daddy, but she was the power behind the throne. He was the power, don't get me wrong now. He called the shots. But she ran everything.

I never knew my real parents. But my adoptive parents used to tell me the story. How I found out about it was when I went to school and a teacher called me by a different name and I couldn't understand that. We were in kindergarten and I really panicked. When I came home, I explained it all to my mother. She tried to explain it to me by showing me this birth certificate that I was this person. I didn't understand what adoption meant. Now I understand what adoption is, but then I didn't know.

But my adoption was never legal. Mommy knew my mother and from what I hear I would be better off with Mommy. I'm saying it wasn't like I was given away to strangers. See, Mommy had been known for having foster children. Matter of fact they were known for taking care of adopted children. Plus Mommy ran a day care center, that's how she made her money. There was always a bunch of cousins. We always called each other cousins and brothers and sisters and stuff.

So Mommy and my mother made some kind of a deal. I think my mother was supposed to come back and get me, but Mommy said that if she was to have me, start raising me, that she didn't want her to change her mind to come back and get me. I think she had a certain period or so, and when she did come back, what she seen she felt that it was better off if I stayed there. They didn't try to make her sound like a terrible person, but they also spoke well for themselves.

I know very little about my real parents. I'm supposed to have had a uncle. Now this is how I knew that the teacher was calling me by a wrong name. He had sons too. This boy Kevin Housemeyer used to always call me his cousin. See, my real name is Marion Housemeyer, okay. But the adoption was never legal, so my name was never changed. I was raised under Ralph Daniels. See, I couldn't understand, me having this uncle on the other block. I just figured that in that community everybody called everybody aunts and uncles. So when I did like get interested in my own family, it was like too late to go back, like even try to find the Housemeyers because they were gone. I had already blossom to the person that I was . . . that I liked myself, being myself.

My mother died a year ago, in '90. She was seventy-one years old. My father was much older than my mother. He was almost like eighty-two when he died. My father just died. These were the parents that raised me from the time I was three months old. Mommy was from Seneca County and her father, they're all from New York to New Jersey. And my father, he was from a place called Columbia. I don't know if it was Georgia or South Carolina. Must've been like a little township called Columbia or something like that.

They had other adopted children too. Well, they were relations too. Some of them were cousins. I think me and Jane like were really only the real outsiders. I was a very special child to my mother because she always wanted her own little boy, which I think that's what soften me up so much. We were like very spoiled, very sheltered. Plus she was a much older woman. She was like forty-eight years old when she got me. And she was more like a grandmother than a mother in her affections. Mommy was very overprotective. She was sweet as pie, you know. Anything you want, if she could give it to you, you got, you know. By her being little settled then and able to afford adopted children, we grew up pretty much, you know, not middle class, but I mean we didn't hurt for anything. At least in my younger ages. As you got older we started having more responsibilities.

Things started coming down on me kind of hard because I was a little different. I didn't care for basketball and rope climbing. I didn't like getting dirty. Plus we stayed in church a lot, and we had enough people in our family, which were mainly girls anyway. So what went on a lot of times was a lot of bickering, a lot of chitchat, a lot of chatter, a lot of cooking, a lot of home basting. So there wasn't a lot of sport, active sports family, where there was a lot of male dominance. Even when I was put in those type of situations I would find myself uncomfortable and request my mother that I not return.

But nothing really happen before the age of nine, because I really had a cherished little childhood. I didn't have a disturbed childhood. It was no family beatings, no mother and father romping and raving and fighting. They barely cursed. They were church-going little people. Everything was really family. It was Christmas eve, big Easter celebrations. There were always family picnics and gathering for the summertime. We were always closely knit. Like we used to have family reunions at Uncle Buster's, that was my mother's youngest brother. He was like the well-to-doer in the family. He drove one of those trucks. He had a big family too. Anyway, he made a lot of money. So every summer that's where family reunion would be held, because Uncle Buster had a nice, real big home in Franklin, in Seneca County. My mother was crazy about all that. We used to go there a lot.

I didn't get along with Uncle Buster at all. He was the one that told my mother I was gonna grow up and be a little sissy and sent my mother home crying one time. I was about five when that happened. Because his son had one of those bicycles I used to ride all the time and he had took the training wheels off it. So Tommy knew how to ride his bike, but I didn't know how to ride his bike without the training wheels. So Tommy was holding me on the bike while we riding. We were just kids. So when he let me go, like his father lets him go—you know he's imitating his father—and I only went like twelve inches away from Tommy and fell and I skinned my knee and I cried. And Uncle Buster held this against me because I cried. And then because I cried, then my mother came running to me, you know with all this extra attention and stuff. "You gonna make him a little faggot," you know. Now I can remember that back at five years old. That made a real impression, especially to see my mother crying too from him saying something so mean.

So there wasn't too much going on before the age of nine. My first turning point I think it was my cousin. Aunt Jackie lived up Eighteenth and York. Mommy raised her too. This is how much older my mother is. My older cousin, Derrick, was like a teenager, but he was a real big guy, so he looked even older. I went up to Eighteenth Street to spend the weekend with Aunt Jackie, and she had to go to choir rehearsal or something. Left me down the house with Derrick. Derrick wanted me to mess around with him. I didn't understand really what he was really talking about, but I knew that it was something different, that it was something dirty.

I was about ten or eleven, and Derrick gave me fifty cents for me to follow his lead, to do just what he wanted me to do. It was a lot of touching and feeling and rubbing. I doubt very seriously if he really knew too much about what he was doing. This happened, but see there was no real penetration.

He had like a deck of cards, right. And when you flipped them over there were pictures of people doing things. These were nude pictures, but it was a deck of cards. So first we played cards and we only played a game or something like "War." So as we played "War," each time like he would win or something, he make a suggestion about something.

I don't remember exactly everything. I can still see the pictures with the cards. Somehow another we ended up nude. I think like every time he won at "War," or something—I think that when I first heard about that's how you play strip poker, that's when I first heard that phrase—then we ended up nude, and it was getting close to the time for my mother . . . and then like I was ready to put my clothes right back on because all of a sudden I got frightened. And I didn't want to play this game no more, and that when he bribe me with the money. Only thing I can remember is that we just got in the bed together. I don't actually remember no real penetration. There was only sex foreplay.

Then Aunt Jackie move down in Georgetown. That's when . . . it was maybe a year later when we were down there then and Derrick did want to penetrate me. I was scared, but I had been penetrated before from a boy up the street named Frankie Bailey. I was about eleven, 'cause by thirteen I was . . . in junior high. I was quite active then. I made him give me a dollar. So every Sunday, Aunt Jackie would be going to church and I would be all dressed leaving like I was going to church. Instead of going to church, I would head around Aunt Jackie's house with Derrick. And then as each weekend went by, maybe a month or so, then I would start asking like for fifty cents more. Till I got about thirteen years old I start wanting five dollars. But I realized that you could get money for doing it, right, and Derrick was like a steady trick then. I realized I could get easy money for doing it. It became more . . . it became more . . . more of a regular? I mean an expectation. I could do so and so and so. Everybody didn't have money and stuff all the time. So when I end up having extra little cash nobody really questioned it because they figured that Mommy always gave it to me, you know.

I don't know what to really call me and Derrick because I got to the point where I would say I was using Derrick. First of all, being . . . keeping it quiet, you know because he was so much older. He already knew better. Really with Derrick it probably would have been that one little affair. He was bisexual and he liked sex. And then knowing he was getting it on a regular basis, every Sunday, you know, like he was expecting it himself too. It was mostly with Denny and Frankie and them. Boys that I really liked that I had little encounters with, like under the schoolyards or in one of the school bathrooms. And then we could do this while we're here and then the rejection I would get afterwards, like when we were amongst our friends, you know, in public. Then label our ass with, "Here come the sissies!" But yet just two hours ago, you know, you were all over me. You know, dealing with the mental effects of that.

So up until the time I was ten I was pure as the driven snow. I wanted to discover myself, but I was afraid of myself. Because I wasn't into women. I didn't sit around and talk about girls and stuff like boys do, you know. I knew there was a lot of difference to me anyway. A lot of things that were supposed to be—I suppose what society would call normal—wasn't normal to me, you know. I always wanted, I always desired to . . . even through watching television, watching my sisters with their boyfriends and stuff, to be laying up in a man's arms, you know, having a boyfriend. There was always a fantasy with me. I would sit around and think about it. That was always the case, as early as I can remember, even before Derrick. So it didn't really have nothing to do with him.

It was all ideas and—I'm not going to say expectations—but I knew some day that I was going to have a chance to get involved with something like that. The dream was just too for real and certain things that I would do I knew would get certain attention. I knew that something was going to happen to me, but I was cautioned by what I would hear from like older folks about things that happen. See, they wouldn't say "gay people" or "homosexuals" or stuff like that. And see then they didn't talk that much around me, but they talked about people that were different, like gay people in my neighborhood. Like when we would see them and somebody would just say something about them, we would be sent to another room. "Go in the other room, mind you business. Leave so and so alone." Like we were being held, sheltered from it, which aroused my curiosity even more. "Well, how come Stevie looks different?" You know, "Why you always send us out the room?"

Later on I did have an incident where I got caught in the park with this guy when I was in the seventh grade. I was thirteen then. And this cop caught us. Then my mother came up to the police station and when they found out everything that was going on so many people were trying to say that they always knew or that they had some idea. It hurt my mother, but it really wasn't that much of a shock. I don't even know if my father found out about the incident in the park. I don't think he knew anything about it. I think my mother and them kept that away from him. Even if he did know anything about it, he never said anything to me about it. So I don't think he ever really knew. Because after that scene I didn't get into no more trouble. I was definitely afraid of being in trouble. That little ordeal of going to jail and then see all the things that you heard about it. The way they try to scare you out of it. In my juvenile years, it worked!

But I had all these fantasies. My sisters used all this nail polish and shit, all kind of feminine things. We were always getting dressed up and done up and something, you know. And that was it too. Always wanted to be getting pretty, and then, like we would go running to the television to see something like the Supremes. I mean everything was so glamour and so thrilling. It seem that it had to be easy, you know. It was . . . it was life. It had the kind of pizzazz. I would just yearn, you know, to . . . you know. But I didn't know what was what.

I was different from other little boys because it was by me being more outgoing and mature, more intellectual. See, I read more and I sat down more. And then I was always around grown people, you know. I was more mature. The majority of the guys, they wanted to have some kind of fierce gang war, standing on the corners drinking out of wine bottles. These little things totally disassociated me with those boys. I didn't see males as nothing positive. For real, coming along during then, I already figured that you will be dead sooner or later, you know, you just a no-good person. I only trusted older men.

I always liked being a girl, you know. The girl role to me was the better. It seem like you always got the best if you were a girl. I can see even as I was coming up you would always see things sacrificed for my brother for my sister, you know. "Oh, he don't need that 'cause he's a boy!" So to me being the girl was always . . . you got the best if you were a girl.

Women were good. My mother dominated her family and stuff. She took care of everything. My father, only seen him when he came in at night, and when I was to wake up in the morning, he was gone. The only time I seen him was when we were in church. I mean, my father lived there with us, but I'm saying he worked all the time. I was also surrounded by my sisters and we were running around then. My mother didn't do too much running around, but she ran the house. She was the matriarch. She did everything. And I was right there and she told me everything. She would show me how to work out a project on the stove and I would perfect it. Once I learned how to fix the egg I would try seasoned salt or the new kind of this or that. So I was pretty much a homebody, moreso than a basketball freak or wanting to run the street. Later, when I got older, these things did start happening, you know, me staying out. That's when me and Miss Sammy, Miss Ali, we all in

Coleman Junior High, well, we all knew who and what we were. We were all outgoing homosexual personalities. We didn't subdue ourselves, you know.

I lived in Castle Rock, West Georgetown. It's terrible down there now. But when I was living there it was perfect, with the DePaul College just right up the street there. See, the teenage and stuff then were moreso into their wine and reefer. They were wine guzzlers and reefer smokers, you know. During my younger days I think the worst thing then was probably during the gang fights or somebody's husband beating up their wife or something. I seen more domestic violence and stuff. Come round the corner, you see Schooky beating up his wife, all drunk up and stuff. Murders were gang-related problems. I'm saying it was not like the time it is now. The robberies, the . . . it wasn't that often then. Crime was light. Didn't have much of a problem.

There were things that were important to the people in the neighborhood. They were community people. They all valued their neighborhood. They were very competitive. The biggest thing that was going was Calvary Baptist Church. There was competition for choir, best choir, best churches. And they were in it for the teenagers—the black groups, dance records, and best block parties. One up the street may be rallying to get their potholes fixed, and the next street neighbor would support it. Georgetown was like that.

My father worked at Hampton's Bakery. So his job paid him very well, real good. He came home with all kinds of pastries for us every day, fresh pastry. That's what blew Mommy up, why she was so heavy. The times I was with him, me and Daddy used to have fun. We didn't have much to talk about though if it wasn't a TV program. He was a very quiet man. He was a Southern man. He enjoyed his solitude. He didn't even sit around my mother that much. I think what turned her whole life was her children.

When we were growing up we were our own little clique. My sisters were very protective of me. I couldn't have a problem with anybody or they couldn't have one because we were always there for each other. Even like as I was growing up like maybe one or two of the boys or some in the neighborhood that I might have a problem with, didn't want the problem with my sisters.

My oldest sister, Melody, was fourteen when I was born. Jane was a year younger than her. See, all my sisters were big sisters. Me, Holly, Pamela, we all stair steps. Carole, Holly, and them, they only like six or seven years older than us. So we always had bigger sisters. We always, you know, fell under that type of protection. My sisters had boyfriends and stuff. We didn't have no problem with nobody in the neighborhood. Plus I hung out with hard-core Stud Angie, who would knock the . . . who had two brothers herself. And one of them was Al and he ran a gang down there. So we didn't have no problem, you know, with our neighborhood, with nobody picking on us and bothering us. Not saying that we didn't have, but not too often.

I was closest to my sister Melody, you know. She was already married by the time I was ten years old. I would end up staying over her house, and she end up sending me to school. She talked to all my teachers. She would be there, you know . . . when I was out of school she would be there to pick me up. My best friend was my sister Melody.

Melody died when I was very young. I was ten when she died. I think that took a whole lot, a whole lot away from us. I think that's what actually threw me and Mommy a little closer together. Mommy was the brain, but she was like Mommy's arms and legs. And she had gotten married and she was pregnant. Right after she had delivered birth her rheumatic fever acted up. Her heart stopped on her and she died, and that took a lot out of us. My mother practically died. I think that's what made me want to be her strength. I didn't know too much about my sister's relationship with her husband, but somehow or another Mommy managed to get the baby with his approval and that kind of soothe some of her pain. I loved Georgie, my sister's baby. I just disliked him sometimes when I would think about some of what my life would be like if he had never came along. When she died I tried to make her baby my best friend, but I kind of resented him. Because I figured if he had never been born my sister would still be alive.

It seemed like me and Mommy were even more so . . . more tighter when Melody died. That's why I had . . . not really to sneak and do everything but I would . . . that was during the time when I was turning into a liar because I would have to work my way around things, you know. Get Mommy, you know. And she would check up on things and then I would start involving other people in my projects. If my mother calls, so and so and so. . . . It got difficult like that.

Because of my sisters Mommy would talk about men. I had a lot of sisters and there were always boyfriends and stuff. Mommy was the type of person she like anybody, but if she had something to say about you, nine to one there was something about you that wasn't too right. In general she would never talk negatively about men. My mommy's attitude would be, "He's nice, he does this, he's respectable." You know, she looked for the better qualities, especially in a man, especially if she could get a favor or so out of it. She never talked down on men, no. Not until my boyfriend, Joey, 'cause she didn't like him.

I left Joey one time. I was about twenty-one and I had a black eye. Mommy was, you know, upset about that. Then what really pissed her off was I left the house with him to go back up to the apartment that him and I had. She cursed me out. "Don't you come back no more." Yeah. If I'm gonna leave with this nigger that's beating me all up like this, don't come back. Maybe about two months or something I left him again. She had the opportunity to throw it up in my face again. "Uh-huh, the nigger done beat you up again so you want to come running back here." Ain't nothing like that.

She was a lively person. She would have an occasional cocktail once or twice, but she was always throwing the book at you. I mean for right and wrong. You have to understand my parents were much, much older. You know, already settled in their lives than a lot of younger parents. . . . We had to be in bed by eight-thirty. My sister Melody enforced that. When I thought I was grown at thirteen, with that man in the park thing, I was docked like ten o'clock for like about six months. I was about sixteen before I could come and go again. When I first turned thirteen it was alright whether I came and go. I would never hang out really late. If I was out, I would be like right out on our steps or, nine to one, already in the house because I didn't run the streets that much.

When it came to the house that's just what it was. Her house. You did what she said do or . . . you know. Although she wasn't the type that would throw you out but she was going to deduct some type of privilege from you. If you couldn't do this, then you couldn't have this. She wasn't mentally abusive. I can't never remember a real beating, beating. I can remember like pinches or pushes or maybe even a knock on the back of the head. But I was never thrown down flights of steps or beat with sticks, or you know. Some of the thing that these child abuse people . . . broken arms. . . .

She had us sweeping up. We didn't do everything. We were showed one time how to do it and . . . you didn't work detail until you were qualified and capable of doing it. Like my sister Lisa, she never had work detail because Lisa had poor sight. She was always, you know, getting special glasses. Her eyes were operated on several times. Now she sees perfect, and she never had no work to do simply because Mommy didn't want her bumping around.

I mainly worked in the kitchen. See, I was always in and out of the refrigerator. On Saturday we cleaned the refrigerator. This is normal. In the summertime we all wiped down walls and fingerprints and stuff. Mine was mainly making sure all the dishes and stuff were all in the cabinet, right, and I scrubbed the refrigerator and I would just have to do the kitchen floor. Then my sisters would have other floors and somebody else would have the bathroom.

I also had to do my homework. Mommy used to get a lot of static from my teachers about my work, about poor work habits. So she'd try to fill in my leisure time, she would try to buy me books, you know always. . . . I was terrible with my times table. Like I was twelve years old before I really got them down pat. I was supposed to know them right off the top like between the ages of nine and ten. I was drilled so much to school where I started resenting school so much that I wasn't learning anything.

At one point I was sent to Lake Platt. I was thirteen years old then. Oh, Lake Platt is where they had a little diagnostic clinic because I wouldn't go to school, right. And it was called a diagnostic clinic. So the judges, they wouldn't send you . . . you go there for like . . . the sentence was supposed to be sixty days. I spent more than sixty days. They evaluate you, you know, on your education—you know, how you get along with others, and they keep you there. It was real nice out there in Lake Platt. They also have like a little juvenile camp out there too. Where they keep little criminals! But this was the diagnostic hospital that I was in. But some of them criminals are some of the patients too. So you would find yourself sometimes trapped there and a lot of them were cute and I was young and impressionable. I had gonorrhea there. Yes! That when they had me at Lake Platt.

Anyway, when I got home from school I would watch television, and I would stay in all afternoon. Sometimes I would go out and play. I was a favorite one for games. I was friendly with everybody on the block. Mainly the girls. If there wasn't a game of jump rope or a game of jacks or we would sit there and play one of the little famous card games. Then I would be sitting across the street with my girlfriend Angie. We weren't smoking reefer yet. I was fourteen when we first started smoking. At twelve all we did was a little wild running around, punking the street.

They were pressuring me so much about school. This was like between eight and twelve. School was a breeze for me. I didn't start messing up in school until . . . I started getting C's like about eighth grade. Before you know it was a D. I wasn't being absent from school. I was just not totally going in, you know. Then when I would go, it would be like make-up courses and I was scoring low because I wasn't studying, but just enough to get passed to the next grade.

I didn't graduate from school. I dropped out in the eleventh grade. I was promoted to the eleventh grade. I never went back. I was too busy growing titties and strutting my stuff on the stage.

I was thirteen when I first got to Coleman. I knew Sammy already, and I already knew we had something in common, but when he left Carver School about the fifth grade, I went on to the sixth grade. So I didn't see Sammy no more until the seventh grade. Just in that year, Sammy was much more flightier than at Coleman, which also helped me come out more. And we met a new friend too. She's a sex change now, Ali. So the three of us were all there in Coleman Junior High together. So then, as we would put our ideas and stuff together, we would like hooky school. Maybe at Sammy's house because his mother wasn't home. And we would be having like maybe guys or something over. And then we started having our experiences. I remember one of them was with Dean Conway. We called him Ton because he had a big head and him and Sammy . . . usually after the sexual performances we would end up in a fight or something with him because he would change up on you after he had done these things.

Going through that period like I began to change. We started meeting like older queens who were like, "Hey, breasts!" The things that we always wanted ourselves. And then after that we became drag queens and we got more involved in perming our heads. These things were coming on as we were in junior high school, you know. Then they started to seeing changing in us. My mother didn't want to accept it, but she would say it was to be expected.

From about eleven until eighteen, nineteen, I was very sexually active. Very! You know, 'cause I wanted to. . . . Alright, I would be more so a leader than a follower. You know, trying the things that I've learned about, like from people that I would meet, like older homosexuals or where I would manage to get some of their books and borrow . . . like with Derrick . . . the card thing. Things that I've always seen in myself but wanted to put into practice. I wanted to be a part of it. And the problem was not everybody was ready for it. But I was susceptible to some things that Sammy wouldn't do if we were out with two guys. Let's say that he might say "Yeah" to anal sex but he might say "No" to oral sex. Whereas he would say "No," I would say "Yes." I'm fast! I was a schemer, conniver, a little plotter, you know, set up little things. Really, I was not a perfect angel, but I wasn't a terrible child either.

I learned that I was capable of having a baby underneath the schoolyard with Charlie Thomas! He lived across the street. I'm serious! I had never experienced nothing like this in my life. 'Cause see he wanted me. I didn't know what this was. It trickled out me. It felt so good, it must have been a sin, but I was scared to death because it kept running out of me and down my legs. It was so watery. At first I thought it was pee. He made me come on myself and I was scared to death.

Well, usually me and Charlie used to do it in the laundromat and go behind the dryers, but I don't know, I didn't want to go. I was getting older then and I didn't wanna . . . must have been about thirteen then because I stopped wanting to—this was after the incident—because I didn't want to be seen in no public places no more and see he just insisted, kept, you know, sweet-talking me. Kind of knelt me down and make me do it, do it, right here in the schoolyard. I was telling him, you know, these kinds of places get you caught in. So we went into one of the little doorways and I had never experienced anything like that. We were kissing and grinding, that's what we were doing. We were all wrapped up. There was a real Sharif-Streisand scene. I mean, like, Lord, I was never gonna see him again in my life, and I mean we just . . . all this hugging and loving and dick bumping and . . . and I started coming and didn't know what to do. I didn't know what was happening to me. It scared me. I was frightened but it felt so good.

I had on a pair of light-colored pants and I could see it through my pants 'cause it was thin and so watery. And it was like running down me and I went running . . . I broke away from him and ran and he didn't know what the fuck was wrong with me. I guess he . . . he leave me the fuck alone because I'm going crazy. I had never experienced that. I went home and I hurried up and changed my clothes. Luckily I got in the house that night without arousing too much suspicion to myself. When I got upstairs and I hurried up and changed my pants, I came back and I just sat at the top of the step trying to figure out if something was wrong with me. It was on a Sunday night too. They were watching a Sunday night movie. I remember that music to the ABC. I kept hearing that. I was sitting there just trickling. "Oh, God, I hope, you know, I'm not gonna die." It was supposed to be the best experience in my life but it was the most frightening.

No one had ever talked to me about my body and what happens and stuff like that. Not even Miss Coffman or Miss Sammy. I guess them bitches probably never knew nothing about coming. We're so busy chasing a dick, we didn't know what happened with a dick. I realized all of that after I started talking to older queens. Miss Hennessey and them. Girls who hung on with Miss Serena's buddy. Miss Hennessey explained it to me one afternoon. I went over for rehearsal. We had a little singing group. I went up for rehearsal and I was telling her about it, and she laughed. She hollowed! She told me just what it was and everything. And then she told me the next time I do, you know, what to expect. "The older you get, the thicker it was going to get." She said, "Actually it's probably gonna be thicker the next time. Because that was probably your first little trickle." And I told her how scared I was and how I ran home. She said, "He probably thought you were crazy."

From the time I got arrested and the time I met Joey, I was still seeing guys like Charlie Thomas, oh, what was his name, Mark Taylor, these were basically neighbors. Denny Pritchard. You know what I mean, boys that were . . . like older guys in the neighborhood. Like when I was thirteen, Denny was seventeen. They would be like three to four and five years older than I was. Mark Taylor was like the oldest one. He was like about eighteen years old. Matter of fact he was out of school when I was in the sixth grade. I was eleven when I was messing with him. I went around to go get a paper route, I had my teacher fill out this form. Then when I took it back, Marky wants me to wait until everybody was gone to discuss this paper route he was gonna give me, which was only one little block so that I could go and drop them papers off and come right back. So he could get to do his thang. He was eighteen then and I was eleven. Because he was out of school. He fucked my brains out with that little dick. It's little now, but then I thought it was something. This was like the year before I went to junior high school. I was becoming a little cut-up then. I was messing with Charlie Thomas then too.

Like I said we were hunting for dick and getting dressed and going out and being the Supremes and . . . you know. There was more talk about getting dick than having dick, because we would run from a dick quicker than . . . than more so . . . especially Miss Sammy. We did more talking about it. We used to write love letters and stuff to guys and stick them up in their lockers and stuff. And put things on them like "Mystery Writer." We would never sign our names. You know high school girly shit.

I think it was around fourteen years old, me and Stud Angie, girl I grew up with . . . Angie's gay and I think that's what kind of had us close too because both of us understood each other. But Angie was three years older than me, so by her being older she . . . and by my mother liking her . . . being into Angie, kept me up, like out in the open. I remember the first time Stud Angie gave me a drag of joint. We went down to her basement. We're down in her basement 'cause they fixed everything up with blinking lights and peace signs, incense. We were teenagers now. We were growing up, Earth, Wind and Fire freaks, and rock group freaks. We would smoke. The first time she gave me a joint I didn't know whether or not I was high. We repeated it again the next night.

My mother seemed to feel safer with me being out with one of my girlfriends than just being out by myself. She didn't care too much for Sammy or Miss Coffman either when she had met them. But Coleman Junior High was one my biggest turning points. My girlfriend, the one I hadn't seen for a year, one year we were separated, it seemed like almost three years to us. And then making a new friend, Miss Coffman, and all of us had so much in common and that was the buddy system there. I think that was one of the major turning points when I started junior high.

I grew up like overnight, you know. By the time I was fifteen, sixteen, I had little jobs, like I would work at Woolworth's. Just mopping up or cleaning up. I like having my own money, my own independence, and I was talking about coming out of school already. Okay, and that's where I went through a big thing with my parents because Mommy called and got me fired from the job. We had a little confrontation there. I told the people that I was much older than I was. She used to have a habit of going through my things. Not because of drug or cigarette or anything but for women's clothes. Because she would hear how we would be dressing up on weekends and stuff. When she used to find things like that, I would steal little things from my sisters. There would always be arguments. "If you're gonna wear stuff, you've got to buy your own." She knew I had no source of money so then when I got my little job at Woolworth she was thrilled at first. Soon after I got the job, I started buying things. Everything that I was getting I wasn't letting her see, like brand new wigs and stuff like that. I would stuff it in a drawer and she would never know nothing about it. And then she did find out, go up in my drawers. So she realized that I was buying little things, like little panty girdles, bras, and stuff. She called up and got me fired from the job. I guess she figured this would break me, since I couldn't get women's clothes. Called this truant officer on me too. Now that I think about it, we went through a doozy too.

By the time I was seventeen, I was getting my hormone injection. I had an older friend, Stewart Buckner, he's dead now, who was on welfare. I was using his medical card. I would go with Ginger Hope. I had met Ginger when I went to Georgetown, and she took me to Dr. Thompson and he would give me my hormonal injections.

I was still living at home, during this whole blossoming, this whole changing. I think I left home right after, around Christmas time, to move in with Miss Chapman at Fifty-sixth and Cedar Falls Avenue to be in her show. She had you dress up like a character and you would pantomime the songs from the records. We worked in several bars, some at the prisons, and at nice nightclubs. Some were gay bars. The biggest thing then to me was being this ultra-perfect woman and trying my best to be Diana Ross.

Yeah, I was shoplifting too. This was when I was about twelve or thirteen years old. We pick things we would want, like eyebrow pencil or a tube of lipstick. Might steal a panty girdle. Things that we were going to use, you know. Not even maybe that next day but we knew somehow or another we were going to find use for it one of these days. We used to make a big production about the Halloween Ball. We were only like thirteen-year-old sissies. Knowing damn well we wouldn't be able to go for at least another five years. But at least we had this.

So when I was twelve or thirteen I was hanging out with Miss Coffman, Miss Sammy, and Stud Angie. We would cruise men, being sluts like Mother used to say I was going to be. We would make up an excuse to say something to a man or something. "Can I have a light, honey?" Hunting for men in the afternoon so we could get back home before our parents know where we were.

We would hang out with older queens too like Miss Hennessey. They were older and they were into things too. They would show us different little ropes, you know. They like started out with singing groups, from singing groups to makeup artistry, to how to steal. . . . Go in the wig shop and how to roll a wig up and stick it in your bag. Just showing you how to go into Blair's and clipping an outfit to busting a store window to snatching out a coat and jumping into the stolen cars and riding off. I was a little older when all this happened.

So on a typical day, we might all be standing right at Eleventh and Main Street at the little cigar store after getting our little cigarettes. You know, just pacing up and down that little area. One of us might have a jump rope, one of us might even still be carrying a book, somebody always got some kind of food or something in their hands. We were always out there and all of a sudden guys might walk by. You know, some guy that all y'all think is cute and "Oh, child! Who's gonna be the first one to say something to him?" Oh, oh, silly things like that. That would be in the afternoon for us, you know. We were out just trying to have a good time. I can remember sometimes we even used to get chased and that was really a thrill. We would be chased by a gang of boys . . . but don't let one of them catch you. Go swishing past them, let them start attacking, "Get the faggots." And we go flying off running. Because we can run then, we were young. I'm saying, you get away and all meet at a certain corner and stuff and talk about how we flew and how we did this. "Baby, if they had caught me, I would have cut them." Little punks! That would be fun!

To me my friends were exciting. Plus we all liked men and all lived close, and we all in school together. We had a lot, too much, in common. I felt liberated when I found them, I preferred to be . . . it would be like separating me and my sisters 'cause I didn't even want to be around them. I would rather be with my friends. You know, it was almost like I found something better and it was more to my liking.

My mother was concerned about the people I was hanging out with. She always wanted to know what they were like and what they want you for. Have they tried anything? 'Cause Mommy wasn't stupid, but she couldn't prove anything. And then she was under the impression that I was the type that would tell. You know, she be, "I don't worry about them 'cause Ralph would tell me." She would ask me if they were funny, this was once I got into junior high school. Before, she never questioned nobody I messed with or hung around, but that didn't happen until I got real flaming and outward. This was after I was arrested. Then she started questioning everything. She got very involved then.

It took her about a year to get over the arrest. Well, not really a year's time—it only took a couple of months—but I'm saying it was a while before she finally got it out of her system. But those first couple of months were like doozies.

Well, this is what happened. We were over to the park. . . . These cigarette had came out, these new cigarettes, and we had gotten like several free packs. So we were over in the park. We had on our little rabbit jackets, me and Miss Sammy. Miss Coffman wasn't with us. There was this guy in the park, this older man, and we went over and took our little cigarettes out and just got a light from him. So he gave us a light and so he liked us and so we wanted to know which one of us he liked.

We had men's clothes, but we had on the little girls' mink coats, little wigs, and our little hats. We weren't totally in drag. Smoking my cigarettes and trying to act like Doris Day. Sophisticated! One trying to be better than the other. So then we got him to show us his dick. And to me, my heavens! he had the dick of his life. I don't know how we got him to show us his dick. Somehow or other that old pervert didn't take long. We sat there with him on the bench for a little while talking to him and told him to show it. And before you know it we were down there behind this tree and he was showing it to us.

After he showed us his dick, we left there. But then we came back the next day. We came back the next day. And it was the same man. And so Miss Sammy decides, put her coat down on the ground. This is in the daytime now too, and squirms on the ground for him to come and get it. Alright.

The old pervert jumps on us, but before I know it Miss Sammy is crawling from under him, right, wrenching with pain. So I'm saying, "Oh, child, you can't take that. I can." I . . . I can't wait, old hot ass. Pulling my pants down. Laid down on Miss Sammy's coat and let this man start penetrating his thing in me. Well, then when I looked up a cop is running this way. So he hurries up and jumps up off top of me and then the cop runs straight, but keeps running right behind him. I get up and I keep on going, but when the cop comes back I'm gone, but Miss Sammy is with me and the cop grabs Sammy's coat, picks it up. And I'm saying, "Shit! They just wanted him. Let's go and get you coat back from the cops." That's how stupid we were. So I go and asked the cop, "Can I have Sammy's coat back?" So he can see that it ain't mine. I got my coat on. He said, "Where's the guy at?" I said, "There he is right there. He wanted his coat." He said, "Oh, good." So he catches both of us. So then by me having on a coat, I'm saying, "Well, we can tell them that the cop is lying. I already got my coat on and I could say that in a minute." We're trying to create Perry Mason and we ain't even old enough . . . we ain't even seen a real court case.

Before you know it our parents come up and get us and we had to go back to court to say what happened. And we had to make all this sound like this man had raped Sammy. It was really a lie, but the only way out of it—oh, God! I never think I would tell this story again—the only way out of it was, to clear us, was to make it sound like, to make this man sound like a rapist. We were children.

It was my sister Jean's idea to say that the guy had seduced us. After we cried . . . after they came and got us, they were like, "Lord, you know how they would put you away." You know they scared us. Jean came up with it, "When you go up to court"—when you're a juvenile you got to go to court right this next day—"when you go up to the Juvenile Detention Center tomorrow for this hearing we tell the story. . . ." They kept us up all night long drilling this lie into our heads. And he got sent up on seven to something years. He was like thirty-six years old. He was in his thirties and we were just little kids. We were still in seventh grade. We're thirteen years old.

My mother went to pieces. She didn't take it very well. She was furious. I mean she said a lot of things to me that she would have never, have never said before, you know. "What the hell is wrong with you? Want somebody digging in your ass?" I mean really letting you have it. "Some kind of sickness. Don't you know you can get cancer?" She was awfully terrible. She told me I could never get a damn thing from her. I could never get a damn thing from her. She was quite upset. And then she would be a little harder on me with my work then too. "If you don't do these dishes, I tell that damn man when I go up to court." To have me scared. I was a good child for awhile until that case was over with. And then once it was over with we never talked about it anymore.

They were scared that we would be sent to jail. Because Mommy was very upset because of what she heard, what little she knew about jail, what little she knew about homosexuality. She was afraid I was going to jail, go in there and get killed or something. And then the more she hears from counselors and all them people molesting you and so forth. Mommy really thought I was going to be in the penitentiary. She cried almost every time we went court. That's how scared she had been.

As for me, it didn't bother me too much, you know. You know, I knew the real truth about it. I knew we were over there fucking around with that man, trying to get us some dick, and we done got caught and you know and that was the way out of our situation. . . . Alright, here the truth, so it didn't bother me that much, but everybody else was so shamed that we were associated with. Hell, I loved the attention. I loved the limelight about it, but I, you know, I was even more sheltered then. For weekends at a time I was constantly questioned, "Where are you going?" You know, have to be seen, verified every place I've been. It took awhile for that to die down too, now that I think about it.

It did hurt me to hear my mother talk about somebody digging in my ass. It hurt my feelings, but that was the way Mommy felt about it at the time. I mean . . . I was so trapped up in mixed emotions, of guys, the police, then Mommy coming down on me hard. I'm ignored. My sister is drilling this lie into both me and Miss Sammy. I was shattered with emotion that I just became numb. I didn't know how to feel, because I didn't know what was expected of me, you know, to feel anything. I was afraid to show gladness, you know, relief about the stories that I actually got it down. And I didn't . . . I refused to show too much shame because that seemed to put more pressure on them. . . . It was like, "Well, it's all your fault," once I would show I was ashamed. If I showed fear then it was, "You better be scared." It was a shaky year. I was under a bunch of different emotions, and I think that even moreso it helped me to escape to where I was determined that I was just going to be me anyway. It actually ·helped me prepare myself a little for this world that I was getting ready to come out here to attack. If I could accept it from these people I loved, won't bother me so much out here with the people that I don't care too much about.

When the encounter with the guy in the park first happened I didn't feel freer, because they made me feel like I was so wrong. You know, and everybody, you know, going through their own little personal changes about it. At first I felt like the worst thing in the world, but after it was over with and the story in the newspaper and everything had died down and after Mommy had got me fired from the little job and stuff, when I was about sixteen years old, I think that's when I started becoming totally free, free-flowing, free-feeling.

After this happened I had toned down a little bit to take some of the attention off of me. It was getting to the point that some family function, like my Aunt Jasmine's, the one that lives in Pennsylvania, or even like if her family came up, it was like "Where's he at?" This made me want to withdraw. So it made me not want to be on certain teams at certain times. I did shelve myself for a little while.

It took a lot . . . it took all of that mental anguish that I had to find . . . I had to re-accept myself a little bit, okay. I had already freed myself up. I would let what people say run my life, you know, worry about it, but then during that time I did find myself trapped up in that and I was worrying about and mainly worrying not wanting my mother to get hurt no more. Finally came to a conclusion, "Well, huh, I have to live my life. I'm sorry if she didn't like it, but I mean, you know, but she's not me." It took me about a good year and stuff to get that type of attitude back.

I always did what they wanted me to do. When I started doing just what I wanted to do, I did it where it could be acceptable because first I presented it like . . . like a joke or something, you know, to laugh. And then before you know it, I eased on out the door. Then after I started developing my little body and stuff, this was the way I was always going to be. My mother needed me more now because, see, I was older. So she took it pretty well. At first she used to tell me, "Well, if you got to dress like that why have you got to look so whorish?" you know. Then she started being more helpful instead of attacking me more. "If you're going to do it, at least look halfway decent. Be presentable enough to be out, don't look so that you can only go out at night."

At about seventeen I stopped listening to them and started doing what I wanted to do. I was going to the doctor. After awhile it would have been too late to try to tell me anyway. I was going to the doctor to get my hormonal shots and stuff. The hormones provided a balance. It builds your breast up and slows down other processes. I haven't been on them now for two years. See, they stop the hair from growing in your face. They soften up areas and swell up your breast and they develop. And if you keep you hormonal stuff going, you get your castration, you won't ever have to worry about another male hormone. So while you're on hormones, keeping your therapy going, you'll have the perfect woman's body. You may spend about three hundred dollars for some silicone to fill in certain little spots. You're good to go.

The hormones allow you to start thinking like a woman and feeling like a woman. Therapy makes the conflict between the male side and the feminine side worse 'cause, see, you becoming so hung up in knowing that I am a woman. Once somebody slaps you with that reality, it can affect you mentally so desperately. The hormones are telling you you are a woman. Yeah, those hormones be telling you that you're a woman and that can affect you so terribly that it can snap you out if you're not a strong-minded person. 'Cause I've seen times that somebody might have known, found out that I was a guy, and I cried when I ain't no crying type of person. For real! But I'm saying that I was so disturbed that they found out. So you really got to be in control of yourself. The battle is not male-female. The battle is all female, especially if you're having castration.

Yeah, that's a snapper right there. If you really can't take it, the best thing to do really is just not to argue with that person at all. The reality of it is going to take you through a chance. Unless you're strong enough to say, "Yeah, but I look like what I want to be." You have to have that type . . . you have to be witty too and snappy. Ready to pop back on . . . you got to be a reader, you know. Hormones quiet you out though, they soften you up a bit too much. And it makes you vulnerable too. You're easy prey.

See, that's your first step towards your sex change operation. You got to have your hormonal stuff set first, and you have your castration. In step three they build the vagina and do all that stuff. There's a lot you go through before that. You got to have mental therapy. You go through like five stages. Well, the quicker you put your money down, the faster you can get on. You go through three stages before you get one. See, every sex change ain't ready for a sex change.

I thought about doing it, but I think it was. . . . After Mommy's death . . . I don't . . . I think it was my downfall with Joey. After I stayed with him three years and we didn't really work out. That was just a heavy heartache, and the introduction of drugs. "I don't care" affected me then. That's what it was. I stopped caring. Somehow or another it didn't matter to me anymore. After I broke up with Joey, I just run home and took care of my mother. I had gotten away from everything, and then I started getting high.

The therapy didn't start because I was hanging out with Sammy way back there at thirteen. No, 'cause see Sammy never turned into a drag queen. But we had . . . during our high school, junior high and high school years, we always had dressed up and went out like on our weekend and stuff. But I'm saying we developed into our adulthood, Sammy stayed in school. He's still in some school and he didn't turn into a drag queen. Ali has had a successful sex change. And I'm still the one who hasn't made a move yet toward sex change or turning back.

I guess what made me take that first step was the determination of wanting to be . . . seeing other transvestites and wanting to be like that. That helps to push you into it. Just like I'm saying, if you want to be a football player, what you do is you sit there and watch a couple of games and see how the game is played. You develop on your own. It was the dream! Don't misunderstand, not all female impersonators are drag queens or transvestites. Not all of them go through it. Some of them bodies reject hormones, some of them . . . they all have their reasons why they don't, but taking the hormones is like one of the major steps.

So I started hormonal therapy about ten years ago. Oh, back then, honey, everybody was thrilled to have titties. Oh, you were a real freak then! Had titties and a dick. Honey! Oh, child! You were a specialty. Nowadays, honey, people expect . . . they already know that you can get titties. It's not that much of a biggy. It's a thrill to have them, then you were real special. Especially if you had real nice, big ones, you know. Yes! To work in Metro Center, that's what some men . . . I mean, just to go out and buy a prostitute, well, you really ain't got to go out the neighborhood. So when you come downtown, you can get paid top dollar in Metro Center. You know, you were a specialty then. Specially men like you would meet that would be like from out of town.

Some would be looking for drag queens. Not all of them. Some of them would be looking for women. I'm not going to make it sound like they're coming out just looking for a drag queen. But I'm saying some of them could take it once they would found that you were a drag queen. I mean, that was a thrill for them to have somebody who had tits. And then you have some of them that would totally want to snap on you, you know that figured you were a woman. Who was thrilled with you! You know, who would treat you like royalty. Whereas you come home to a husband like Joey who treat you like shit, you know. Used to feel like shit. "I'm more appreciated by my trick than I am by you." To this man, I'm nothing.

I'm usually attracted to men's physique. Everybody like certain things about people that turn them on, you know. I don't want Arnold Swartzeneggar, or this freak type of muscularly person, but I mean I like a well-built man, a well-stacked man. I like a fairer skin. I mean we have our own little, what we think are our little sex gods. As for race, I have better times with white guys. I don't know why. Maybe it's because I like white men better. So if I was out on the stroll and I had to choose between a white guy and a black guy, I think I would take the white guy. I think I would have a much easier time. I would have a better time. 'Cause see the black man just try to be a little bit more . . . much more aggressive than most of the white guys I've been with. I'm not saying that there aren't aggressive white guys, but I'm saying that the ones that I'll be with I prefer to go out with the white guys.

Now, as far as a lover and relationships, I don't know nothing about. I lived with this white guy, Harold. He was fifty-seven years old. I loved him dearly, because he spoiled me, you know. I stayed with him, and I was smoking cocaine, and this was in the beginning when I smoked it. All me and Harold did was ride back to Jefferson and buy cocaine. And Harold had this cute little hangup that I used to like. Like soon as we walked in the door we just started stripping our clothes off, and as we were getting high, he would walk around like picking them up, folding them up, looking at me. That was his goofy . . . I loved it. Yeah. I loved it. You know, I'll be sitting there smoking and Harold would be folding clothes. Oh, I loved it.

As far as age, the older the better for me. Because when they are older, they already know what they want to do. They not always about playing any games and going through the bullshit. They done already been through all of that. So they already know. They're pretty well established.

As far as sex, they can go vice versa or I just perform the way you want me to, you know. I demand nothing. Just pay me. Doesn't matter if I'm working or not. Like with Harold. With him too. I mean, you know, I prefer for you to let me know how you want things to go, and then I'll tell you what I like and how I like things. I could deal with that.

Actually, you know, sometimes things like this can bring you closer. Make it better for your relationship.

When I says the word "gay," that means that you're a feminine-acting male or either a lesbian. 'Cause not all gays want to play the part of a woman, that's when people, you know, get mixed up. The only way I would say that he was straight is if he . . . I could accept the bisexual . . . if he is having women and men, you know. But if he is only having men, he's gay! I mean, that homosexual, only having sex with men. As for me, I don't know if I could be in a relationship with a man who likes to flip flop. I used to say I couldn't deal with it both ways like that. But I . . . I'm not gonna say I've changed but . . . it's not of my preference, but I could deal with if it was something in it . . . had to be a little more to it than love. There would be reasons why I would be dealing with the person. My preference—no. I would prefer him being on top. I would be more submissive. If I have to deal with one of these flippies or something, I could put up with him for a couple of months if there was something involved, some money or something like that. That's not what I would want in a relationship. A flippy! That would be like going to bed with Miss Sammy! I am saying, one of my sisters. One of your girlfriends or something, you know. A flippy! I done heard plenty of that stuff too.

To me a gay person is a bisexual person or a person who just prefers to have sex with the same sex. Yeah, I know some queens say that the people who get fucked are gay people, and if you go to bed with a man, if the man is the one who is the fucker, then he's not gay, but that's not true. I don't believe that. That's not straight to me. I mean, just because you're on top, even if he's sleeping on top with another man that doesn't make him straight. He's gay too. I mean that what's people don't be realizing. All gay people don't want to be effeminate.

So when I'm looking for a relationship, I'm looking for a gay man who always plays the massive role. I ain't got time to teach nobody nothing unless they got some money. Then it's worth investing your time in it. But just to stand 'round here and be bothered with one of these nuts, just to try to make a life out of it. No!

I was always out of the closet. I don't think I ever went into the closet. I mean, to actually have the balls and go on and get . . . come out dressed like I want to . . . you know, to do it the way I wanted to do. Even when I do it and those who can look at me and still know I don't care. They even know that, you know, that I know they know, and you still doing it. Then you got nerves! I don't care. I'm not living your life, I'm living for me. But it took a lot of studying other queens. I couldn't wait to get old enough to dress and do things I first wanted to do.

So I became accepting of my homosexuality very young, very, very young. That's what was so especial about myself is that I knew it and I didn't try to hide it. I moreso flaunted it and that was definitely a no-no, you know. It was like I didn't care whether or not you knew. The majority of the people I dealt with, was coming up around, family people or right there in that little villa we lived in . . . it wasn't too many noses turned down on me because it was like in a family area where I was already accepted, you know. So to hear something about me having an affair with somebody across the street would possibly be true or might be some lie I done made up.

I always liked men sexually. The mystery of a man, I think it probably started like when my mother first took me to Boxhill Park and they had this big swimming pool and this was where the first time I was left by her, you know, to go like in the boys' entrance and you would be getting dressed, you know, getting undressed, you know, to run to the showers and get into the pool. This was like my first time. Even though I knew she was right out there. I already had my swimming trunks on, you know, to go in and take my clothes and fold them up and see all these naked men. It was like "Oh, my God!" This was like then, "Oh, have mercy!" I found myself mesmerized, you know, hypnotized by the male body. Then all I could see myself was like being Erika Cain swept up off my feet, you know. Carried off by this man up here in the great big bush and these big thick muscles, you know. Oh, my God, these long, long, long dick was hanging, was draped from these musclebound legs, Lord have mercy! This one guy I could still see. I mean he was just so perfect!

I can remember this. Oh, yeah, Lord! It was the first time I ever seen somebody dry their back. He took the towel, you know, he then just fold the towel and rub his back to dry it off. I just stood there and watched him do it. And he paid me no mind at all. I couldn't have been no more than about six, but I mean, you know . . . oh! I just quivered. I watched him the whole time. At the time I could only sit on the edge of the pool and paddle my feet but every time you turn around I was looking for this man. And when swim time is over, and they blow the whistle, you know, and they round up, I would be flying in. I couldn't wait. And I think I missed him. He must have left ahead of time and stuff.

I can still remember this man drying his back and that was exciting, erotic, and . . . I wasn't even near puberty. I always knew that I like men. When I were growing up I was always plotting when I could act out what I felt inside. Oh, I always plotted that. Used to play like roles and we used to play house and stuff. Alright, with my cousin and stuff, they would go 'head and play Mommy and Daddy and I would have to be Miss Ward, the lady from across the street, you know. I always had to have a female role or I would be grandmommy. I would come in and give all the kids candy, and then I would always have to have me a female role.

I never thought about why I was gay It never even bothered me. I never even given it a second thought, but I know that I can't make nobody happy but me and living my life to make me happy this way, then I was going to do it. I'm not always sitting around thrilled with smiles, but I'm content with myself. I'm at peace with myself.

The most difficult thing about being gay is being accepted sometimes in certain situation, you know. It's almost like the racial thing. You know sometimes, soon as they discover you're gay, the door is slammed right in your face, you know. So I think that's about the hardest thing about being gay. As soon as something goes wrong, "Oh, well, they wouldn't give it to me because I was a queen."

I think it's hard being black and gay. You have less advantages being black already, you know, and then to be gay and black, I mean, there all the more reason to give you a no. Even if they say you're qualified because you can and you're black, but because you're gay, this could be an excuse.

When it comes to dealing with being gay, I hate having to deal with other people. I mean, things like as far as you getting jobs or sometimes even like the lady at the checkout line when you're at the supermarket.

And she looks up and she sees you're gay, so she feels as if she doesn't have to give you a double bag. You know, small things like that, but I'm saying people do little wicked things like that. Well, you can kiss my ass, bitch, because I'm not going to sleep with you whether or not I was.

I deal with the rejection politely, and fantastically sweet as I possibly can. That can be in any situation. I'm not gonna disrespect you, first of all, and I'm not going to be verbally abusive. Well, maybe I might be a little verbally abusive, but I'm not going to disrespect you and I'm definitely going to treat you much better than you're used to being treated, by saying, "Yes, and thank you. And by the way, I think that's just a lovely blouse you have on." When it might just be totally disgusting. You know what I mean? It satisfies me.

I don't know somehow or another it used to bother me. When I was in situations where I was trying to be impressive, you know. If I really wanted this person to like me. You feel it. You're only human. You know, you put up a big freezer in front of you, because you got to shield yourself from this whole world sometimes. But I'm saying somebody that you care about or, you know . . . somebody that you personally feel that you want to impress, when you're rejected by them, it hurt. But other than that, honey, anybody else, "Later for you."

You know, if I get on a bus and I'm walking through the bus and people whisper or people begin to snicker, I know they're gonna do that to anybody. But the thing is, you don't let it fuck with you. But the times when it does fuck with you, you just try to keep as much self-control as possible.

Courage! You have to have it from the jump street. The courage to come out, you know, to deal with. If you don't have the courage, first thing somebody says to you, you'll run back in and do what they want you to and still be unhappy. You know what I mean? You've got to have it, and you've got to want it, you know, to be yourself when you come out here. You got to start with yourself first. You have to got to like you, first. You have to look at it from the standpoint that there has to be some realization of self-love. You ain't gonna last but so long out there without it. That just like trying to be a ballplayer and you know damn well you can't swing, you can't hit this motherfucking ball coming at you this fucking fast. But you're gonna go out there and fake that you're a ballplayer, and you're gonna have your little feelings hurt when they tell you you're a wimp and get off the field. You know what I mean? You really thought these guys were your friends. You know what I mean?

I've never had a sexual relationship with a woman. Oh, well, nothing funny about me. I would never do a thing like that! Laying up with no woman. What kind of fool would be laying up with a woman? Dikey old broads! Never! I loved to hear my sisters and them talk about that. When they get to talking about Stud Angie across the street. "Something wrong with that bitch. I want me a dick. Why would I want my face stuck all up in some pussy?" They used to be terrible about talking about people. Oh, Angie grew up with all my sisters. I'm saying, they don't talk about her like this in her face, and they're actually friends. Every time they need a car ride or something like that. . . . And plus my mother was real close to Angie because of me. They would never hurt Angie's feelings. Only a couple of other people called her Stud Angie. And we only do it like when we're sitting around having fun. Other than that she's just Angie. I would never disrespect her. Angie is my girlfriend. Times when we were younger . . . in the mornings, when we leave for school, be sitting around. . . . She'll be calling me "little Miss Sissy Ralphie." "Come on, Miss Ralphie, child." "Oh, Stud Angie, please." You know. But I'm saying the moment we left the house, she was Angie and I was Ralph. Amongst ourselves and other gay friends of ours we could cut up then. Now that we're older, to hear me say Stud Angie it would be like, we would be reminiscing, you know.

In between that time after the park thing and the time I met Joey, I was running around with Miss Sammy and Miss Coffman. That's when I was . . . cooking up our little female impersonator attire. We were growing into blossoming young queens then. By the time I met Joey I was full, in bloom. I started meeting older queens. . . . Miss Sammy took me over to meet Miss Hennessey first, then I met Miss Serena, then I remember Miss Bianca, Miss Dinky. They were all older girls. They were going to Kennedy. Yeah, I knew tall Detra too, . . . Bianca. These were all older girls. They helped, you know, boost you along.

I was at full drag by seventeen. It was always my desire to go into full drag. When I was very young, I always wanted to be a drag queen. See, my mother had plenty of time to get ready for me going into full drag. I

wanted to be Diana Ross, a drag queen. I wanted to go right out there.
. . . Honey, when you're coming along then, honey, the Supremes
would make up people. . . . You know, you would break your neck to
see Ed Sullivan just to see them. We did anyway. And we were just kids.
So I always wanted to be a . . . somebody to . . . some type of entertain-
ment or something.

So this was when I was learning a lot from older queens. Hearing
about their lovers, you know, their relationship with their boyfriends
and stuff too. I'm saying I was growing up because I was getting away
from relationships like running around with Charlie and Mark and them
'cause I realized that they were just using me then as a sex object, you
know, as a sex tool.

So when I was growing up, I wanted to be like . . . I don't know . . .
like a TV personality or something. Now that I'm older I say I wish I
could have been like Oprah, you know. 'Cause she is worldly acceptable, you know, outspoken. I like that type of attitude. And she cares for
others, but she's catty too. I like that. All that realness, you know. I
watch her show, and some of the things you see that she just wants to
laugh about her damn self. I'm saying there are very few times, and
Oprah will look into the camera, and you know, old bitch, you want to
laugh. And she'll cover it right up, you know, and go on with her show
without trying to insult anybody. I love somebody who can do that,
with that type of attitude.

Before I left the house, I was only smoking that marijuana with Stud
Angie. We were still going to school, right. She had started going to this
business school and . . . somewhere near Sussex Street, something and
Sussex. I was going to J & M Vocational. It's at High and Southbourne.
And see by me missing so many days out of high school, and by them
not wanting to send me to a disciplinary school because my only problem was attendance, my mother signed me into one of those. And then
this would keep my interests. I was taking up a nurse's aide course there.
They would give you like carfare and lunch money at the end of the
week, which was only nine bucks. It was really like going to school and
getting a little pay. Plus we were only seventeen years old. I mean for
that weekends that would be your marijuana money, your little eyebrow money, little lipstick money, and then carfare wasn't that much

either. I think it was like sixty-five cents to ride the trolley back then. So you didn't have that much of a problem. . . . You know, money wasn't a big issue like it is now. We would . . . in the morning when we would get up and go to school—Angie's brother sold joint, so she always had marijuana—so when I would get up to go to school, we would run over there, we'd smoke joint first, maybe play a few records at first, and then run and grab a doughnut or something and run and jump on the subway because both of us took the subway. We would be high all morning long. Even to the point where we got to school. We done got to the point where we started carrying it with us, alright. My problem then was learning how to roll it.

I was seventeen when I left my mother's home in Georgetown. I was in female impersonating shows and Miss Chapman helped. Chappy was a dancer. He used to dance with the Edgar Eames dancers, and he was pretty organized here in Jefferson. Everybody would do like a character or a star that they were familiar with. So you had to express some kind of little talent. Alright, we already had talent for dressing up, so it was getting down to see how good you would work in front of people. It didn't bother me too much to express myself in front of people. I did songs by Gladys Knight. We would put the tape on, or the records on, and then you would, you know, sing like that.

I met Chappy up at the Club 101 one night. Me and my girlfriend, Ginger Hope, it was on the weekend and we were wearing sizzlers then. That's the name of a dress. They were real short and they had matching panties. But they called them sizzlers. We were wearing sizzlers and we were looking real, real cute that night. When we went to Club 101, which was like an older club, like an all-night-long club. It was a thrill for us. And coming outside, Chappy spotted her first, and took and asked her if she ever did any show work. It interested me. Then after he kept on talking, "I heard of you. I know who you are." And he gave us both his cards and told us to call him. Ginger didn't call him right away, but I think I called that first thing that Monday morning and he took and told me to get my girlfriend and for us to come out there that Friday.

Ginger's dead now. She was stabbed to death in Georgetown year before last. I wasn't still close to her because we had stopped seeing each other. Ginger had even stopped coming downtown that much. Ginger had converted back to wearing men's clothes. She, you know, had even was supposed to have left town when I was still with Joey. So Ginger and I didn't . . . we would either bump into each other or I would see somebody that knew her and tell them to have her call me or I would call her. We would still spend time together, you know . . . our reunion with . . . was real great because then we have so much reminiscing to do and then Ginger was into getting high real good too. And we would talk about our shoplifting days. I don't know the whole story. By the time I heard about it, Ginger had been dead and buried.

Anyway, we got all the way up to Chappy . . . we got up there and . . . I auditioned, okay. . . . I forget exactly who I wanted to do, but then he . . . it was somebody like Dionne Warwick or Melba Moore, some big star. They already had somebody doing Diana Ross, which totally kind of . . . at that time I was saying, rather blasé about it then because I couldn't do what I wanted to do. It was around "Midnight Train to Georgia" time, and it was a real big hit. So I swore to God that I could do Gladys Knight.

He would supply you with everything. He bought records for us and this, that, and the other. So this was a thrill for us. And then we were using marijuana, and we could get high. And we could go into our routine. And when we would get out to Chappy's house, then we would do dance steps and so forth. He supplied the outfits for us, the gowns. He had us sewing. He was a real business type of person. There was not too much messing around or playing around. Only on the times they gave you off. They paid you well. Whenever you did a performance with Chappy, you did get paid. So was no need to mess up. And if you did mess up, he was kind of hot-tempered. We were nervous something too. We're little afraid of him.

By that time I had just started using drugs. I was first introduced to cocaine, snorting it, by a friend of Chappy's. He had a thing for young queens. Towards the end coke was really becoming real publicly known, a lot more than it was before. You would think that it was, you know, quite a big deal. His name was Toby. So Toby would give you, you know, a few snorts of coke. Having performed, and the more you would perform, the more, the more drugs he would give you. Okay, my first time with him, I really wasn't too familiar with the effect. I didn't know whether or not I was high. I didn't know what I was really feeling. And then I felt . . . I was trying to get in good, so I didn't want to be a flop. So I went along with the program. But then the next time I did do cocaine with Toby, I knew what to expect. I wasn't really, really all that too much thrilled with it. I'm saying it was no biggy to me. It was like "I already did it." I was more of a marijuana freak. I would, you know, go across town to find a good bag of joint. Or a larger amount of joint for a lesser—if I could get a nickel bag—get a bigger one somewhere in North Jefferson, I would travel here and go out East Jefferson just to have more. I wasn't that interested in cocaine. It really didn't become too much of a fade until I started smoking, I guess.

So when I was doing the drag stuff and snorting cocaine, that was like my first little experience. I'm saying it wasn't no biggy then to me. I was moreso trying to just blend in with the friend of Miss Chapman, Toby. And I mean it wasn't no thrill. It was a thrill because I was doing something hip. I was growing up then. I was trying to hang in there. I was thinking, you know, trying to be one of the girls. I didn't do it very long at all. You know, actually it was like really a one- or two-time thing then, you know. Other than that, just give us a joint.

So after he took me into the show, I lived out there in East Jefferson with them at Fifty-sixth and Cedar Falls. There is where I met my first boyfriend. No, I went back home first because we had stopped doing . . . we were like on a little hiatus then. He didn't have no more booking for us for a month or so. And things had starting really getting separated with our little group because then everybody was going here and there. Some people were finding work other places, some people weren't that interested no more. I have a lot of energy and stuff and I still wanted to keep on kicking. So it was at clubs like on Eleventh Street, and I would be trying to get back in clubs with some of those bigger, like whiter queens that had bigger productions. During that time hanging up there is when I met Joey.

I had moved in with Chapman when we were working. And then after we stopped working, me and Ginger both came back to Georgetown. We stayed with our parents. And we were just going out on our regular old weekends. Just started to getting warm then too, because we had broke up like about March or April. But I stayed with Chappy for about a year. We went through that whole summer, me and

Ginger. We be worrying about getting to our doctors for our hormone therapy. Then we would worry about our clothes. Okay, money wasn't so plentiful for us. So this is when we started dressing up and we started at Oakbridge Mall and we would find outfits and we would like take two or three outfits in the dressing room. Wrap up two of them or either we would even put them on underneath our clothes and walk out the stores with them. So I guess that when like we really started getting into little thievery, so we would have outfits. And we would steal things like . . . we were stealing for ourselves then, you know, like silk hose. Then we started meeting people, 'cause we were mainly like getting into bathing suits and stuff because we used to go up to Richardson Lake. That's right off of Butler Drive. We would go up to there, you know, swimming. So then we would meet some people would like some of the things we would have. And then we would tell them we can get you these. And then we shopping in malls. And then the Marketplace opened and before you know it we had started meeting queens like from North Jefferson that were shoplifters too and they would like drive out to different malls. And we started, you know, shoplifting with them, and that was the first time I had got arrested was in Blair's for shoplifting.

My mother kind of went through it. I already just turned eighteen. "Now, you got a record." I got six months' probation or something like that. So I had to be pretty easy, so we didn't do too much. We stopped shoplifting just during that period. And it was around the end of October or the early part of November, we were in town. We going back to Club 101 again. No, we're going to Club Christine. While I was walking down there, this guy had stopped me shortly before we had got up to the club. His name was Steven Charles Davis. He told me his name was Joey. We just started talking. You know, he gave me his number and everything. I was attracted by his hat, this brown hat with this thing up on the side of it, and this long coat he had on with it. I thought he was fine, and I liked him but I couldn't really stand there and talk too much to him because Ginger was standing there waiting for me.

I don't know. I guess I was just trying to really get away and I don't know what I was trying to get away from. I knew I didn't want to go home sometimes. Sometimes I didn't even want to be bothered with Ginger. And running in and out of the club just didn't seem too much because we never seemed to like any of the guys anymore, you know, we were running into. And then we were out of work and then . . . the next thing we had heard about Chappy, he had got a brand new bunch of girls and they were supposed to be working somewhere in New York. I was feeling like we had been cheated.

Anyway, I called Joey. He asked me to call him. I don't know when he asked me to call him, but I didn't call him exactly when he wanted me too. I had called one night and he told me to come on up to his house. I thought he had a house. He met me at the bus stop at Twenty-ninth and Cramer. Only to be living in the projects! But he was real, real sweet to me and real, real . . . he was real different 'cause he wasn't like any of the other guys I knew. After I slept with Joey, I would go on back home and that would be it. But he wanted me to stay, and I wanted to stay. So before you knew, I ended up being there like all weekend. And then he went home with me and that just started. You know he bought one of those little blue like travelers' bag and asked me if I had a suitcase at home.

Well, it was his sister's house or her project. She had four children already and a crazy little mental case of a husband. And we all up there together. She had three rooms. Three upstairs rooms, living, dining room, and kitchen. And me and Joey stayed downstairs, in the living room. We had like a pull-out couch and we stayed there. We stayed there all way up to May before him and his sister really start having hot and heavy, you know, little heated little arguments. Plus his mother used to come in. So she knew nothing about me being a gay person. So one night when her and Joey were arguing the mother found out. Other than that Miss Julie use to treat me real sweet. Soon as she found that out, seems like she got a little distant towards me. So me and Joey moved out.

We first went to Atlantic City and that where things started separating between him and I because we would be like running out of money. Then Joey wanted to hustle. He was a thief hisself so he would want to steal things and selling and that seem like it would take too long to get things done. When I really had no hustling ability. But then like I was meeting . . . Brandy, Charity, Coco, queens that, you know, that would be down there on the beach and so forth. So at night . . . one afternoon I went into their hotel room with them and he couldn't find me and I had my dress with me and had went to a club that night. So I had even met some guy down there, you know, that was teaching me the 'ho stroll down there, the 'ho stroll, the strip. It was almost like I had totally forgotten that I had came here with somebody because I start having fun and I was having a little money of my own.

I even started staying with them. It was only like two nights, and then one night I came out to come down and somebody just came up behind me and attacked me. I mean real viciously. And wouldn't you know, when I got myself together, I realized that it was him, and he was having a fit. I don't know . . . first I thought maybe because he didn't know where I was or because he didn't know what was happening. It was because he heard or what he thought or he didn't approve of what I was doing. First, I was real stupid because I figured he was right, so I took and gave him all my money, like a fool. Thinking I'm doing the right thing.

We left and we came back to Jefferson. And we took and moved right back in with his sister. I got all my stuff together, all my paperwork, and I went and applied for welfare. I didn't know Joey was using drugs then. It was about two weeks after we had got back from Atlantic City, and I had gave like his sister some money and he had got mad. He had took like the rest of the money that I had had and he was gone like two or three days and his sister took and told me that she was glad that I gave him some of this money. And she waited like a day or two 'cause he didn't come home that first night, before she told me. She took and said, "Joey out there with Hipster." Which was his cousin. I was, "Yeah, they're probably running around doing all kinds of things." You know, really things that were total bland, and she was, "And you gave him all that money." I said, "Yeah." She was like, "Okay, you know when he come back, he would barely gonna have any of it 'cause you know what he's out there doing." I didn't know Joey was a drug addict. He used drugs intravenously. I didn't know about this. She was telling me what not to do, because if you do this, you give him money for this and he does this. She's making it sound like I'm really stupid. That's when we started having conflicts.

Other than that, me and Joey used to get along perfect until other people started getting in our affairs. Then Joey figured the best thing for us to do was to move. We stayed there all that summer and September the fourth we moved into this rooming house at Nineteenth and Sussex and that's when the only thing we had going for ourselves was my check and his check. He got to the point where, you know, to me it always seem like he was always tired. It seem like he was always sleepy. So I would like take these opportunities, like run up to Ginger's, you know. Then maybe might be gone . . . maybe like come home two, three o'clock that morning. Joey would practically be in the same position or didn't even know how long I was gone. So I kind of like used this to my advantage. "Oh, he don't know what . . ." you know.

When I was with Ginger that's when I was running. Me and Ginger were smoking marijuana, and we were running around with guys before I knew Joey. This was a sexual thing and I was being paid to have sex with them. I called myself putting up a stash, which Joey was finding, and that's how he was staying high so much in between his check period other than taking our rent and food money. I wasn't even aware until I went to go find something. Anyway, something came up, thinking it was the Halloween Ball. I went to go get my money so I could go and buy all the things that I wanted—you know, so I could really look nice for this Ball—and I had something like twenty dollars in the pocket in the closet that I was keeping my money in. Not knowing that he was going through my clothes, you know. Like he knew about it. We had really started going through it then, and it was from then on that me and Joey started having really brutal fights and arguments. So, for the Ball, I had to go back into the stores again and start lifting clothes and stuff just so I could go to the Ball.

I met Joey when I was eighteen, and I stayed with him all the way when I was twenty-one. The abuse started from the second year. I couldn't even remember all the times I was injured in that relationship. Every time I turned around I was abused for something. My mother was to the point where she hated him. I wasn't fighting back at first. It wasn't until I became so afraid . . . I mean he had messed me up so much. Every time you turn around I was bandaging. It took all that before I actually started fighting back. Because I was afraid that he might, this time, if he started attacking me, he might really hurt me again. It was then that it seemed when I started fighting back, our fights got worse.

The physical abuse made it easier for me to say yes to drugs. Alright, my mother couldn't accept that I was beaten so many times. One time I left him and I came home to my mother's house, and she wouldn't let him in, but then I opened the door and let him in. And then I left with him, and she took and told me not to come back, and so I realized that I didn't have no support there. Then even after that when we would have fights and stuff, I would use the drugs as an excuse.

The fight with the wine bottle was the most serious fight I had with him. He attacked me. I think he had . . . I don't know what we were fighting about, but I can remember the actual fight because when I went to go hit him, I grabbed a wine bottle to pick it up. And he turned around just in time, that when I threw it up, he turned around real quick to catch it and threw my hand into the wall, and the bottle broke and it all just came down, sticking all in my hand. I realized then, this had to be it, you know. This all got to stop.

I still was with him, like maybe three, four months after that. My feelings for him had really like started taking a turn. And then, as I got myself together . . . still realized I had friends that were still interested in me, and I could get away from him. He realized that too, and things even started getting even worse. Every time you turn around, we were fighting over not even seeing each other. Like Barry would come and see me, and I would tell him about it. Barry was my cousin, so he knew I wasn't lying because he knew like the majority of my family, my intimate family anyway. We were like fight over that. By now, if he was to hit me, I was hitting him back, you know. It seem like every time you turn around, we were fighting about something.

After the fights, it seem like we would turn into lovers. I don't know, and then I guess after he would do his little, his little drugs and stuff. But he would try to make up all the time. Like sometimes I would say, like, "Well, I did make you mad." Like I would start like I was really at fault. He had that way of really making me feel guilty.

I stayed through this abuse because I didn't want. . . . His sister was like the first influence of like to get away from Joey would be the best thing. I was determined to prove that I could . . . that this thing would work, you know. Even after family relations even felt that it wasn't going to work. Even some of my friends would see us would say, "No, that ain't for you. Get away from it." I was determined to prove that this would work. It took abuse before I finally realized, "Well, they are right." You know. It's time to bail out, and then, when I wanted to bail out, Joey almost made it almost impossible. He was chasing me around town. He wanted to attack me on the spot. I had to actually get another boyfriend to keep this man away from me. Somebody I had no interest in at all, just because I knew they could handle him, you know. Plus I knew he was a regular at the club and he was a nice guy, and I let him know I got a problem. He'll help me get rid of it.

Our relationship ended after we finally lost the apartment on Seventeenth and Spring, when we both went our separate ways. Then he wasn't allowed at my mother's house. I wouldn't be in places where I knew he would frequent, where he could run up, you know, and see me and so forth. Plus it was like in the wintertime, so it was a little easier then.

We lost the apartment because Joey wasn't paying none of our bills. First, the electric went. One thing at a time. You know, he was having any kind of Tom, Dick, and Harry could come there. He would allow any of them to come and use the apartment for drugs or sexual affairs. And our landlord wasn't going for all that. Then every time you turned around . . . the majority of the times, we were fighting ourselves, then it even got to a point where somebody was up there fighting with a trick or something. The place started getting abuse. "Y'all have to roll!"

After I left Joey I went back home with my mother. My sister Shirley just had a baby. My baby sister, Lisa, was pregnant. Mommy was really glad to have all of us home. My sister Jane, the oldest one, she was home. A lot of us were home that year, and we had a lot of kids, lots of nieces and nephews, and it was real thrilling. It was almost like a Christmas that she had always wanted. I was really depressed up, because I was like the only one without a boyfriend or without a baby's father or whatever. You know, everybody had something going, but I had Mommy, my mother, and I had my father there too. I played a big part in the children's life then too. 'Cause they all trying to get to know me too. But then Stud Angie still lived across the street. This was before her and her mother moved. So then I spent most of my day across . . . and we had started getting into acid and that's when I was snorting cocaine. I was really into getting high then.

I didn't stay at home too long, because I gotten back into another show, well, one with Kitty Lonique. I met Miss Kitty at our show, at our cabaret. She was given a free ticket to come by this guy who called hisself being our manager. She was given a free ticket to come and see us, because Miss Kitty worked with the Solid Gold and Miss Kitty had a lot of connections in Jersey anyway. Right after that show, things picked up real fast. 'Fore you know it, we had flyers going out. Meeting Miss Kitty was one of the better things that happened to our group.

Miss Kitty worked with the Solid Gold Revue. This was a bunch of professional drag queens. They had traveled a lot of places. They were real known. They have an album out and everything. They did things live, they didn't do things like off the record and stuff like that. So this was a big opportunity for me, Marissa, Clarice, Sissy, Bev. Who else was with us? Sherri traveled with us, but she didn't do anything. Miss Tiffany, . . . Josie, calls himself Cotie now, and Celia. This was a big . . . customer with a whole lot more money. Our little entourage ourselves, I think we had like say about five hundred dollars between ourselves per night and working with Miss Kitty. So we were really making. . . .

We started out with this guy named Ed who thought he knew what he was doing. We did a show at a cabaret. That was the show where Miss Kitty was supposed to have seen, right. She did show up, and we all did our little performance. I did this song called "The Devil Is a Liar." I performed on stage in this little red costume. Well, Miss Kitty was up for that because it was real comical and the audience really liked it. So she definitely wanted me. She liked the LaBelle act, which consisted of Clarice, LaTanya, and Marissa. Of course she always like Tiffany. Tiffany did this thing by Milly Jackson. By this time we were a lot more advanced with show business, our little drag shows. We knew how to dress. We knew what we wanted. We knew what we wanted to present. It wasn't like we were told to do it, like it was when we worked for Chappy's. You know, this was on you. You did that, you know, "Go out there, kill 'em." Now we were doing exactly what we wanted to do, and we worked for Miss Kitty for about two years. And it was a lot fun with

Miss Kitty. The only thing with Miss Kitty was that Miss Kitty was an alcoholic. A lot of times we stayed drunk. It was a lot of drugs and sex around us. We always had money then to get drugs and we used to shoplift a lot then over at Concord Mall—not at Concord, but Cleveland Mall in Somerset County.

So I worked with Miss Kitty for two years. I was twenty-four years old because me and Sharon got the apartment. I was going on twenty-four when I started going with Monique. Miss Kitty was paying us well. Me and Clarice, one of the other members of the group, she was in the LaBelle act, we had got us an apartment off Thirty-eighth and Main. Clarice got busted in Blair's because she had got caught stealing this dress, and then when the security guard tried to stop her, she hit him. And she hurt him! Other than that they just would have beat her ass and then just locked her up. This man pressed charges for being attacked too. So Clarice had to do a year and half or so. Plus she like was having a probation problem. So I'm saying then I was stuck there at the apartment by myself. But I still had like group members. Marissa staying with me a lot, and Anita used to shoot meth and that when we . . . I started using the needle then with Anita. We were shooting meth together. I'll come back to that.

I was going with this guy named Butch. He used to stay in and out of jail so much that it left me a lot of free time, and then hustling was real good too. I would be in and out of Club Christine, where all you would have to do is sit in the bar and johns would walk up on you. I would, you know, always want bigger drugs, which means that made my hustle a little harder. Whereas I wouldn't start dealing, I would start clipping them, leaving them in hotel rooms, taking their wallets, trying to use their credit cards. A lot of time I did do these things and like I was lucky that I never got caught trying to do anything or I never got caught going into one of their pockets. Although I have had some scenes where once they realized that, you know, but something had happened and I was gone. So there have been times like when they came after me. But I've always managed to escape from them. I was never caught. Then I guess slightly after that, I realized that I couldn't always sit in the bar, because one of these guys might run up on me. So I started hanging out with Miss Clarice and them, and Dawn, and North Jefferson girls, and they were all big shoplifters. Plus they all had big customers. And they would drive around like to different malls, like to Cleveland. We ride out to Cumberland County. We would go to a lot of different places.

You know, we had a bad scene at Blair's one time, that time Clarice got caught, and she hit the security guard. But by me personally carrying the package, it was best that I walked on out with what I had instead of trying to go back to help. It was scenes like that, after I seen what they had done to her, this kind of made me leery of going into the stores.

They had beat her up something terrible because when she tried to pull away from them, they got rougher and then she got nasty and then one thing led to another and before you know it they had drugged her on off, which gave a few of the others leeway to get on out the door. And then I felt a little guilty, because she was my roommate at the time, about not standing there beside her, but then what was the use in both of us going to jail? So then after she went to jail—she had gotten really high bail—I done slowed down a lot then too. I started having more time on my hands. Plus my boyfriend was in jail. I used small excuses like this. . . . Then my mother was mad at me. Which really hurt. . . . I mean these were things that made it really easier—you know, like who cares, you know—for me to use drugs. I got quite involved in them, and the more drugs you got involved in, the more you schemes and plots and plans.

I was like a totally different person compared to my childhood. The person I am now, I think I'm kind of a little better—I think converted a little back to my roots—to the person that I had turned into because those drugs. Then it got to a point where I would get high and knew that I couldn't be able to have money to have another bag of meth. And right after I would get high off of that, I would get evil to the point where getting high gave me an attitude. Because it wasn't like I had it before when I had money to keep on getting high. And then the fear I was putting in myself scheming, plotting. I was scared to go out to turn tricks sometimes because I was afraid that somebody would come in and see me, somebody I had clipped. I was afraid to go into the stores to shoplift because they might recognize me. I mean all this kind of stuff was starting to come out now. You know, you were hearing about surveillance cameras. You were hearing about decoys walking around the store looking like shoplifters. You know, you heard about under-cover policemen and stuff.

While I was living with Miss Kitty. . . . When we were in Jefferson, I was still living with my sister, okay. She was living in South Jefferson, and my girlfriend Clarice, the same one we got the apartment with. Then our other girlfriend, Sissy, had an apartment on Wicomico Avenue. So I was either at my sister's or my mother's or like if we had . . . our group was coming back in Jefferson and probably going back to Somerset County within the next two days or so, it would be a possibility where we just might stay at Sissy's because she was with our group too. So we would come there and maybe like rest up and do some shopping or something or maybe come back to Jefferson to get high. We didn't have a lot of connection over there in Somerset County when it came to drugs and stuff. Plus we needed Anita and you know other connections for our drug use or our reefer. I'm not going to say we didn't get high. We got high. But I'm saying we weren't so apt to getting high as much as we were insisting on having some reefer or sitting up in a doctor's office because I had to have my Valium. The Valium is what really started me off into this smoking scene. I just got into smoking a year ago.

By this time me and Clarice had had the apartment out Thirty-eighth Street. I stayed there for a whole year and then I moved from there . . . by Clarice being locked up and everything and wasn't handling that heavy rent by myself. Plus I had started going with this guy named Butch. Well, his name wasn't Butch, but I used to call him Butch. And we moved to Forty-fifth and Brookside. I was twenty-four then. I stayed there two years.

Well, he was a doozy! See, the majority of the time he was a clumsy old cocky old robber. I was hustling then. I was prostituting then at Club Christine then. He was a robber, and he was a junky too. It seem like that's all I met in my life was freaks, bums, and junkies. Joey wasn't a bum, but he was a junky that specialized in shoplifting. But then again, Joey would do anything that it took at the time. It all depended on what he needed.

My relationship with Butch was as abusive as the one with Joey.

Much more! Because he thought he was down with everything, you know. But he was . . . he had a lot of sex appeal about him, you know. And he used to swear to God that he was this macho type of guy although he did all kinds of other things in bed. He had like this complex about himself. He felt a little disrespected. It was maybe because of what you knew about him that he might have thought others knew about him. Like, that he would play a real macho manly part, but he wouldn't want to give off the impression that he would do the same thing in bed that I would do. He was just as passive as I was in bed, and he didn't want anyone to know that. So I'm saying, he was always on the edge, you know, he was always afraid that somebody would get him confused . . . like call him a sissy.

Joey on the other hand was very, very masculine, very, very dominant. Joey wasn't a flippy like Butch was. I would have never gotten involved in a relationship with Butch if I had known that he was that complex. And then see I had a lot of girlfriends around me a lot of time, and see he always thought he could like read between the lines of what they were saying. He had a hell of a complex! It's easier and simpler when you are in a relationship and you know who's doing what. Because see then he could identify with himself. By me being older, he always felt that I knew more and I was always trying to make him feel smaller. Or especially like in a public situation, like I was trying to make him feel dumb. He was very complex.

I was really attracted to his body, his physical. . . . He was good-looking anyway, but I liked the way he was built. I had no idea that he wanted to be sexually passive sometimes. It wasn't difficult for me until I realized the effect it had on him. You know what I mean? For awhile there I was thinking that I had the perfect thing going, you know.

The first couple of months we were like inseparable, you know. And then that was . . . like one time this guy, Nicky, brought me home one time. I knew him from Georgetown. I grew up with him. I was living at Forty-fifth and Brookside then. We drove up, and he was waiting outside the building and happened to see me in the car with a guy. I got out right in front of him. Lord, he accused me of doing all kinds of things with this man, right. I'm trying to tell him, "He's just a friend." First, I'm really giggling it off, you know, like, "This little fool is jealous." I was saying, "Naw, that's nobody. That's a friend, Nicky, from so and so." I mean, out of the blue, my God, he tried to murder me.

It was a lot more fights with him than with Joey. It was like a fight with him almost every other day. Oh, child, it was common. I always badgered by him. I took a lot of mental abuse from him too! I could calm him down more easily with a bottle of Thunderbird and a few . . . well, he like joint too, but he used to shoot these things called ritz and tees. They weren't that expensive to buy then. I could let him just go on with that and I might not have to see him two or three days. That got to the point where there was like a little relief.

My mother finally broke us up. My mother had gotten real, real sick. This was just before she died, and I had to go home. I was more than glad to go home, you know, because this was a relationship. I was really in love with this man. I really hated breaking up with him but it was for the best. Plus my mother . . . she was to the point where she would be needing a nurse and then I was nervous because of, you know, . . . wasn't but one of my sisters home and Jane worked at night. And then my nephews, they were pathetic. They were like, you know, running around selling drugs and so forth. Somebody had to be there to keep an eye on my mother. This was a way for me to get high too and not have to worry about paying rent. And I moved all my stuff out of my apartment into my sister's basement out Fifty-third and Green and I went on home to my mother, and I lived with her right up to when my mother died.

When she died, first, I stayed there at my mother's house. Then my father died. My mother died in July and my father in November and it was last year. My parents' deaths were very traumatic. Who's there for me now? Oh, do I give up here or what about me? I was very selfish. How dare them die! Especially my mother. And he really got nerve, you know. Then my mother's death took a toll on him. I'm still going through that.

Right after their deaths I started staying with my Aunt Jackie 'cause my mother left the house to Melody's Georgie. It did need like a little work on it here and there. So my Aunt Jackie, she was going to help to do it. I was staying with my Aunt Jackie for a little while. Then I came up here to North Jefferson and I'm stay with Keisha and that's where I'm living now. I've known Keisha, oh, ever since we were little girls. We were, you know, young little queens.

Like for gays, those who are using drugs are the hustlers. I would say the shoplifters, the prostitutes, the street runners, they're the drug users. I know drugs are a substitute for whatever they feel that they are missing moreso than just to use drugs and get high for the enjoyment. Then you find those that are just like regular junkies, they abuse drugs just to be abusing drugs. Sometimes you do drugs to get high, to enjoy yourself, to have fun, you know. Which means you don't have to do this every day, but when they do it every day, like that, then I feel they are doing it to replace something, to fulfill something or escape something, to run around. It's a reality maybe about themselves that they can't face, and they use it to forget. I used to think that was why, after my father was buried, I was drinking a lot then. I was drinking to forget. Then, you know, I said, well, fuck it because I'll never forget, and then I went back into smoking again.

I've used them all. From the marijuana to the cocaine to the heroin to the Valium to the regular old nicotine addiction of cigarettes. That's about it. Oh, to the crack. I stopped mainlining about two years ago. You know, this epidemic has gotten too out of hand. It's too scary now. It's bad enough doing one thing, but I don't want to double my chances. I already being sexually active out here for money, you know. And then the drugs too. I've lost three girlfriends already from AIDS. I can't afford to be losing no more. I even give condoms away. I used to carry four or five of them with me. A lot of them I have given away because I know that they are working and too lazy to even stop to get them. Not that they can't afford them, but, you know, just too . . . or don't think about getting them until it's too late.

My experience with the heroin was just that, an experience. That was with Joey because I think we had an argument one time and I was telling him that I knew about him and his dope. I think like he spent the last money on it or he either stole money from me or something and I was having a fit. By this time, see, I was fighting him back. So he was like, "What, Shontae? Come on here. Here, let me give you some." And he had shot some of that in me. I enjoyed it, and a couple of times I had did it with him, but then he kept . . . he kept gnawing into me after he give it to me, he be like, "This is the last time I'm gonna give you this. You can get hooked on this." He kept on telling me. And I would look at his arms and some of the other people and stuff, you know, known junkie, I could see my mother going off. She was so through with me being with Joey.

Valium was like my first addiction because I was taking the Valium and drinking when Club Christine was a big thing going on then. We were going to Club Christine and between the dance floor and the Valiums and a couple of cocktails, I was cool. I was good to go. I only would take two at a time. And I remember it only started with one. I would take, oh, about eight Valiums a day. Those were ten milligrams, the blue ones. The strong ones. So twenty milligrams at a pop, and eighty milligrams a day. It took me maybe about three weeks to get up to eighty milligrams though.

I remember like when Angie first gave them to me. Not Stud Angie, this was another Angie. She and my girlfriend Megan had came over to see me and Joey that one time, she had gave them to me. I knew them from Club Christine, and they seen him totally . . . like the whole time they were there . . . was trying to enjoy their company, but he was totally unstable, totally an animal. She took and told me, "That dude . . . best that you get away from that man. But here, here is something that would keep your nerves calm." And she gave me these little blue pills. My nerves were shot, and I had only took one, 'cause I didn't know what this was, but I liked it, you know. And then the next time or so . . . I think later on that night, 'cause you know the effect from Valium doesn't last very long—but it hung in there on me 'cause it was like my first time— I say about eight o'clock that night I took another one and I think that one like put me to sleep. And then like I got started the next day . . . you know, my regular routine. Wasn't even thinking about them. I think maybe I even like left them alone for a couple of days. I think like maybe me and Joey had an argument or something like that and seeing that I was upset, I took one of these pills again and, you know, it calmed me down like right away. It seem like that's the point where like every time I got upset, I would go and do one of these pills. And I think then it started talking with my other girlfriends, and then even Angie then too was telling me I like them pills! She was like, "Child, your doctor will give them to you." And then you start hearing the stories that they would tell you. "Child, I took me two, honey, and had me my drinks and. . . . Shit, I was fucked up." Then before you know it I got into wanting to get fucked up, you know. It started like that. Joey got sort of sweet then about it. I would tell him like instead of buying a six pack of beer, because at first I didn't drink that much beer. I was such a good little girl when I was first going with him. I wanted to be the perfect little housewife, and that's the kind of shit he like. Now see that's the kind of stuff that stopped happening as our relationship progressed. "Like you don't do this, you don't do that. What the fuck wrong with you?"

Once we got to the clubs . . . my drink then was Champale and grenadine. This guy Butch I was messing with at Russell's Lounge, he started me on sloe gin and milk, you know. And sloe gin and milk and two Valiums, oooh! Honey, that was a shot! And that was cool. Well, Joey, he was wino. He like wine, but then . . . I would say like I wanted a case of beer, then he would be like, "Well, solid!" You know, but that make more sense. Like okay, on our check days or something . . . like I got my check first, then he would get his like the day behind me or the next day, and that would be solid. He would get like a half-ounce of joint and he didn't even smoke joint. This was when he was a sweetheart. These would be the kinds of things he would do for you. He gave me reason not to run the streets, you know.

See, a joint high then was more of a party high anyway. Because if you smoked joint, you get the giggles, you know. You be feeling good about yourself. So to smoke a joint by myself, see that it would be alright while I was watching television. I mean because "The Jeffersons" would be funny. You know, things like that. Then to smoke joint with Joey, you know, once we got home, that was easy 'cause then they would give you the munchies, so then I would want to cook, you know. So I'm saying things like that kept us on the level. And then as our fights and stuff would go on, then I didn't have no joint, and then my nerves would be shot. Angie seen me one time and seen how my nerves were haywire. "Here, take these." I think she gave me like about six of them. No, it was ten of them. She said, "You take these." I guess automatically she thought I was gonna start taking two. And she said, "You'll be alright." She said, "Child, 'cause you're gonna have to get away from him." Then once I had me a Valium, Joey could do what the fuck he wanted to do. Yeah. Go on!

So I started doing Valium, and then it was the methamphetamine. We were speeding a lot then. I started that hanging around Anita, my girlfriend Anita. This is one of the ones I used to work with. She was shooting stuff and it just looked so exciting to me then, you know. I was going with Butch then, and I think he was like in jail then at the time. And I had Anita staying with me. I called myself reading her. Start telling her that she should stop that shit. And she was, "You never tried it, Miss Shontae?" And I was, "No!" "Well, you should try it," you know. And then the experience of just the needle going in your arm and seeing the blood and then the effect. And then before you know it, I was running around my house cleaning up everything.

They had big thick veins. No kind of missing nothing. They be sitting up and she wouldn't even have to tie up. I would be so jealous when we be up Fifteenth Street, you know, hitting, getting my little shot, and she would have no problem. It would be a half-hour working on my little arm. You know, trying to find a vein. Now, that's what helped me stop too. All that poking and poking and still nothing happening. That also helped me to stop real quick. You know, I always had to have somebody with me. I got to the point where I knew I could do it by myself, but it was . . . but my nerves would go haywire with the idea of me sticking myself, you know.

It took me about six months to shoot myself 'cause see you got to a point where, alright, you were getting high with people who were also getting high. See, the less you know about it and the more they know, the less you get out of it. So I had to learn how to hit myself because first of all they would load your works up and they were thinking, "Well, you don't need this much because apparently you don't know what you're doing 'cause you can't hit yourself." You know, they aren't taking responsibility of you doing too much, you know.

My use increased once I learned because I could do more. The more I did the more I could do. Whereas I started out with like a half a dime bag, within a year's time I could do a whole dime bag. Where I might break down in shots, like maybe half here and then do the other half like within fifteen or twenty minutes. I had to learn because people were messing me up. You know, somebody would call theyself hitting you and before you know it your arm is all swollen up because they didn't know what they were doing or they pushed it in too fast. That's what messes you up. That's what got me into doing myself. And then, the frustrating people when they can't get you and it's blowing their high trying to get you. The frustration and the attitude.

When I was using IV there was a lot of needle sharing with groups and stuff. There was a lot of that. And see then where I was down on Dover Avenue, down on Fifteenth and Dover, you could always buy needles. You know, they had—Dean and Tamara—they had supplies of things like that. So if you didn't have one yourself and somebody just finished with one, you would go 'head and rinse it out and use that needle too. AIDS was just started to get popular. It was still like in magazine articles and stuff. Hadn't like . . . you hadn't start hearing about the deaths and stuff just yet. But it was after I had stopped though, I had started hearing more and more about it.

Oh, I loved meth when I first started. Plus it was the circle that I was in this time. Get high off some speed, I mean I really loved it! I mean, we would wake up, instead of wanting to know what was for breakfast, she wanted to know whether or not who had the works or if you still had yours. I've seen times when I went tearing up drawers trying to find some works I had hidden, you know, because I knew I had them, and this would be more important to me than a cup of coffee in the morning.

I stayed on meth for awhile, at the most a four-year span. After that period, well, I'd gotten back into Eleventh Street then. Me and Bianca. . . . When Somora and I was living together. You might have heard about Somora Jackson. She was the one, her and Sidney, they were taken here from Jefferson and their bodies were found out in Plymouth somewhere or somewhere in Washington County somewhere where they were shot and chopped up and burned up. Somora was one of my roommates. Me, Somora, and Bianca was a barmaid at the Night Works then. That was a bar at Eleventh and Main. Now, this has been like a good four years ago. Somora got killed in '87. Yeah, a good four years ago. So we were still dipping and dabbing in and out meth every now and then.

But see I went on and established myself on welfare. You know, we like had backup money. You know, like to keep our rent paid, and then we just hung in the bar and occasionally go out with our john and stuff. I was living at Nineteenth and Roberts and at Sixteenth and Hubbard was where Miss Cyd was selling meth. Alright, right up the street from her, Miss B.K. was selling reefer. So it got smooth for awhile. All you had to do was get your money and run around the corner and then right on back home. So we had like a little get high little feast. There was a lot of harmony there. If I didn't have it, Somora had. If Somora didn't have it, I had. Bianca was always a sure thing because she was a barmaid. She would come home with her little tip money and if she didn't get high that night, she would like loan you money, you know. Something like I was the only lifter there then. And we had another roommate, Darvey, he stayed in the front. He just recently died last year of the virus, AIDS. He was a good seamstress though. I could steal like sewing equipment or something for Darvey and either use it as a deduction out of my rent or either money in the bank. If he couldn't give it to me right then and there, soon as he would make something for somebody and get paid, he would give me, you know, my little ten or twenty dollars or whatever was going on at the time. Actually, we weren't having no financial problems there other than our little once and awhile shoplifting sprees or going down to the bar and running into a date. Then see, 'cause we had a phone and everything, so some of our dates were like regulars. You know, just call us up, find out if you're going to be home at so and so. It was plentiful because it was three of us there. One girl wasn't there, there was always somebody there. Or then Bianca worked in the bar so she could always call you up and tell you that so and so is down here. Things were running pretty kosher for us then. We had no problem getting to our drugs.

I was still on the meth. All of us were then. But then Somora started doing ritz and tee. She started going with this little boy named Alex. And it was such a cheap high and he was . . . I don't know, we started losing contact with her when she started dealing with him because we weren't that crazy about him. But we tried not to disrespect him. Although there were times things would get out of hand. And somebody would just have to voice their opinion.

I had gotten involved with Curt too, this guy Curt. So that's how me and Somora started getting closer because my boyfriend and her boyfriend were hanging out. So as soon as we would get rid of them, we would go out on our little sprees and we were doing drugs.

I would have been with Somora that night, but I took and told Somora . . . 'cause we had two bars we were going to then. She was hanging out with another ritz and tees named Dolly. 'Cause I had left the house that night with Bianca and went straight down the bar with Bianca. And Somora finally came down, must been about one o'clock she came in the bar. And she waved and she said that she was going down the street to Rose Gardenia's. That was the last time I seen her. I took and told her, "Okay, but I'll be down there." I wished I had pursued calling her. Maybe if I had stopped her there, she wouldn't have ended up where she ended. I felt a little guilty about that too, and somehow or another I took it . . I made it my fault that I didn't stop her. But then she went down there and from there . . . Somora didn't come home that night. But it was getting close to the Fourth of July holiday. Somora always liked going over her mother's house for the pool. You know, the show-off bit. Either get her mother's car and come over and pick us up and then take us back over. Well, Somora didn't show up, but she usually makes all these plans like a day or so before. By the third we hadn't heard from Somora. Somora been gone since the first, since the thirty-first was really that night. And I hadn't heard since the thirtieth of June. We hadn't heard from Somora, and Somora hadn't been home. So then we decided to call on over to her mother's house. Her mother said that she hadn't seen her. Then all of a sudden this thing came up about the Candlebrook Park. That's this park out in Washington County somewhere where they found these bodies. We called up and reported our girlfriends missing, and then that's when they started putting those case . . . you know, from the missing girls here, we were missing in Jefferson. But none . . . none of us bother to pinpoint Sidney until we got in town. And Lisa and them were saying, "Somora went with Sidney that night in a car." Sidney had rolled around the corner and had said . . . the guys that she was with, that they got money.

Alright, well, I know Somora is famous for sticking her fingers down in somebody's pocket. She was a major clip artist. I remember one night I walked into Somora and she took and told me, "Miss Shontae, don't even bother to go back there to your room. Wait for me to put my shoes on. We're going around Miss Cyd's. Here's a hundred for you, Miss Shontae. Here, I clipped him of eight hundred dollars." She had eight one hundred dollar bills. She gave me one of them. I was, "Lord, have mercy!" She was my best girlfriend. She just used to get it like that. I wish I had like a little tape of what really went on out there that night with them, to actually know what really happened. But I know both them. Nine to one, one of those men caught them going in their pocket or they stole from them and they couldn't get away from them and drove off with them. I know Somora too, she wouldn't have went that far out of the city, you know, just to turn a trick. So they had . . . they had to either been hurt here, while they were here in Jefferson, and then taken out there and dropped.

That was one of the worst things that ever happened to us. Everybody was quite upset. Everybody was quite mystified. Everybody was scared to go out and turn a date and everything for a little while. Because of these maniacs. We just developed this little group called "Heart" because of Somora and Sidney. We were taking donations, and shortly after that, that I had gotten in a fight with the guy that I was living with where he broke my jaw. So I was like laid up in the hospital for a long time when the group was getting started. And then shortly after I got out, there was very little unity. It was scraps here and there, separate groups, conservative group, drag group, but at one time everybody was willing to bring everything together. At first they went into it wholeheartedly, because they were really feeling the bitterness of this tragedy. It was helping everyone to appreciate real togetherness— "Heart." More like a support group, but it just, you know, fell apart before you know it. The meetings got more distant. Instead of every week, like we wanted, they were coming every two weeks. Our membership start coming apart, you know, you go to one meeting and you might have twelve people and you come back the next time, it might only be seven people. You come back again might only be you and two other girls.

Well, I really stopped using methamphetamines after Somora's death. I stopped because after I had went through this thing in the hospital the doctor had took and told me that they couldn't operate on me right away because my body was so broken down from needing things like potassium. I had like three or four days just to be pumped up on all types of health fluids so that I could be just operated on. It had put a lot of scare in me. And then I was scared to death because I wanted to be tested, but I wanted to . . . I didn't know whether or not I wanted to know or anything. But then I was tested anyway. So that wasn't a problem with me. I was tested for HIV, but I didn't have no HIV problems. Everything there came up negative. Thing about it was that I barely had any blood at all. It was like iron poor, no blood at all, and then all the blood I had lost from the actual operation.

After the methamphetamines I was still smoking reefer, and maybe I might have dibbled and dabbled with it once in a blue. Or maybe like I might have been out and ran into somebody like Brandy, Sharon, or one of the girls out in East Jefferson. I might even, you know, had a little special occasion. Just myself. Let me run over to so and so and get high, you know. It was like that, but it wasn't a daily thing then. See, I did drugs so in between then that once I got high, I'd be high for awhile. I wouldn't have to go right back to needing another shot. And then after that high was worn off, I had something to do, you know, to take my mind off of drugs, anyway. I always stayed busy.

Then the cocaine came in. I started smoking. I was over my sister's. My mother was still living then, and that was the thing with the pipe. 'Cause my sister, her husband James had gotten her into it too. Smoking, it was the fascination with it. Watching this smoke come all up in a glass bowl, you know. But really, we were still marijuana heads and Colt 45 girls, me and my sister. It took awhile before we really got involved in smoking, you know the cocaine. But we did enjoy it. I was twenty-five the first time I used it for the first time, and then it was like a year later before I used it again.

So that first time I did it with my sister. Her boyfriend was a dealer. He had like a lot of marijuana connections from New York, because my sister used to buy big then, because she distributed it too. They were into drug sells. He was already into smoking it and stuff. My sister wasn't and it wasn't until they started going together. My sister kept it very quiet herself. And one night I came in late and they were sitting downstairs and I seen that thing on the table. I was, "Lord, have mercy. I have never tried it." She said, "Shut up. Here." She thought like I knew what I was doing. Which I didn't, and we sat there and before you know it the sun had rose. We had a cute session that night. Now, the next night when we did it, my niece and stuff were over because she couldn't do nothing while they were there. And they had left, and then we were getting high then. And I, you know, felt the effect from it, you know. The difference. I don't know, I was always slow get higher. I felt the difference and I was, "Oh, my heavens. I liked it."

After I was healing from my jaw being broken, I was going with Calvin then. After my wires and stuff came out, I was up at the Night Works, and this guy came in. He was a trick, and you know, I was turning him. And we got out to my house. I was living at Fifty-second and Corvier then. He had this little red bag, with a pipe in, his little cooker and everything, and he had cocaine. Well, we got high. He was flippies, but he was a trick. But we had a ball, and he had went to sleep, but I was still up sucking on this pipe and getting all involved in it. And I even ran around the corner and you could only buy bags then for twenty dollars. I ran around there and got me another bag. My girlfriend next door, she knew how to cook the stuff up. That morning when he jumped up, he had to fly out of there. Well, he flew out of there and left that little red bag. I think that when it started. 'Cause I had a pipe, a cooker, got me all the equipment. He has left me that little thing.

So I started using crack when this guy came and left his little bag, that little lovely fellow. The woman around the corner—I was unemployed then—she sold drugs and stuff. Well, her house was a mess! I mean, it was disgusting. Alright, I was a good domestic, and I came around one day to get some drugs for somebody or something and I talked with her. She took and offered me a hit, and by me having my own little pipe and everything, I really wanted to get in good with this woman 'cause she sold smack. She had nothing but white customers coming to her house. This was money! She sold cases of beer. This was nothing but money coming through here. She see me do like another little hit in the pipe, and she took and said, "Now, I'll never give you another hit again." This blew my mind. I felt this big. I was never so hurt in my life, because I wanted to be impressive here, you know.

She said that because I was doing everything all wrong. So she took and told me, she said, "The next time you get fifty, you come around here and I'll show you how to smoke." Alright, that was the first lesson of it. Letting me know that coke costs money, and what you're doing is throwing away money. That was why she said that. "You ain't doing nothing but throwing away money. You ain't gonna be throwing away my money."

Alright. Well, that night I came back with Victor with three hundred dollars. Victor is a guy I had met up at the Night Works. With the first fifty dollars, I learned how to cook. I learned how to smoke. So she taught me how do it. Plus and then I was hired by her. I did her whole downstairs one time in one afternoon and she gave me fifty dollars for it. She was highly impressed. She came downstairs and she thought she was in a different house, you know. Plus I was out to make an impression that time, and I got the job. And I worked for her, you know, on a regular basis. Every day I came around there, and that was fifty dollars. Twenty-five of it was automatically, I would, you know, buy drugs with it from her. Whereas and then with the other twenty-five, I would either like stash it towards my rent or sometimes I would end up running right back around there buying more drugs.

From the times I was working for her, which was only a couple of years ago up till now, I had never seen like these little vials coming in now, these little caps. Never seen nothing like that there and everybody there when we're getting high always used pipes. Now they just use little, you know, stem things.

Vera sold drugs. The lowest you could spend in Vera's house, and you had to be somebody close like me, would be twenty-five. But the majority of her customers were coming up from Hastings, East Conwall, some of them were out Southwest, you know, 'cause she sold heroin too. She didn't use needles but she supplied them. Like then you could rent one of her rooms to shoot your stuff up in.

I guess I had worked for Vera for about eight months, and this was like almost like routine where I did crack almost every day. That would have been '88. In '88 I realized that I was hooked. And I had started like the beginning of that year. Oh, see then there was no telling how much I was using. Considering the quarter I would do a day, and then in between what I was getting from other people, helping. I could never like really actually measure it out. I know for a fact that I was doing at least a quarter a day. So like after he left the pipe at my house it was like only about a week and a half before I was doing a quarter a day at Vera's house. And that was like after New Year's when he left a pipe at my house. I remember one time we had like eighteen caps all at one time.

In the beginning, I always had like either welfare checks coming or either had me good tricks lined up or whatever to support my habit or either I always kept me a husband. Which turned me into a conniver and a schemer because I couldn't always let him know what I was doing with their little money and stuff. Which would be some of me and Joey's fights sometimes.

When I first started using crack, see, you were cooking it yourself. We spend like maybe like about twenty maybe about forty dollars a day because I was just beginning. It only took maybe like about two weeks before I was spending up my whole check on it. By the time I started getting into caps, right off the top, I would say maybe about eight caps a day if I could afford them.

I get high, I get high to get high, to enjoy myself, to enjoy getting high off of drugs now. It's not like it's a necessity. There was once upon a time like during my Valium days when I felt I needed it. It allows me to cope. It helps in so many way. The most difficult thing in my life right now is worrying about the next day. What am I going to do tomorrow? Or feeling the guilt of not taking care of responsibilities. Knowing that I was supposed to do so and so and you know, and didn't do it because I did the drug instead of going to pay the electric bill or, you know, something like that.

For me the drugs and the hustling came together, you know. Because I always . . . well, actually I think the hustling came first because I already knew, you know, how to hustle. Yeah, I was turning tricks first. Because I liked being picked up. I liked running around. It was the rush. I can still feel it coming on, but what I hated about it was not being able to turn off like if you smoke a couple of joints and after awhile you go and eat some ice cream or something and lay down. You couldn't do that with the meth. I don't care how hard you try to sleep, you were not going to sleep. It took so long to wear off. As I got older and got more involved, you know, involved with it, I was finding out just as much that I didn't like about it—the kicking, you know, the pumping the blood back and forth.

I've exchanged sex for drugs. I've done that several times here recently.

It all depends on how many caps you want to buy me. Either I'll give you a little blow job or, you know, if you really want to lay up, then, that's twenty dollars or thirty dollars you may as well go 'head and give me, you know. I know that you have that many caps, you know. Five dollars apiece is just like giving me thirty dollars or forty dollars.

I'm usually not up until like the later hours of the day now. See, like now, like me and Christie, she lives in the house with me and Keisha, we'll do our little cleaning up and stuff from like dishes and stuff from yesterday, you know. We throw our little lunch and stuff together for our breakfast. And we'll be getting ready for our stories. Somebody run around the corner to grab our little snack, like little cookie. Grab our little snack, and then all we'll do is plot and planning. Start laying out our clothes and so forth of what we're going to wear tonight. Talk about how many yappies we gonna get tonight. We call a caps, yappies. Talk about how many yappies we're gonna get tonight, and what we're gonna do and then call it a night or . . . you know. We don't start getting high until like the later part of the day, like later part of the evening. You know, any time after nine in the evening.

Now, Keisha got a boyfriend, you know. So she's down there in her room, so she might go out ahead of us or something, or she might not go out at all. There is always somebody home. It might be a movie or something on, because I'm the television buff and I might be the last one to go out. Sometimes I might not get out until like maybe one and two o'clock, you know. And then if there a movie coming on after that, and only if I feel like, I might get up. And then there is days like I'm definitely gonna go out, like Friday, you know, Saturday. Like tonight is Friday, and I'll be out earlier tonight. I might be down there as early as eight o'clock, come in, and I might go back out, because I'm close enough to the house.

I usually go straight to Metro Center, downtown on Eleventh Street between Mill and Sussex, usually on Eleventh and Beaumont. I'll be working, baby. Well, now see if it's the weekends, I won't be down there too long before I be done turned me a couple of nice ones. What I be hoping to do is wanting to meet somebody who I'll take home with me and then hope they want yappies too and then that way I can spend their money instead of spending mine. By the time it's over with between me and them, I still got money if I want more yappies or I got money to get started the next day.

I stay out until you're ready to come in, you know what I mean. Sometimes, you might not get a date at all. Sometimes, you might be out there doing so well that you want to keep staying out, you know. There have been times when I've stayed out to like ten to twelve o'clock, and then there are times when I stayed out from nine o'clock to five o'clock. I mean I used to tell Butch . . . I used to tell him that I was going to work. I would tell him, "Look, honey. I work from nine to five, nine at night until five o'clock in the morning."

As for the price of a trick, we start it at twenty dollars. Sometimes, on a day like a weekday or something, like a Tuesday, Wednesday, Thursday, you might have to suck a little dick for, you know, maybe a ten dollar dick or so, you know. I'm saying 'cause the money ain't that flourishing or either it's just some cheap motherfucker and you just want to hurry up and get some money because you're totally broke. I usually start like . . . my lowest date level, like a night like tonight, I ain't starting, the lowest I'm going is twenty, and that might just only be my first one. That's just to hurry up and put twenty dollars in my pocket, and then I wants thirty dollars, then I wants forty dollars, and then you know. If the trick is right, you want to blow and lay, you can spend forty dollars or fifty dollars doing all this, a blow and a lay.

Fifty dollars is a cute price to get it for a night. I'm saying, you're in Jefferson, and with so many piping-ass bitches, what you want forty dollars and fifty dollars for, they can get for ten dollars sometimes for it. So I'm saying, you might have to scrinch down to forty dollars. You might even have to scrinch to thirty dollars, you know, for both. But that don't mean you have to give a good performance.

On an active night, I might be out on the stroll for about two hours, three hours at the most. In that amount of time you can make a cute little . . . you can make between sixty to one hundred dollars, which would be substantial. If things are going poppy right, you can make close to five hundred dollars, you know you're going to stay up late.

Eleventh and Beaumont is my favorite area, for me anyway. It's more of a known area for our type of girls, you know. When they're coming to Metro Center, you're good for spending thirty dollars, forty dollars. Out on High Street, they try to cheat you with their eight dollars bullshit. They're try that shit with you and they'll have hundreds in their pockets. Besides it's worse now that crack users are out there too. Where they would pay you twenty dollars, thirty dollars for it, they can go and get it for five now just 'cause this dizzy bitch on this corner down here wants a hit. I don't reduce my price.

Some of the people on the stroll are watching each other's back. That's that little unity there. Especially if the cops is hot, you know. Even if it's somebody you don't like. "Watch out girl, 'cause Maggie is hot!" That means cops. 'Cause you always got to cover each other's back as far as the cops is concerned. But it must be a lunatic or something out there and some girl might know and let somebody else get in his car, you know, something like that. But I'm saying, it the working relationship. If you're amongst some of the workers out there, you know, you'll get support.

Locating a trick is not a problem. You know, you don't have to do nothing special. I mean nine to one they're going to see you. They out there looking for it. So all you got to do is be available. A little smile helps and a decent approach helps. 'Cause see, everybody don't like you looking like a slut. You know what I mean? And that's where you have advantage over some of the girls out there, because they only hang out there with dresses up to here. And then sometimes you can't look too churchified, you know. Because they're gonna keep going right on past you because they don't know really what you're up to.

There are all kinds of gimmicks out there, you know, that work. You got guys out there looking especially for somebody like you, you know, or you just cruise on down the street yourself. You know standing all the time can be so obvious, you know—what you're standing there for? you know—and that can make you look cheap. 'Cause see, they can ride by and offer you anything that they want to offer you. You know, people find you. I mean you know what areas to be in and they'll come up on you. I mean they'll ask you what you want. It's not all the time they can give you what you want, so you might have to take what they can give you. More than likely I like to run into a regular. Somebody I've been out with before.

Nine to one if he pulls up on you, he knows what you're about. So I'll ask him if he's a cop. He has to identify theirselves. All of them don't though. But you would say something to him like, "You're dating?" "Spending twenty?" "Twenty for a blow?" "You want to go out?" "Hey, honey, what are you doing with yourself?" "Come here. Let me see that. I bet it's a big dick." "Come give me ten dollars, I'll play with it." So I'll get in his car, and we pull into a little spot that is convenient for you. I already have these places in mind. You know, you have your own little parking lots, little alleyways. Unless you luck up on somebody who's halfway decent and spending a decent amount of money and it's early enough to go to a hotel. 'Cause they loads up on the weekends real quick. If he's alright, then you take him home.

One guy, we went half a block one time before he told me he was a cop and the car behind me was his partner. It was a doozy! I remember one time I was just in this Mitsubishi wagon on Eleventh Street. And by the time we rode around to Tenth Street, the other guy pulled up. His partner was there. When they want you now, they'll get you.

Cops definitely don't want to be touched. They have their little ideas about whores and prostitutes. They think you're poison anyway. As soon as you go to touch them they pull away. "Okay, baby, let me out right here." This is prior. If you had already done quoted price and stuff like that, they're gonna try to insist on busting you anyway. But I'm saying, if you get in, you know, and you automatically went through, you know, "Now, how are you doing, baby?" Touching them, that gives you pretty much of an idea. "Honey, let me know." See, they can't prove that you're a prostitute.

I was never sentenced to jail, but I remember in '83, I sat in the jail from March to June twenty-third. They had me for burglary, larceny, and receiving stolen goods. And that wasn't none of it. I was in a gallery. The only thing that it was, was in the wrong place at the wrong time. I was in a shooting gallery down at Thirteenth and Clarke. I was a juvenile too. Oh, God! The cops came up there and I mean they just kept on coming. I had never seen so many cops in my life. Lord, have mercy. And all the people that was up there, honey, that was shooting up—Lord, have mercy—and was nowhere for them to run, honey, because it was on the third floor. I was up there in this little halter dress with all this hair coming down my back with this other old whore up there. She was so old! Oh, Lord, she was so old. And she was trying to tell me. She said, "We just tell them cops that we were up here just turning tricks." But she was right though. She said, "That will be the best for us, to get us off easy." Well, Lord, have mercy, they went to pulling the wood and everything out. They found somebody's credit cards and all kinds of stuff. Well, didn't they blame that shit on me. And I sat there for that whole . . . about a whole four months. They kept me locked up, and I was . . . the worst thing was that after they finally got me out of the police station I had to come right back to court the next day. Me and my mother went right back and then they transferred the case over to City Hall. I was the only juvenile and the rest of them were adults. And then we had to go back from City Hall to what they call a further hearing. Well, I ran away. I went out to East Jefferson. I was scared. I didn't go back to court. I ran away, and they came down looking for me. They had the bounty hunters looking for me. Well, when they locked me up, they took me to an adult prison 'cause sixteen was old enough. I was old enough then. They took me to the Falk Corrections Center. I had never been so humiliated in my life. Lord, have mercy, they had me in these handcuff all through a belt like I was really this . . . oh, my God, this outrageous criminal. It was absolutely horrible. And then, honey, took my clothes off in front of all these men just standing around gaping and gorking at you. Oh, making you feel like . . . oooh!

I had long hair, and they took it off me. Oh, it was a piece. They took it off me. Oh, it was awful. You hold your hand all up in the air, and they search you, and then they make you spread your cheek, and they looking all up in you. Then they send you to this doctor who just tosses you around like. What he calls an examination is moreso like being put through a spin dryer. Oh, God, it was horrible. Then they don't feed you for hours. To when they do feed you, the slop they throw at you, you're so hungry that you eat it anyway. Oh, God, it was the worst. It was the worst thing that ever happened to me in my life. And I don't take too kindly. All I ever did during my prostitution days, they would like arrest you, pick you up, right, write you up a citation, and they would hold you six or so hours or sending you home. Or either if you had a warrant or something on you they would hold you and then they would send you to the Police Headquarters, and then you wait to go upstairs to see the magistrate. Nine to one, the charge was simple little prostitution and they give you like ROR or nominal bail.

Jail was absolutely horrible! Well, what was good about it was as soon as I got in . . . they ask you all about yourself. When they found out that you're a homosexual and before you know they put you on the block with all the rest of the girls. Well, I was never so relieved to see a bunch of faggots in my life. All the horrible things you hear about jail when you're coming up, I just knew these people were going to be in here beating on me and just fucking at random and just doing what they wanted to do. And there were a couple of them that were just as young as me and Miss Courtney, Miss Brown, girls that I knew, Brenda, Miss Sarmie, that I had hung out here with on the street, and they were there too. And then it became like a little kiddy playground. Other than that the only thing upset you was being locked up at eleven o'clock. Not having you privileges of just wandering like you wanted to.

When I was younger I was in shooting galleries. I used to hang down at Fifteenth Street. They're not really much more different from crack houses. But they're a little different because you want to shoot your shot and it's not all about passing and sharing, you know. It seems like the cheaper the high, the more trouble you have.

Yeah, I've been in crack houses. Sometimes you can go in a crack house and have a nice time, and sometimes the only things you want to do is get up and get the hell out of there. For one little yappy, there might be four people who done put a dollar to it. And that one person who done put like a dollar and seventy-five wants the most, and you'll see a scrap over that. Something that small. And that can mess up everybody in there. I have been in one crack house where the cops came through, honey, and tore up everything. I mean, looking for the crack, and for everything they tore up, they never even found it. They did more destroying, but took everybody down and ran them through and they ended up letting them go. That's a hard one.

I've seen them fighting over such a small ridiculous, you know, hits. "She got more than me, or I got more. . . ." Oh, I remember one time when this girl got caught in the bathroom sucking this. . . . His wife was already there, but I guess they thought they could run in and get away with it real quick. I think like the phone rang or something and she wanted to call him for the phone. She wasn't even thinking that he was in there doing something. She pulled the door open on them, and there it was. So her husband got himself a little bit of head. 'Cause he was selling drugs too, and giving this other girl a cap for it. She went off, 'cause she was pregnant too. She tried to kill Vera. This wasn't the Vera I worked for, this was another little girl named Vera. She ain't had no money or something and she was trying to get a hit. The other girl wasn't pregnant, the wife was pregnant. Vera had just lost her baby. They had took her baby because she was on drugs. She was like recently out, she was maybe like three hours out of the hospital. Already there, you know, in somebody's house trying to get a hit.

I don't schitz. I guess my schitz is watching others schitz. Sitting there talking about what they're doing and why is they doing it. I guess that's my schitz. I get a kick out of watching them feel around and look for things when I know there's nothing there. I get simple when I smoke crack. I'm a giggler. I find everything funny, really. I'm a simple bitch. Especially when I get high. And I find everything funny and I become quite the conversationalist just like when I used to do speed. It was almost like I'm on "Oprah Winfrey." I would get talkative and joyful. Where somebody gets high and gets cranky, gets evil, gets attitudes, and I couldn't understand that. What was the purpose of getting high if you're going to get high just to get upset? You get high to feel good, you know, to change your attitude, you know, to make yourself feel good.

Now I don't get high every day. During the weekends, I'll get on. I'm beginning to feel like I'm really drying myself out. I start not smoking every day at the end of last year. Then I went through the summer, well, say the last of last summer, you know. I don't know why I started doing that. Just seeing some of the changes you be going through sometime just to try to get something. The older you get, the wiser you get. And you see some of the things aren't really worth it, you know. And you'll say, "Fuck it, because I'll get money tomorrow, and that way I can get high, right."

So my life has sort of slowed down, but it's flexible. I bounce back and forth, but I'm moreso in control now. I know how to adjust to slow myself down. I know what to say to myself, you know, to ease the burden some. I'm not going to say that I ain't gonna want no more. I know how to "Oh, well." Condition your mind to get involved into something else. To take your mind off of it so that you can . . . like pacify yourself with, "Oh, well, I'll get so and so tomorrow or by Tuesday." Plot on it that way. That way you can get things accomplished that ordinarily you would set aside just to get high. You know, work on it like that.

I didn't bother my parents too much with my drug use. I guess there were times maybe when I wished I hadn't called. I used to go and cry and call my mother up, and she would ask me what was wrong. I would tell her I don't know. I would be at my mother's every Friday, right, but by the time I would get down there, I would be totally drug free. The only thing my mother knew I did was smoke reefer.

There are things I wish I hadn't done to my friends. Just like the situation with Somora. Maybe if I hadn't been using drugs and, you know, I might have been able to speak moreso on her using drugs, you know. All of the money that was right there with us, that we threw away on drugs, maybe we could have put in something, and had a lot more going for ourselves now than just throwing it away on drugs. I have some regrets.

Like my boyfriend, Burney, was like one of the best men that I ever come across in my life. And it seem like as soon as I got a good man involved in my life, then there was drugs, you know. Even got him involved in it. He was a drug user and he had stopped using drugs. He was trying to go straight and I would like kind of encourage him back into using drugs. He was, you know, a peaceful person. Before you know it, him and I were having little scrapes and he's the one who busted my bottom jaw. I got this scar from that fight. He hit me in the side of my jaw. I didn't know it was broke, so I didn't immediately go to the hospital, which allowed a lot of poison to set in down here in my jaw. They had to cut me after they had set my jaw and wired it like six weeks later to go in and draw out all of this poison.

As far as the tricks, I only regret the tricks I turned that I let get away with murder. The ones . . . in my younger days . . . that was dogging me and only giving me five and ten when I should have been getting top dollar for the services I was performing but was too young and didn't realize, you know, didn't know the special "T" that I was performing was a top dollar specialty. But they were getting over on me. Those are the ones I regret. I only regret not working them, but other than that, a lot of my tricks, especially like once I got involved in Club Christine, a lot of them were, like, became regulars and stuff. Almost like became friends.

If turning trick wouldn't have been so easy, you know, then money wouldn't have came in so easy. And then I just said, "Oh, well, later for school and so forth." Because I could do this. If that didn't come along so easy, then maybe I would have been forced to maybe go along with some of the ideas of the more positive people. Because I'm saying the older you get, the rougher it gets out here. When you're coming along younger then, when all the opportunities are there at your feet, it was fucked up, because I could just go 'head and stand on this corner for five minutes and what you're working for all day long, I can get in five minute. I regret that I was living the fast life, thinking fast and being fast and not really caring. That affects you. Not really realizing what was happening to me. Sometimes you're thinking that these people are actually thinking something of you, but once the money exchange hands that's the whole story right there. I'm standing there stuck with twenty dollars and a promise that you'll be back. Knowing that sometimes maybe when you do come back, you don't even want me. You want my girlfriend. That takes a toll on one. You get mentally whipped a lot out there in the prostituting game.

Oh, I mean they rob you. They'll rape you. Yes, and these things have happened to me. I've been raped. I remember one time I was in a car with these two white boys. They drove all the way out past Ferry and Barnes somewhere and told me come on and get out of the car with them. "Leave your pocketbook in the car because we don't know if you're carrying a knife or anything." I'm thinking these two little young dumb white boys, and you know, I get on out the car, I guess to roll in the grass. Before I know it, one goes back to the car and the other just jumps on top of the car and they leave me all the way out here in this dusty field.

And gets my pocketbook snatched. And I'm stuck all the way out there. I'm so far the fuck out that when I finally get to a street, and it's so dark out there . . . when I finally get to a street . . . the cop cars, I don't even recognize them, such different colors. Then the one car that finally did pick me up and took me back to a subway area, the man wants me performing all kinds of things just for carfare. I had to do it. I didn't know where I was at. I did a Somora on him. I dipped into his pockets. I mean, I came with a hundred and something dollars, but I was still upset because my pocketbook was gone. It's gonna cost me just this much just to replace what I just lost. I had no regret like clipping him. And then I felt good about it because he gonna try to have me do all kind of things, he's gonna take advantage of the mere fact that I was out here all the way lost. He wanted to do all kind of sucking and nipplings, you know, screwing, you know. He knew I was a man. We got that together and then he really felt that all he had to do was to give me carfare, you know. He gave me that real quick. That's why I knew where his money was. So when I got out the van to get on the damn subway, all the way out at Ferry and Barnes, thank God, as soon as I got up there, the train was still just sitting there.

I remember one time Liz was in the car. We were younger then. This was a long time ago. We were all the way back around High and Beechwood. And I think we like got in these guys' car a block up from High and Wicomico and they were supposed to give us the money as soon as we got in the car. So then the one in the back, he's really the fast one, gonna hurry up and pull down his pants. But the one up in the front is the talker. Me and Liz finally come to the conclusion, "Well, if y'all ain't gonna give up the money, then fuck it. We'll just get out the car." He took and threw this knife right to Liz's neck and slashed it down the side of her face. And still took and told her that she better go 'head. "You don't want the same thing to happen to you, you get busy on my boy." Well, I had to threaten to bite the man's dick off. "If I put my face down here, I'm gonna bite this motherfucker off and y'all gonna just have to kill me." I was already frightened, and I felt that he was gonna do something to me any fucking way. He got me trapped back here. If he's gonna do something to me, I'm gonna fight my way out of here. And the other one, "Well, fuck that, man, let us out." I'm sitting up in Jefferson University's emergency room all that morning with my girlfriend Liz while they stitched up her face. She insisted that I stayed there with her while the doctor stitched up her face. I think that was one of the horrible experiences and it didn't even happen to me.

As for me, I think the worst was when I was up on Andover Heights Drive. Parked in like the lovers' leap section. I was so high and so outdone, I don't know really what went on. I was out there with this one-eyed guy. This is the one that pistol-whipped me and left me out there because I wouldn't perform the services before he gave me money first. First he tried to scare me with the gun, you know. He did scare me, but I tried to hold firm. All of a sudden before I know it he took the back of that gun and went upside my head. He was trying to put out an eye or something. He had beat me ungodly, with that gun, all across my head. It took me a good two weeks before I really healed up completely. I think that was one of the worst trick episodes I had. It's some rough shit happening to you out there.

And then when I was in Club Christine, some of the things I used to see up there like happening to people. Buddy and Walter Lee—he was the owner of the club—I seen him get killed right up Club Christine. Me and white Brandy, this little white drag queen. It wasn't too much action going on up at the club that night. It was like on a Monday or Tuesday night. We were up at the club, and Buddy—he worked there for years— he acts like he owns the club or something. The owner was up there that night, and these big black guys, look like a football team or something, had all went down into Club Christine. Me and Brandy had came upstairs and went over to D'Alonzo's and bought pizza. And we were sitting in there eating our pizza and we were giggling and taking our time. But as we were coming back across the street we seen these big guys all coming out of the club. And as we came down the steps—first you come down the first two, the first landing, and then you turn and go down—even before I turned to go down the landing I seen Buddy stretched out on the floor down there and he was bleeding from his head and as we came on down the rest, Walter Lee was laying over here and he was dead. They had killed him. They had beat him to death with their hands. By the time me and Brandy got down to the bottom of the steps, Buddy had jumped up, started slinging his hair like he was still wanna go and do something. And he went in the back and was saying something and then Vinny was standing over Walter Lee's body, kept saying, "Call the police, call the police." Me and Brandy was down there stunned, like shocked, like we didn't know what to do. So finally when the police got there, they were trying to ask us if we did see anything. So we just left it on Vinny and them, but we seen the guys coming out, but my God, we got to work these streets and stuff. We couldn't pinpoint nobody. I always felt a little guilty about that I just didn't say nothing.

I used to see people in Night Works, where Bianca worked. Honey, I see people in the bathroom, and see the bullies go in there and seen them come out where they done went in and robbed them, beat somebody and . . . some of them ain't even come out. Where you had to call the cops and stuff, which would make it hot on the bar for the rest of the month.

And then I remember being with Miss Illyana, coming around the corner, this is a girlfriend of my sister's and at the time I didn't even know her. We're up on Eleventh and Mill. This guy was messing around with these whores. This whore named Tracy. Tracy was a big whore 'cause she used to be right up there in the club with us sometimes. I just be in the bathroom. I just stood in the same mirror fixing my hair with this woman, smoked reefer with her and everything. But I always knew she was a dangerous-ass bitch, you know. She wasn't that crazy about queens anyway because they were like a threat on the block when it comes to turning tricks. But this other girl was down there arguing with the guy and the guy was also going with Tracy too, I guess. We looked across the street and we seen them arguing, and I kept hearing her call the other girl, "You, bitch, you." And before I knew, all I could see was this little silver thing, once they got together, when they started battling. All I could see was Tracy with this long . . . looked like a needle or something . . . but I guess it was a knife. The girl died. Right there on the spot. Stabbed that girl like several time in her gut and she fell, she went right out, and then the cops were looking. The next time I seen the *Herald*, they had Tracy's pictures right on the front of it.

I survive a lot of these tragedies by pretending . . . really, you know, you try to block them out. You try to forget them, but you don't really want to forget them because you always relate them to something else, you know. Like when you see something getting ready to happen, like almost a little déjà vu because you've seen something happen just like this before. And you knew the outcome of it. So either you get yourself out of it or you turn your back on it, if it's nothing you can do about it. If it's a situation that you think you can help, you offer advice but you don't enforce nothing. You don't try to stop it, because that's how it can happen to you.

When I look back on my life, I would say the significant turning points are deaths, drugs, and adulthood. I couldn't say, I did so and so because I grew up in a broken home or I was beat, you know. Whereas I hear . . . like some of the stories I hear, some of these people I'm almost inclined to believe that they had reasons for doing some of things that they did do. But actually, I think mine mainly came out of loneliness and being misunderstood. I was either trying to fit in or I was trying to escape, trying to run away. I was moreso escaping. I felt as if . . . what people were saying, what society was saying was what you're supposed to be like. I was made to really feel guilty, because of my upbringing, because I didn't follow life as some expected me to. Like going straight on to school into another school . . . being basically the all American guy. Like when I was at Lake Platt. Well, they recommended me to the JBA School, the Jenkins Beauty Academy. I didn't go through with that. I guess my own guilt feeling and really, I guess, caring about how some people looked at me, not all, just some, I think it helped me to use drugs. I think I started with it. It was the sense to belong because here was an atmosphere where I could try to feel totally comfortable and was actually recognized by some of these people.

It was the more they told me I couldn't or where it wasn't so acceptable. I think that's where transition came in. It was moreso where I had to prove to myself that I could, you know, and say "later" for what they think. That I'm gonna do it anyway. It was the fight of being me. Because I was doing what I wanted to do for me. That's what it was. Instead of trying to be like what they said I should be. I think that's where the whole separation came from. Whereas when drug use came in, it may have been a little easier because I had already, as far as they were concerned, I was already a failure. Whereas the drug use was a substitute to help make me feel important to myself, too. To help me fantasize more, I guess so. That's all they do.

*"Hey! It ain't all about bragging.
It's all about, you know, being
honest and that's that."*

China

Nothing really happened to me that was significant when I was growing up. I lived a normal life, okay. But I chose this life. I was given the tools. I just didn't use them.

I grew up in East Jefferson Heights. There was a lot of loud music and neighbors there when I was growing up, but there wasn't a drug or crime problem. Now it is! 'Cause this crack is taking over.

You know even when I moved away from home the neighborhood still looked the same. Everybody mind their own children, kept their houses up, whatever. My block always stayed clean, and was more like a fashion statement. It's like every week somebody was working on their house. Somebody had to have something new going into their house just about every month, something new. We not talking about grocery bags or bags from the shopping mall. I'm talking about something material, new, going into their house, and we was the same way.

My parents wasn't married. Both of them are still living but unfortunately they're not living together. My mother still lives in East Jefferson Heights, and my father lives in South Jefferson somewhere. I don't know exactly where he lives at now.

My father is forty-five or forty-six years old and he's a drug addict—a cocaine smoker. He's been a drug addict since I was the age of thirteen, and I'm twenty-three now. He was in and out of the house. The longest he ever stayed was a week, and he was just in and out of the house. He was always there on my mother's paydays though. So that was like every two weeks. In and out the house and . . . just didn't care. I would have little part-time jobs and I found him asking me for money, whatever. It was really hard.

There was a lot of problems—a lot of tension in the household when he was there. So I didn't really care if I ever seen him. I never really spent any time with my father. When he was there I was either out that door or sitting on the steps or whatever. I didn't want to listen to his shit. He didn't care. He didn't care. I felt kind of bad somewhat about not having a father around when I was growing up but then with the type of father he was I rather deal without. Because my mother was the father and mother.

My father played no real important role in my life. The guy my mother is marrying now I consider him as a father because he's good. He's good to her. He's good to us. You know, even though we all grown now, he still respect us and ask us how we're doing. It's not a time I don't call my mother's house today he don't ask me how I'm doing. You know, do I need anything. He don't have to do that. I'm not his child. You know what I'm saying? Today, I don't even know where my father is at—what he's doing right now. I don't even know if he's alive.

My mother is forty-four. I'm closer to her. I always wanted to follow in her footsteps and do the things she did and, you know, whatever. Seems as though she was always a role model for me. Even though she was my mother, we were friends also. I always felt like she was there. She really did care, period, the bottom line. And I'm very grateful to her for that today.

My mother taught me my basic values and what kind of person I should be, what I should and shouldn't do. She was the mother and father to all three of us. I know my mother loved me. Very much so. All of us, the same way. She didn't have any favorites. She loved us all the same.

So when I think of my parents I would like to be the kind of person my mother was. She was like a role model to me. She was happy with her job. You know how some parents bring their job home. She never did. I know she done had problems on her job. Okay. We always kept it good for her as far as the house being clean, and taking out trash and everything. So that wasn't no problem.

I wouldn't like to be the kind of person my father was because my father ain't shit. Now, I know that he was on drugs 'cause I done been through it and I see the symptoms that was in him. He was never there for me and it's kinda, it's kinda bad that I . . . I did follow his footsteps in a way. I used drugs. Okay. Like he did I smoked it. And that's one thing I didn't want to do or anything because he wasn't shit!

So the things that I learned most from growing up in my family were from my mother. I learned most of all to be a good person. To be honest, try to stay out of trouble, but then again I did get in a lot of trouble. I learned to be a clean person, stay healthy, stay in school. I did graduate. She wanted me to go to school after that but I didn't. That's when I met my friend.

She told me not to be naive either. When I was a child I can remember her talking to us like we were adults and I learned a lot from that because it wasn't where she was talking to little babies. She always said, "I don't have any more babies." Okay. And she didn't.

My mother didn't never have a lot of men around the house either. Twice I can remember her dating. . . . Well, the first time the guy she was dealing with, it didn't work out. But this last guy she dealt with she's engaged to him now. Matter of fact she's getting married to him this month. They've been going together for years. I was about eighteen years old when he moved in with her. So she never had a live-in lover when I was living with her.

But when my father was there, there were arguments. That's it. Never fights. Like I say, he never put his hands on her and I know that for sure. He never hitted us either because to him we wasn't really his children. Well, he didn't act like it. So it was never nothing violent.

There was no affection and stuff between them. No, not that I can remember. No. He always slept on the couch and okay, see, I was a child then, okay, but I wasn't slow either 'cause I always hung around an older crowd, but you never know what goes on behind closed doors, okay. I'm not going to say that they had a sexual relationship or not, but as far as I know they didn't, because I could see the arguments and stuff. How could you go to bed with a person like that? She just really felt sorry for him.

I wouldn't say my mother was a religious person, but she had a deep sense of what's right and what's wrong. She was always like that. I mean she went to church every now and then, but she wasn't really no church-going woman or whatever. She would drink occasionally, but she didn't do drugs. She was always at home and took care of the kids. And Grandmother was always there because she lived in the house with us. She helped out as far as food, babysitting, and things.

My mother was a very good housekeeper. But you know what? We really did most of the housekeeping because she would work and come in and by the time she come in from work the house was clean. There was a requirement in the household that I help out. I mean, I had to live there too, you know. It was just natural. I'll get up some mornings and just start cleaning, especially in the summertime, just start cleaning. Like I said, I love to clean and cook. I love doing housework.

My mother never really interfered and she wasn't strict at all. I mean, every mother got their little rules, whatever. Yes, I have got my butt beat many of times because it was me, I was hard-headed. But I wouldn't say she was strict. She gave me my freedom or whatever. I was allowed to have company in the house when I was fourteen. Most of my company was guys but I mean she didn't really say anything about it, but she was getting to think, you know. Everybody come over for me was guys or whatever. So when I told her when I was fifteen that I was gay, she already knew. She didn't disrespect me about that. It seems like it brought us closer than what we was.

But my mother would get mad if somebody else disciplined me, though. That happened once, come to think about it. A woman across the street and my mother aren't speaking today because of it. I got caught stealing an ice cream sandwich at the corner store. I'm on my way out the store. The Korean . . . you know them Koreans, they watch everything. So she was like, "Wait, wait, wait, wait." And it just so happened the woman was in the store at the same time and she found out. She slapped me and I ran out of the store and went and told my mother. I told my mother that Miss Catherine slapped me. She said,

"Why?" But I just kept crying and everything. She was upset. I told her Miss Catherine slapped me. "She slapped me because I got caught taking something out of the drugstore." We called it the drugstore. "I got caught taking something out of the drugstore that didn't belong to me and she slapped me." "No, she didn't." My mom went outside. Matter of fact, the woman was coming up the street. And I never forget it. My mother slapped her and told her this my child and Miss Catherine put her bags down like. . . . She always thought she was the bully of the block anyway. Like she was the shit. Well, that day my mother showed her who was the shit. She did not raise her hand back to my mother. My mother slapped her right in the face and that kind of fucked me. Oh, they went off. But to the day they don't speak to each other. To me she was more jealous of my mother than anything. But I got a beating for it after all that. I did get a beating for it and I end up going around taking it out of my allowance, out of my piggy bank. I had the money for it. I just took it just to be taking it, seeing if I can get away with it. Somebody ate the ice cream sandwich, but I didn't eat it.

So I got beaten like when I did something . . . like I said about the ice cream sandwich. If I hooky school or something and she found out. Not really dramatic, nothing. I was usually beaten with a belt. Sometimes with my clothes off. I was about . . . guess about thirteen maybe when I got my last beating. Well, she knocked me upside my head when I was eighteen, but that wasn't no beating. The worst beating I remember is when she took all my clothes off and beat me with one of the extension cords. I hooky school. I hooky school for a whole month. Me and my cousin Buffy. We hooked school for a whole month and it was near my birthday. Well, I got a birthday present. I was beaten with an extension cord. And I deserved it. Hookying school just to be doing it. Hanging with that fucked-up crowd. Just to be doing it. Young! I was about eleven.

When I hookied school I would just ride the subways. They had the old subways then. I was riding the subways, eating all day 'cause I think she used to give me four dollars for lunch money. I always had lunch money every day. So it was no problem. My mother had a good job and my grandmother helped. My mother key punches.

If I wasn't beaten she would talk to me. Yeah, she would punish me too. The longest I've ever been on punishment was about three weeks. And it was supposed to have been a couple of months, but she gave me a break, whatever. I don't remember what I did. I know it was three weeks. I think I stayed out late.

So she wasn't really strict, but she had her rules. Staying out of trouble, hang with the right crowd were important rules. Go to school. Stay in school, do the right thing. She always helped us with our homework. She didn't want none of her kids to smoke. Okay, or do drugs. Me and my twin sister we used to smoke joints a lot. And she stopped, I kept on going.

Like I said she was the mother and father. I mean she was always there. She was always there. And as a child and even as now I feel as though I'm a very lucky person because I can call my mother right now and tell her what's going on with me and my life which I'd do anyway, and I try not to ask for money that much, okay, 'cause I'm twenty-three years old now, I need to be making it on my own. But unfortunately I'm not. I'm a little down and I'm trying to recover off of drugs. But like I said, she's always there.

When I was growing up, I had one friend. I guess I could consider him as my best friend because we both came out of the darkness that we was in. We went to parties together and went to movies together. We did our homework together a couple times. He was intelligent. I mean I was smart, but he was smart. Okay, and he never gave me the answers. He helped me get the answers, okay, and that's what I liked about him.

So he was my first friend. I guess I was about twelve, maybe thirteen. We were in the sixth grade. Graduated together and everything. He sought me out because we dressed alike, we acted alike. He was always feminine. I was always feminine. We always dressed nice going to school, whatever. So we just combined it with each other, you know, started speaking. It seemed that we likeded the same things, you know. Even at lunchtime we would order the same things or whatever was similar. We would sit together and stuff like that.

I feel as though I brought his out. 'Cause I was always out there. I knew what I was, okay. I said something's wrong. Why is I looking at these guys like this, you know? Why is they coming around me? I seen myself feminine. The way I moved and talked and walked or whatever.

And I liked it. I really did. I was psyching it. I got so much attention. And somewhat I love a lot of attention. I liked it more back then than I do now. Okay, 'cause sometimes you get too much attention, okay. So I feel as though I brought his out.

Back then it seemed like the guys were always around us. Some girls would get jealous of that or whatever. A couple times I got into fights with girlfriends of mines 'cause they fought after their boyfriend or whatever. I'm not bragging anything now, but during my younger years I looked just like a girl, okay. I was always stand out like that. And a lot of times people mistaken me for a girl. Even today they do.

I didn't dress boyish or I didn't dress girlish, okay. I always dress casual. So it wasn't like I looked like a little boy going to school. But see I never had no problem with my mother out of that! Well, she always wanted my hair cut but as far as I dressed, no. 'Cause I always lookeded nice whatever I put on. I picked out my own clothes, always the newer fashions, you know.

I told my mother I was gay because I realized I was gay and I never hid it from her or whatever. She was upset, but she knew. I wasn't sexually active until I was eighteen but I told her at fifteen because I felt myself liking boys. Always wanted to be around boys all the time. And not just to play with them, just to be with them and whatever.

When I told my mother I was gay she cried. Told me that she knew, but I'm still her son. She loved me and whatever I be, be the best. She always told me that, even before I told her I was gay and after. She told all her kids that whatever you be, you be the best. Simple as that. Don't let nobody never knock you off your pedestal, whatever. So she didn't really take it as hard as I thought she would.

My sisters didn't take it hard at all either. They knew! I played with their stuff. I always played with their babydolls and stuff. But you know what scared me? It scared me that my sister was going to be liking women. But she didn't. She's got two healthy kids today. She's engaged also, and she with her high school sweetheart. I thought she might be lesbian 'cause we were twins. You know what I'm saying?

My father wasn't never there so I grew up with a bunch of women anyway. There were times when I thought I could have prevented being gay if I would have been around my uncles more. I don't know. It just that I could have prevented it if I wanted to. But I didn't want to. I knew that I was a boy and that a lot of things I got for Christmas I didn't want to play with. I always wanted to play with my sisters' things and everything, dress in they clothes and whatever. Me and my twin sister are the same size anyway, period.

I really think I was born gay because I never really had feelings for a girl as far as to go with her or to have sex with them or anything like that. My father was never there. I never really had a person I could really depend on, a man in my life, okay, until my older years as I went on. But that was through a relationship, you know.

Now, I wouldn't say that being raised with a bunch of women was the reason for being gay because today I'm grown enough to realize right from wrong and to know if I want to be gay I could be gay. If I don't, I don't have to. But I chose this type of lifestyle, and I'm happy with it, you know. Even though it's wrong, but for me, I'm happy with it.

I had problems in school because I was gay though. Yes, I did. Ninth grade when I went to Bishop McMahon it was a lot of guys I had problems with. The first year of high school there were seniors and juniors, it was sophomores, and they thought they were shit. Here comes a freshman, and then he got the nerve to be gay. Yeah, I had a couple problems. Never fights though. You know, faggot this, little notes on my desk, shit like that. Faggot this, faggot that. You know, little bullshit, but I didn't pay it no mind. They weren't painful for me because you know why, because someone was paying attention to me. That's what I thought. I used to say, I used to be hurt sometimes but I say, "But shit, they must like me, 'cause they're paying attention to me." As a matter fact, one guy that was throwing little notes on my desk liked me! Used to always want to come over to my house. "Where do you live? What's your phone?" and things like that. Yeah. As soon as we get in class little notes used to get thrown on my desk. "You faggot, pussy this." Shit like that. I had more trouble out of the black kids. Yeah, black kids, uh-huh. But this guy who I said liked me, his name was James Edward or something like that. Well, anyway, we became friends after that, after all that. He see'd that I was no joke. That I would hold my hands up to you. I may be feminine and all that but it is some man in me.

Okay. So we became friends after that and a lot of that ceased down. I'll say about the second semester that I started getting friends, all of this little faggot stuff ceased, just like that.

When I left Bishop McMahon and went to Kendall High I didn't have any problems. You know why? 'Cause that was the neighborhood school and everyone knew me from around the neighborhood. Okay, there was people that I didn't know, but that got to know me, knew I was a nice person. So I didn't have any problems. More or less the guys were really coming for me then than they were back at the other schools because I hung around a lot of guys but I hung around a lot of girls too. And some guys may been liking a girl and they wanted to get close to me to get close to them, you know what I'm saying. I was feminine in high school. Very much so. Yes, I was. I went to their little parties and things, rallies and stuff. I knew people on the football team. Enjoy myself, have a good time. I almost went out for a cheerleader for real but I didn't. . . . I didn't have enough heart to.

About when I was seventeen I had my first wet dream I was really starting to get into boys and it was a dream I had. My mother would talk to me about sex. Especially when she knew I was gay. Okay. I was fifteen when she first talked with me, and she was telling me that, you know, if I liked men, don't rush into nothing. Get to know a person whether it's a male or female, don't rush into nothing, and believe it or not she told me about condoms. She told me that it was good to have these, to use them or whatever. That's when VD was popular then. You know she told me about VD and stuff like that. It's a vernal disease. How it could hurt you, maybe even kill you. I mean she used to tell me a lot of things. I don't remember specific but I knew about condoms before they really started getting popular. That's why by the grace of God today I don't have AIDS or the HIV virus. Because I'm not going to say every time I had sex with a man during my later years I used a condom 'cause I didn't. But I was lucky. Now I do, of course, but I was lucky.

During my high school years that's when I really started smoking joint. But not really when I started, but that's when it got heavy, me smoking joints, stuff like that. So most of my friends in high school got high. So I didn't let my mother know. I started smoking joint at fourteen. I started when I was in the eighth grade. Matter of fact it was the last year of . . . when I graduated from Catholic school and went over to high school, yeah.

I did listen and do what my mother asked me to do when I was growing up, but there was a time when I stopped. She caught joint on me a couple times, which I didn't want her to, and she was telling me to stop getting high or whatever or she's going to put me away and I didn't believe her. Until one day she packed all my stuff and everything just before I moved out. She said, "Stop smoking that shit or get out." Matter of fact that was the first time she cussed at me. I'll never forget it. She said, "Stop smoking that shit or get out of my house."

But I didn't believe her. So I went on to school and everything and I came back. My bags and everything was on the porch. Matter of fact she went out and got a new duffel bag and everything. And I was like, "Well, whose shit is this?" you know. Oh! That fucked me up! I went upstairs. "Thought I was playing." No, she wasn't home. The answering machine . . . the phone rung. It was her. Well, I'm gonna use my code name. She was like, "China, I know you're there, pick up." I picked up. I said, "Mom, you're serious," you know. She's like, "Yes." She said, "I want you out of there. You gonna keep smoking that shit, I want you out of there." She was at work. I said, "I'm not smoking it no more" and this and that. Now, I stopped for awhile, but I went back on. I didn't believe her.

She found out 'cause I was high the night before and she knew. She knew something was wrong with me. My eyes were red and when I smoke joint they get really chinky, okay. You know how Chinese people's eyes get. So she knew. So I came home and she looked at me and she said, "What's wrong with you?" I was like, "Nothing." Then, matter of fact I told her that a guy had beaten me up and made me smoke a joint with him. Why I tell her that, then she really snapped after that. It just came out. Oh, she flipped out. She told me I was lying. I probably been smoking joint for a long time and everything. She wanted me to stop. If I don't stop, she gonna kick me out. I told her I didn't believe her. She made me a believer that next day when I came home from school.

I left home at the age of seventeen. It was really a lot of stress in my family. It was just that I didn't have the freedom that I wanted, because at this time I had graduated, and I wanted to have company. I was going with this guy, Tito. I met Tito at a party. It was more like a get-together. And I had seen him many times, he had seen me, but we would like either walked past each other or maybe seen each other in the store or something. But we really started getting to know each other. It's kinda hard for me to talk about because I still care for that man. I still love him. I had my first sexual experience with him. May he rest in peace, and by the grace of God if he wouldn't have died I think we'd still be together today. I really do.

And I was really into him, and I couldn't see myself bringing him into my mother's house to either make love with him or to actual just sit there and be with him. And at that time he had an apartment, so I just wanted to move in with him. So one day I just up and told my mother that I was moving out, you know. I was going to live with a friend, and that for her not to worry. Gave her the phone number and the address, and I left. I still saw my mother. I saw her about twice a month, maybe three times a month.

He met her on Thanksgiving day. You know what, she really did like him. She really liked him as far as . . . because he didn't try to buy his friendship or love or whatever, but he used to bring her little things, little gifts and things. Thanksgiving he bought a nice house bottle of Reunité, what my mother drank, Reunité wine. And that kind of touched her a little bit. She told him he didn't have to do that, whatever. And I would find myself going outside with my sister Juanita, my twin sister. We used to smoke joint every now and then, and I found myself going outside with her while him and my mother still talk. Mainly about me or whatever. But she took to him better than I thought she would. He would do different things around the house for her, construction stuff, whatever.

We lived in South Jefferson. We were right near Jefferson University's campus, at High and Dover. It was somewhat of a change for me 'cause the atmosphere was different, okay. The neighborhood I come from was very quiet. Neighborhood he was living in was noisy. I mean every day of the week. Now I could see it on weekends, you know, kind of noisy, but every day of the week it was noisy or whatever but it didn't bother me 'cause we didn't go out that much. I really didn't know any of his neighbors or whatever. We really kept to ourselves. Now, his mother lived around the corner and his cousin lived like three or four blocks away. So we really was like over there back and forth, whatever. We'd go to his mother's house for dinner a lot.

Ah, he was strong, he was nice, he was innocent, he was clean. I say he was innocent, because I was the first gay person he ever dealt with and I believe that. To me I sort of turned him around, and he used to always look at me with that innocent face and it'd be for real. It was nothing phony about it. It be for real. He was kind-hearted. He was giving, he loved to share. What I didn't have, I had all of his, you know what I'm saying? It wasn't that I had to give it back to him. I just loved him. I really did.

Well, he had been hurt, okay. The girl he was through with had really hurted him. She cheated on him, and he took it really hard. But I wasn't his sidekick date. He just needed someone to be with 'cause it took me a long time for me to have any kind of sexual intercourse with him, for me to even kiss him or anything. We really got to know each other, and I mean I was a virgin when I met him. And I wouldn't say I had sex with him and fell in love with him 'cause I didn't. I was starting to fall in love with him before I had sex with him. Our relationship started out as friends and we ended up in a sexual relationship.

Tito persuaded me to have sex with him. I mean he did things to me just with our clothes on that . . . I don't know . . . that . . . it felt so good. I was afraid to have sex with him. I gonna be honest. I'm gonna tell you why. Okay. This man had a penis on him that was out of this world, okay. When I first found that out, that was before we had sex with each other, I said, "Well, I ain't gonna pay that no mind." I mean, I want this. I'm gay, you know. If a woman can take it, I can take it. But at first I was . . . but then at that present time . . . just like a woman getting her virginity taken from her. I mean she's gonna feel pain but then she's gonna feel good also. I felt both at the same time and when you combine it together there wasn't no stopping. And it just happened.

I guess he want to have sex with me 'cause I was so feminine. I was so feminine, my voice, the way I walk, talk, act. I convinced him really, but, like I said, when I met him he was straight. He just got out of a relationship with his girlfriend and she's horrible. I mean I'm not bragging or nothing, but if you just compare her with me the only thing that she's got on me is she's got a vagina. That's the only thing. He didn't really feel nothing for her, but I know today he did, okay. Because for awhile he used to talk about her, but I was scared that if I was to have sex with him that he would leave me or if I was to have sex with him I wouldn't be good enough for him. I said I'm just gonna let him wait. When it happens it'll be good and it'll go on from there.

The first time we made love together was in a hotel. Fortunately, it wasn't nowhere sleazy or nothing like that. It was beautiful. It was really beautiful. And if I had it my way, I would want it to happen again with that same person. 'Cause it was beautiful. It was. It wasn't as uncomfortable as I thought it would be. I knew I really wanted it. It wasn't whereas he took it, you know. He was real gentle. Even during our relationship he was gentle, you know.

Tito and I didn't use condoms that first time. Matter of fact, none that day. And I'm being honest with you, I was trying to recuperate myself for about a week and we both went and bought two boxes of condoms and we went on from there. Took me a week to recover. I just felt so good I didn't want that feeling to leave. Okay, I thought if we would have sex again that feeling would leave. I'm being honest with you, I grew closer to him after we made love. I grew closer to him in such a sense that I didn't want anyone looking at him. I didn't take him around my gay friends because he was a good-looking man. He is. He still is. He's a good-looking man.

He didn't care where we went. Even though I was gay, he didn't care. He took me around his family the second week I knew him. You know. I took that to the heart because I have had straight men that I could really talk to, but they only wanted one thing. I didn't want to go for it and they left me alone. You understand what I'm saying? "You just too good for me or something?" you know. Little bullshit! Well, anyway he took me by his family the second week I knew him. His mother, you know, I really took that to the heart. His family knew I was gay.

They took the fact that we were having a relationship better than I thought. Okay. I thought I would be a spectacle in there. They would hold their little noses up and stuff but they didn't. She welcomed me with open arms. I mean she didn't actually hug me or nothing like that, but I ate in her house. We all sat at the table. I was nervous as shit, but we all sat at the table and ate. His mother's boyfriend asked a lot of questions, okay, which I realize today he was just being concerned. I thought he was trying to be newsy. He was asking me questions 'bout my family. What kind of lifestyle I grew up in and stuff like that. What made me become gay. I thought he was trying to be funny and smart. Him and Tito got into arguments about that but he wasn't. And later on down the line I realized that.

Tito and I both worked. He wasn't hustling or anything like that. We didn't have to. We wasn't where we wanted to be but we were financially secure. I found myself holding a lot of money till the next time he got paid and still had money. So we didn't really have to hustle. He was a construction worker and he worked with his mother's boyfriend a lot. So he would make pretty good money, and I was working at Roy Rogers right down the street from his apartment. So that was bringing in money too. But one thing I can say about him, every time he got paid— he got paid every Friday, I got paid every other Friday—he would keep like twenty dollars of his check and give me the rest of it. I get the little bills and things up, get the cable bill and things like that. So I didn't have no problem with that, and it wasn't never where he gave me money and asked for it back.

We lived in that apartment for about two years. We were having problems far as living with each other and that's when his drinking really starting getting heavy and we'd have a lot of arguments. He would walk out a lot. He never put his hands on me. I would mostly do that. Get mad at him, hit him. Step up in his face or something or scratch him up, slapped his face or either punched him or something because of the things that he said. He would call me no good bitches and shit. I ain't shit, you know. He's grown. He can drink as much as he wants, when he want. Shit like that. And it hurted me a lot because I would drink occasional. I mean we had a beautiful bar. I mean we had a nice little apartment anyway. We had a nice bar that was fully stocked and I didn't really know too much about an alcoholic until I really met him. I would find myself every Friday constantly buying something for the bar and didn't realize what I was doing until later on down the line, you know.

He was starting to fade out. I loved him and everything but he just was starting to fade out. You know, as far as being lazy around the house. Don't want to do nothing. I don't like to clean up after nobody, okay. I wasn't brought up like that. You know, everybody chipped in. So I found myself really just losing interest in him but really loved him.

We left there when I was nineteen, and we went to a shelter. That was the first shelter we went to. That's a big jump, ain't it? A lot of guys that was in the shelter was there because of drug-related. We went there because we couldn't keep up with the bills. It wasn't drug-related. We just couldn't keep up with the bills. We was taking more than we could chew. Okay, we started renting stuff, rent to own, and stuff like that. We just couldn't keep up. Like you rent a TV to own it and furniture and everything. We were having problems relationship-wise on top of that. Tito had lost his job. I still had mine, but that wasn't enough to really keep the apartment going and the bills we had. So unfortunately we went to a shelter. We stayed in the shelter a couple months. I was working during that time, but he wasn't. He was collecting welfare. Also I got on welfare also because Roy Rogers wasn't paying me enough at all. But we didn't really do nothing with that money. We got high with it, went out, and stuff like that.

One day somebody told us about live-in jobs at Lake Victoria, through an agency. And one day we just got up and went to this agency and all we needed was twenty dollars apiece for carfare and our luggage and two pieces of ID. We went for it. That's when we went out to Lake Victoria. And living out in Lake Victoria was . . . that was so great. It was way better than living in that apartment, living in Jefferson. It's a whole different atmosphere and everything. It was a gay resort also, okay, that we were working at. Oh, to have money on top of money because I was a waiter and he was a dishwasher, but it was great money. We would hold our checks to the next time we got paid because I had so much money in tips or whatever. We only paid sixty dollars every two weeks. They would take thirty dollars out of my check and thirty dollars out of his because we both shared the cottage, okay. Had our own living room, our room, kitchen and everything. Just like an apartment, but it was a cottage.

It was a year-round resort. You could live there and work there as long as you want to. It was great. But once we moved up there our relationship got worse. Even though we had all that accessories, material things. He bought me a color TV. He bought my coat out there, everything. Even though we had all that, it got worse because his drinking just got very heavy. He would wake up to a drink. He would go to sleep with a drink. It got so bad I threatened to leave him and he told me he'd stop drinking. I thought that would help, but. . . . He said, "I just have one drink and that'll be it. I'll just get one bottle, that'll be it. This bottle will last longer all the way to the next payday." Which it didn't.

He'd get up in the morning and have a drink or have a beer. Even so, I would get up and smoke a joint. I love to smoke a joint before I go to work. I used to love to smoke a joint before I went to school. I wouldn't say it helped me cope but it just relaxed me. It really did. So I felt myself lighting a joint and he was drinking a beer. This is eight in the morning! We both got to be to work at ten or nine o'clock. I said, "Well, shit, he try to follow what I'm doing." But see I wasn't that crazy over no joint. I wouldn't start an argument. It made me feel good. It made me feel relaxed, so I felt him trying to do what I'm doing or substitute what I'm doing, thinking he's doing the right thing. So I found myself hiding it a little bit 'cause he always had to be to work before me. I wait for him to go to work, then I smoke a joint. But that didn't help because he would drink a beer, have a drink here or whatever. So it got worse.

He would just drink a lot during the day. 'Cause this is our cottage and the resort wasn't too far from it, but a couple steps. Okay, so he could walk back and forth and go to the cottage, specially during his break. We always kept liquor in the house, whatever. I threatened to bust up the TV one day. He just bought it for me. I'd had it about three weeks. And I threatened to bust it up. He went in the drawer and pulled out four hundred dollars that I didn't know he had, okay. And said, "Bust that up, I'll buy you another one." I mean it was just horrible. It really was.

One day it all ended. Unfortunately, he was hot one day. He was working and wanted to go for a swim and in the course of him swimming he drown and by the time I got to the pool it was too late. I mean they were doing CPR on him, and . . . that was it.

And I took that very hard. That really . . . to me that really kicked my addiction off. Okay, I started with the shelters and everything. I just didn't care. I quitted the job out Lake Victoria because it was too many memories out there and I was off for the races.

I was twenty and he was twenty-seven. His death was a real turning point for me. He died in my arms. Because you know how they gather around the family and everything. I was holding his head because nobody couldn't tell me that he was not going to come through. Okay, the doctors, family, nobody. I just knew this man was going to come through, and he did not. He went in the hospital Friday night, died Saturday afternoon. That was that. He died in my arms two-oh-one pm on July eighth, 1988.

I miss Tito a lot. I really do. I pray for him every day even though . . . hopefully I pray to God that he's up there. I pray for him every night. I pray for his family or whatever. It'll be three years that he died this year, and it would have been five years we would have been together in November.

He took my virginity away from me. But I did have friends before him but like I say I didn't want of go to bed with them so they left me alone and I was starting to have feelings for them. But I didn't love them. You know what I'm saying? It took me about two months to have sex with Tito. I mean he done offered to take me to the hotel. You know how you hug somebody and constantly hug them and kiss them? You know how you get hot down there? You know what I'm saying? But he stuck by me. He really did. And he done gave me money, stuff like that. Done bought me a ring, which I don't have today, which I'm so mad about. Know what I'm saying?

I sold that ring 'cause of drugs. I just sold all my jewelry that he bought for me or helped me buy 'cause of drugs. Just so much shit. I sold a lot of clothes that he bought for me. He bought me a fur coat. A real fur coat when we were out at Lake Victoria. I didn't sell that. I left it. 'Cause when he died, I took it hard. It felt like . . . I just lost it. I just lost it. I had fifty dollars in my pocketbook and when I left the owners gave me a hundred dollar bill plus carfare to go on that bus and come back to Jefferson. When I come back to Jefferson all I had was two small little bags. I just changed my clothes for a couple days. I left all my clothes and cosmetics and everything. And food and everything. I just left it. I wanted a hit that bad. I wanted a hit of cocaine that bad.

I've had two relationships since his death. The guy that's sitting out there now, he's my lover now, right, and this is not why I'm with him. I love him for him, okay. But he reminded me of Tito so much—even though I had a relationship after Tito and before him—he reminds me of Tito so much it's pathetic, okay. That's not why I'm with him today. That's not why I love him. I love him for being Terry, okay. He do make me sick sometimes, okay. Different things that he do, but I'm powerless over that today and I have to deal with that, okay. We both trying to recover from drugs. It's hard but then again it's okay today.

Well, you know my street name is Jewel. I got that name for two things. I wore a lot of jewelry, okay, off and on. And Matt when I was dealing with him told me, "Damn!" I'm going to tell you exactly what he said. He said, "Your pussy is just like a gem." Okay. "I'm gonna call you Jewel from now on." You know, that just what he said to me, okay. Now, it not the point of me bragging about it. It all about honesty today, and that exactly what he said. I will never forget it. You know that kinda fucks me, okay. But I guess that's why it's so easy for a guy to fall in love with me because I would throw something on them that first time and you know fucks them up, you know. Hey! It ain't all about bragging. It's all about, you know, being honest and that's that.

Yeah, I play the woman role in the relationship. That means walking down the street I always walk on the left-hand side from the curb. I'm not the most attractive one in the relationship, but the one that stand out more, okay. A man is always going to be a man. Comb your hair, brush your teeth, and you know, whatever, wash your face, you're out the door. You know, I like to take time in the mirror. I like to wear mascara, stuff like that, eyeliner. Clothes-wise a man can wear a pair of jeans and a shirt and maybe wear nothing but the same pair of jeans the next day. I don't like wearing the same thing day after day unless I really have to. I like going to the hairdresser's and whatever. I don't like going to a barber shop. I just like doing a lot of things women do. And I know how to treat a man to make him feel wanted. Like for instance especially sexually. I do a lot of things a woman would do to a man to please him. Of course I'm gonna be pleased at the end. I love a man to have oral sex with me. Not the kind of oral sex I'm going to have with him. The kind of oral sex he would have with a woman. Treat him as far as like cooking for him, not cleaning after him, but cleaning with him. I love a fifty-fifty relationship, period. I love to collect money from him when he come home from work.

I know what he want, okay. I done learned from the best, to me. I learned from my sister, my twin sister, and my mother. And it's a lot of things that I find herself doing that I picked up. My mother is one hundred percent woman and so is my sisters. I think like a man sometimes when I get mad, okay. Even though I'm still a man, I'm always gonna be a man, I'm gonna die a man, but I don't think like one. I think sometimes like that when I'm mad and I want to fight, okay. That manlihood comes out. But I would walk down the street, guys would whistle at me. They would speak to me. Be like, "How you doing, baby?" I done had people tell me I'm going in the wrong bathroom or whatever. I done had a lot of people come up to me and say, well, gives me compliments on the way I look and stuff like that. So I can't help but to think like a woman. I just can't.

You know when I think of the word "woman" I think soft. Nice things, dainty things. I don't wear a lot of women clothing. I may wear women blouse, a pair of jeans. I may wear a pair of women's pants that's not too feminine, not too masculine; shoes-wise, you know, in between, not too dainty, not too mannish, okay.

And when I think of a man I think of hard, body building, deep voice. I think of . . . sometimes acting like a big baby, especially when they get sick, okay. I'll be honest with you. To me in my relationships and experiences a man can get sick . . . "Oh, call my job. I can't go to work." "Okay." "I don't feel too good." "What wrong with you?" "My stomach hurt." "Well, I got a sore throat and a toothache, and I'm going to work." You know what I'm saying?

A man needs more sex than a woman. Because, excuse the expression, they're dogs. I mean, come on, they are. I'm gonna speak from my last relationship, from this relationship. I can have sex with Terry for almost an hour straight and maybe two hours later he'll roll over ready again, you know. Sometimes I go for it and sometimes I just don't. I don't think men should have sex any time they want to 'cause sometimes

I don't feel like it. Sometimes my stomach can be hurting. Sometimes I just don't feel like it. I do get headaches just like a woman do. I do get headaches and just do not feel like having sex.

I want the man to be that man that he's supposed to do, okay. I don't want nobody work for me. I always will work and he work. You know, do a lot of heavy things that I can't do or I choose not to do. As far as carrying bags and things, whatever. Take up for me like if I'm in an argument with another man or something. He's always there. Which all my men been like that. That's why I've been so scared to tell them, "Well, Bill said he was gonna beat my fucking ass if I didn't talk to him" or something like that. You know, that's why I hate it 'cause I knew how they'll react to that. You know that make them go off on a warpath. Be hard. Be my protector. Do you know what I'm saying? Be there for me. The way they hold me, okay. I loved to be kissed, hugged. I love to feel wanted, okay. That could build my morale up.

So I been brought up around so many women, I feels like one. I thinks like one, and I act like one. I talk like one. I walk like one. Yeah, I talk like one. By the grace of God I know I'm not one. If my penis wasn't here, if it wasn't there, which it ain't much 'cause it's never been used, I'd know that I would be more out there than I am now. Simple as that.

I would never be sexually active in the relationship. No, uh-uh. So there are different kinds of gay people. There's your butch gay. There's your straight gay that will tell you that I don't mess around with homosexuals this and that. Here they're living with one. Terry is a straight gay. Even though he's having a relationship with me I do still consider him straight because ain't no flipping and flapping. He still get his look twitches looking at girls and shit like that, which I don't like. One day I'm just gonna take his eyeballs out of his head. But I used to mind it, but I say no because see guys are doing it to me and he gets mad. Oh, he gets hot! There's a lot of gay people I know that are just as straight-looking as they want to be, deep voice and everything. When they behind the closed doors they just throwing their legs in the air, you know.

As feminine as I am, what would I want another gay person for, you know? To do things I do, and want the same things I want, you know? Some gay people out here, like meeting a gay, another gay, like as feminine as me. They like fucking each other. I'm not into that, okay.

I've never been into that, okay. I mean it never hurts to try something twice, but I don't think I would like it. I really don't. Me humping on somebody. I really . . . I'm be honest with you. I don't think I would like it.

So I have never been the one fucking the person. I mean I have laid them on their backs and have massaged their backs. I've massaged their buttocks, whatever. That's natural. But as far as putting something in them. No. No, never! The thought never crossed my mind or whatever. I wouldn't say it never will, but from then to now it hasn't. I think, may he rest in peace, Tito wanted me to fuck him. I'm gonna be honest with you. But he never asked me. He never came out and told me, but he used to always love for me to lay on his back. He used to always love for me to do that. And I don't like talking about this because he's gone now and the relationship is over or whatever. But I thinks about that sometimes. Now, I started laying on his back. He didn't ask me to. I just started to. I just like that sometimes. Just lay on his back and hold him or something like that. I do that with Terry. Okay. But as far as actually putting something in him or something like that, no, I just don't.

You know what I like? I like for a man to masturbate on me. I don't believe I'm telling you these things. Oh, but I do, I do. To be honest with you, I do. Matter of fact a couple times I even like masturbating, okay. If he came too fast and he couldn't get me off by coming in me or whatever or . . . I just do.

But if he's doing it right I don't have to touch myself. I just automatically come. Yeah, just the way he's hitting. Simple as that. Home runs and. . . . If I masturbate to get off, most of the time I masturbate by myself because . . . I don't feel self-conscious or nothing, I just, I don't know, want that privacy. It wouldn't turn them off though. Matter of fact I've masturbated in front of Terry before and . . . it was good. It was really great, you know. He really caressed my body and everything to help me get off quicker and everything. I don't have much down there, but the little bit I do have it never gets in the way. You understand what I'm saying?

I never really found a man like this. I mean, I always like tall and dark-skin men, okay. A nice personality, nice smile, pretty pearl white teeth. I like them to be slim, maybe bowlegged or whatever. A nice conversation, don't have to have a good job or big values or a lot to offer, just that love and respect that a woman would want. A good personality. A very good personality. A man who love to work. Someone who is serious about getting ahead in life, that has some kind of goal, something that they can hold on to that they're really trying to achieve, okay. Lot of people don't achieve their goals, okay. I haven't achieved mine. But it's always a chance. It's never too late, okay. Financially stable just . . . just . . . not just making it, but have somewhat extra on the side. Do you know what I'm saying? Someone that will be there for me. Seem like every man I meet is a drinker. He's a recovering alcoholic, Terry anyway.

I'd rather be with a black man. You know I've never had sex with white men, but I have dated them. I have tricked a lot of white men as far as like I say with SSI checks. It's not that I don't find white men attractive 'cause I find a lot of white men attractive, especially at the club. It's just that, honestly, I'm not into white men, okay. And they got some gorgeous white men out here. They do. It's just that I'm not into them. I can't see myself having sex with them 'cause to me they won't please me. They might not have enough . . . they penis might not be the size that I would want it to be even though the size isn't everything 'cause you can have a small penis and know exactly what to do with it, okay. I don't think they could please me, okay. They could give me a conversation. They could take me out. Wine me and dine me. But sexually I don't think a white man could please me.

All three of the guys I've really loved was straight, okay. The little one, which his name is Matt, I talked to him today. But I'm currently trying to get off of drugs. Well, I am. I've been clean for a little while now and Matt is an active addict, okay. I can't be around him. I can't live with him no more because he's still using. I can't live that kind of life today.

It was alright then. I lived in Brookside with Matt. That was a relationship I'll never forget. Alright, 1988, when Tito died, I was twenty. So, from July of '88 until '89 I was in and out of the shelter system. I met Matt at a club in Montgomery County when I turned twenty-one in 1989. I was trying to recover from drugs. I was with a friend of mine and he was from Brookside. One thing led to another. We started talking and he was selling . . . matter of fact he was selling cocaine. He stopped during our relationship. I lived with him in Brookside from the age of twenty-one until twenty-three, until 1991, spent about two years with Matt. As a matter of fact our second anniversary would have been March eighteenth. Well, it was March eighteenth 'cause I was still talking to him even though I wasn't living with him. But our second anniversary was March eighteenth. I came back to Jefferson on March the second to be exact.

At the beginning it was beautiful when I lived with Matt. Just like every relationship, it was beautiful. I didn't want for nothing. I didn't need for nothing. He was really a drinker, but I really got him hooked on cocaine.

His family took towards me, good, real good, especially the kids. Oh, they adored China. I would take them but nobody else would. I would take them different places. I even took all of them to the movies. Living with him was alright until the end of our relationship. It started getting tiresome. I was tired of him. I didn't like the way he carried himself anymore. I didn't like the way he acted when he got high. He put too much money in my hand at one time.

He's an asbestos worker. His mother didn't want that much. He always give it to me, but he'd give me too much money at one time and I would just waste it. I would tell him I'm going around the corner to get me some joint. I'd go around the corner and get me some cocaine. Go in the hit house and hit. Come back and my eyes like this wide and tell him, "Come on, let's go out." And he knew, you know. I wasted a lot of money with him.

When I left him, I came back to Jefferson from Brookside and I was living in a shelter. I moved in the shelter on March the second, 1991. I didn't go home because I was embarrassed. Not only embarrassed I was ashamed of myself. Both my sisters still live with my grandmother. They got kids now. They're doing their own thing. My younger sister is managing and my older sister is a secretary, you know. I was just, I didn't want to go back home. My mother told me to go back home, but it wouldn't have been the same. I wouldn't have had my own room. Even though I didn't have my own room in the shelter, but I'm just saying I wouldn't have my own room. I don't really know my sisters anymore. I really don't know my mother or grandmother anymore. I really don't. I done been through so much by leaving home it's pathetic. Somewhat good, mostly bad, and I brought it all on myself. Drugs did nothing but fucked up my life.

By the time I met Matt I was just tired of the way I was looking and feeling. For four months I smoked cocaine every day. Every single day! Maybe not all day, but every single day I had a piece of cocaine in my system and it was eating me up. Drugs had fucked up my life. Very much so. May he rest peace, Tito fucked up my life, because I chose not to go to college. I chose not to go graduate school or nothing. I chose that, okay. I wasn't naive. I wasn't young or pigheaded, didn't know what I was doing. I wanted him. I wanted to be with him.

Drugs really fucked up my life. It really did. It's so easy hitting on cocaine. But God knows it's so hard getting off of it. I can't smoke a joint today. I can't drink a drink without wanting a hit of cocaine out of that pipe. I cannot do it! I can't go to a house smelling reefer and people sitting around drinking without me wanting some. I'm a addict. I'm always be an addict until the day I die. It took me a long time to admit it to myself. It took me a long time to admit it to other people that I was an addict. I'm not ashamed of being an addict because being an addict showed me that it is a better way to living, okay. I choose to live a better life today. I choose to live a better life.

When I first came here to the Urban Lifestyles Project, I was horrible. I didn't look right. My hair was coming out then. By me really getting off of cocaine that really helps me a lot. To have to really dig down deep inside of what I'm feeling and can express it the best way I know how, but if I had the chance to do it all over again, I would still be with Tito at the beginning. But by me talking him out of doing cocaine, I would take my own advice. I would take the cotton out of my mouth and put it in my ears instead of taking the cotton out of my ears and putting it in my mouth. You understand what I'm saying? I would do it all over again but different.

And he's looking down at me right now . . . it's like, "Well, thank God she's trying to recover from cocaine" because I was on that shit bad, badly. I mean bad. I done hit rock bottom so hard that if I would have just laid my head down I would have been done, you know. I'm grateful to God today that I have a higher power that I can recover from drugs, you know, and stay off them. I know I don't have to use that psychic no more for an excuse. I have arguments with that man out there and have money in my pocket and knowing I don't have to go use, pick up anything.

Now Terry is another story. Yeah, Terry was straight too when I found him. I'm the first one that he dealt with like this that he's ever kissed or whatever. Before I met him I haven't had sex for six months and I was due, okay. I was like a fish falling for his bait, and I fell for it. I do love him. I'm in love with him. I had my choice of men that I could have picked. I didn't. We really picked each other. He had been watching me for a whole month at the shelter we been staying in.

Anyway, I met Terry at a place we used to go to eat, okay. It's for homeless people. It's called Saint Paul's. Terry been watching me for a whole month, the whole month of March. I never knew this, okay. He was doing his addiction then and he felt as though he didn't look right. I was always clean-looking or whatever, was up on my hygiene. So he didn't know what to say to me or how to talk to me. Until one day, this was when he told me he got a fresh haircut and he shaved all the hair he had off his face and everything but his mustache. And I was on the corner of Saint Paul's just standing waiting for it to open and he walked past me. And I didn't have no cigarettes this day, and he walked past. I usually don't like asking people for nothing. So he walked past that day, and I asked for a cigarette and he looked at me and started smiling 'cause that's the first time we combined the eyes together in that whole month he's been watching me. And he gave me a cigarette and he went around the corner and so I went around the corner too. Not to look at his face or whatever or to say anything to him, but I just wanted . . . something just said, "China, walk around the corner," you know. So I walked around the corner and he calls me over to cross the street where he was at. So we got to talking. And the way he was just looking at me, his eyes were so attractive. He just kept staring at me. I just felt these vibes in me or something. It just felt good. So we got to talking and one thing led to another. He was telling me that he was staying under a bridge. That he didn't want to go to no shelter. So I told him I was staying in the shelter and whatever.

We had sex that day too. The first day we met we had sex. I been dying to have sex, and he pulled the right thing out of his pocket and I went for, which was a condom, when he pulled his pants down, I was like, "What!" because I do that. I look at a man face and then it's a habit and I look down at his pants. I'm not no hooker or whore even though I been . . . I've been there, but it's just a bad habit. And I said, "Well, this man ain't got shit," you know. He fooled me. We had sex that day. Right before we went into Paul's.

We went into Paul's, he was like, "Damn!" He starting to have feelings for me. And I said, "Well, wait a minute. You know, I don't want to hear this shit. I just met you and everything. It hasn't even been twenty-four hours, whatever." He said, "I mean you're clean," you know, whatever. So anyway, we got to talking later on that night. I went to the shelter. He walked me to the shelter. He went back under the bridge, and the next day we met up with one another and one day led to another. We started hooking up with each other. I got him into the shelter. I got him into this outpatient program which I'm presently enrolled in. And we've been going together ever since.

We have had a couple arguments, here and there, but nothing extravagant. Kinda dumb stuff. He's kind of upset right now, because he don't have the money he want me to have. He don't have it. He knows I like nice material things. He bought me this ring also. And he knows there's a lot of things he can't do for me, but it takes patience. I got a lot of patience.

So I've known him seventy-three days today. We go out, we go to movies. We don't talk that much though, that's one thing we got to work on. He's been through so much since the age of five it's pathetic. I'm gonna tell you something. His father abused him, physical abuse, okay, him and his sisters, and sometimes he has flashbacks about that, and who's paying for it today? I am. Because he gets flashbacks about it and a lot of his attitudes come from that. He hates his father. He hasn't seen his mother in years. I mean it's a lot of things with him, and it's hard for me to cope sometime because my mother was always there for me and his wasn't. We got a few things in common but not much. But I've grow to like him a lot. I really do think I love him. I don't want to see nothing bad happen to him.

We haven't really argued that often. Probably about four times during these seventy-three days. We argue about stupid dumb shit. I want to see this movie but he wants to see another one. This last one was a doozy though. I wanted to use his medical card to get a check-up because unfortunately my medical card was sent back because I had moved out of the shelter, right. And I wanted to use his medical card. He wanted to get a check-up the same time I wanted to just because I said I wanted to, okay. So I got into an argument over that, and he talking about, "Well, what about me?" I said, "What about you?" He said, "What about my check-up?" I said, "You just wanted one because I wanted one." This and that and one thing led to another and we started arguing. I ripped the shirt off his back and everything. Oh, it was horrible. He just grabbed me and shook me and told me to stop. It was a mess. I better stop that though. I do, because one day somebody's gonna beat my ass. Shit, I better stop that. As big as he is. You know what I'm saying?

Our arguments can be about anything. Like I said we do have problems I mean two addicts in a relationship, you know what kind of problems I could be talking about as far as if I say something wrong he'll flip. If I go out there right now and say, "Come on, let's go," he might get mad. Thinking I'm mad. I'd be playing. You know what I'm saying? Little petty dumb shit. But it's alright today. I don't have to use, pick up, go to use, or go to trick or anything, you know.

Like I said, after the accident I left Lake Victoria and came back to Jefferson and went inside the shelter. But before I went to the shelter I went and got high. I wanted some cocaine. I don't know why this thought came across my mind. I didn't really know how to do it. All I know, I wanted some cocaine in my system.

Well, wait a minute, let me back up a little bit. When we were at Lake Victoria I met a lot of white gay people and they used to snort cocaine a lot. I tried it a couple times but it didn't really do nothing for me. It numbed the hell out of my throat, but it really didn't do nothing for me. One incident I was at a cocaine-champagne party, okay. It was on a yacht or whatever. It was a white gay person that I knew who was still with a very wealthy guy. It was a lot of people there or whatever. We're out in Carlisle and we was out there and you could go on any room you want to on the yacht, any room you want to or whatever. You could either have sex or just go in there and sit down and talk or whatever. Well, anyway, one particular room I went in, it was a bunch of people sitting in there. Some of them were snorting, some of them were shooting cocaine, some of them were smoking. Now, I said my father was a smoker, right? I never seen any of his tools. So I never knew, okay. But this particular time I said, "Well, wait a minute. What is that? You know, what are they doing?" You know. Tito had told me they're smoking cocaine. Smoking, I mean what about that? So I did try it that once and I loved it.

That was my first experience and I loved it. I really did. I loved it. I loved what it did to me, the high, everything. It was, oh, it was really great, and I wanted to do it again and again and again. That whole night I stayed in that room. I didn't have to have no money. The cocaine was there. It was good. It was pure. I didn't have to worry about. . . . Okay, I thought it was like that everywhere you go. I thought it was like that. But God knows it's not, okay. Tito was telling me, "You got me off this shit, now you're get hooked on it. After tonight you're not gonna do it no more." You know, I was like, "This is what you were doing? This is exactly what you were doing?"

I say I smoked about two hundred dollars' worth to myself that night. It was powder and they were cooking it. It didn't take me long to learn to use that pipe either. Learned that night. They showed me how to use the pipe and hold the match, but I was watching too. It didn't take me no time. And the pipes they had they weren't broken up or nothing like that. They were practically new. By the time I got to Jefferson I was a pro. All I had to know was where the stuff was at. That's all I wanted to know. I didn't know nothing about caps until I came back to Jefferson.

See, when I met Tito, he was addict to cocaine, smoking, okay. I knew cocaine was always bad, but I didn't know how bad it was 'cause I never experienced it. But a lot of people had told me not to get on it and everything. Matter of fact a lot of people didn't offer it to me. They would do it in front of me but they didn't offer it to me. . . . I talked to him a lot about getting off of it and everything. He told me if I come with him, he would leave it alone. Which he did. Which he really did. I believed him. He started gaining weight. That fucked me up because I say, "Damn, he was skinny as shit when I met him." I thought that was his regular size. He started gaining weight. He started looking better to me. His complexion, everything. I said, "Wait a minute. What's going on? Am I doing this to you?" You know he told me, "Yes, you are. Yes, you are. As long as you stay with me and continue to be faithful to me and loyal to me, I will stay like this." So I loved that, you know. He was starting to look really good and stuff. Cleaning hisself up and everything. So there was no more talk about cocaine until we went to Lake Victoria.

So at that cocaine-champagne party they had joint, they had Valium, all the drugs you wanted. It started about twelve that afternoon and didn't end. . . . Well it was on a Saturday, I believe it was. It didn't end until that Sunday night. When I came off that yacht I was horrible. I felt so horrible. Felt like I lost eighty pounds. Felt like I was drawn in, but I was going to the mirror and said, "I still look good. Why do I feel like this?" Because the cocaine wasn't gone. It was just that I was so drawn . . . I can't really explain. It was just horrible. We gets back to the cottage and cleaned myself up. I musta took a shower for about an hour. That's how I felt. I felt so yukky. I didn't have to go to work till that—'cause it was on some weekend, some holiday weekend—I didn't have to go to work till that Tuesday and we got back that Sunday night. Me and Tito talked for a long time. He was telling me what I did wasn't right. I got him off this shit or whatever. He felt kinda bad, and I reached for a joint.

What I'm saying? What I'm adding up to? Here, I was turning into an addict and didn't know it, okay. I found myself reaching for a joint. I smoked me a joint. I kept joint. If we didn't have no money, I kept me some joint. Okay, just like he kept his little bottle, I kept me some joints. And I found myself reaching for a joint and when I was smoking it and I felt myself just drawn. Here, I was realizing, "Well, China, you were up since Saturday afternoon and it's Sunday night. What's going on here?" So I slept for a long time. And that was about it. That was my first experience and I loved it. I really loved it.

So the first place I went when I got to Jefferson after Tito died was to get high. Now, when we were in the shelter before, I knew a lot of gay friends of mine that used to tell me about these different neighborhoods where they get high and where they smoke cocaine at and everything. I told them I wasn't into that, but it was in the same facilities where I used to get my joint from. In this one particular house I would be smoking joint downstairs and upstairs everybody else was getting high. Doing things I didn't want to see. So I knew exactly where to go. When I left from Lake Victoria, I knew exactly where to go. That's where I went. Paranoid, but I went. I had all this money on me or whatever. I had a fifty dollar bill and a hundred dollar bill. The hundred dollar bill I broke to have my carfare from Lake Victoria to Jefferson. I went to this house. I ditched my bags. I remember that. I ditched my bags outside somewhere. I just ditched them. All I had was my little pocketbook, my little money in my socks and everything. I knew what I was going to do. I was so hurt. I cried on the bus. I cried after I got off the bus. It was just horrible. So that was my second experience on cocaine that night. Smoking it, and ever since that day, July ninth, 1988, I went on for the races. I went on for the races.

So I say 'bout the eleventh of July of '88, I went back into the shelter system. I applied for welfare. I got on welfare just like that because I hadn't been on welfare for a long time. Okay, and I'm living in a shelter. That's when they started giving out food stamps along with the shelter bed. I started going to the school. They was paying a hundred dollars every week just for you to go to school. It was a gimmick school. A school to get you to take out a loan just for you going to they school. So that didn't help. Because that was more cocaine in my system plus the friends I started to hanging out with. I started losing my complexion. I started losing my weight. I didn't give a fuck about my hair. I always . . . that's one thing I always kept was my hygiene. I just didn't give a fuck. I really didn't.

But I was never in the streets. I always had someplace to go. I went to the shelter. The curfew was eleven o'clock. I always got there quarter of eleven. High out of my mind, but I got there, okay. They had a lot of security guards that worked there. I was so feminine. They were on me. They liked me. I tricked with about five of them. So I always had pull. I could come in really when I want to and get away with it. They had me on a work list, which I wasn't. So I could get to come anytime I want to.

Every payday they got paid I would trick with each one of them.

That went on for about five, seven, eight months. I feel bad about that today because I feel so cheap. But I was getting at least twenty dollars from each one of them. At least. Sometimes more, never less. They likeded me, you know. They didn't know I was going for crack. I was living in the shelter, and the guards used to say, "Yeah, I wants some of that fat ass," you know, and stuff like that. I'd say, "Yeah, you got twenty dollars?" And that's when it all started. One of the guards, he was like, "Yeah, I got twenty dollars." We were right in the guard shack and I had him. And after that, it went on from there. That was the first time and about a week later I did it again with a different guy. I met him in the same place. It was five different guards. I just wanted to hurry up and be over so I get what I have to get and get out of there. Do you know what I'm saying? A lot of times it was oral sex too, and they will pay. Simple as that. Money straight up first. They'll pay. It wasn't nothing, "I'll give you something Friday." I didn't play that, you know.

One particular guard I went over his house one day. Why did he give me his keys? He wasn't there. He told me to meet him there, and I went to his house. Who he gonna tell, you know? I was scared to death, but I robbed him silly. I sold his gold. He had money in the house. I took a very expensive vase of his mother and everything. Who was he gonna tell? Who he gonna kick out, you know? He even tried to get me help. He knew I was on that shit. He tried to get me help.

He kicked my ass too. He set me up. He invited me over to his house one day. He told me that he was sorry and everything. He made love to me. Gave me forty dollars. Yeah, he gave me two twenty dollar bills. On my way out the door, he punched me in the back of my head. He told me that he knew I was gonna get high. He just tested me to see what I would do. I remember him kicking me. He had two more steps going down front of his apartment. I remember him kicking me down them three little steps. I got away from him. He didn't really kick my ass, but he put his hands on me, okay. Took that forty dollars and I went and got high. Yes, I did.

After the forty dollars was gone, I tried my best to get him fired. Which I couldn't. I told them that he raped me. I had his semen inside my rectum and that's how most people do it. When somebody says they raped you, you know they can tell by the semen or whatever. But it didn't work, you know. By me being gay, they said, "Well, it wasn't forced in you," okay. "It was inject in you by free will."

Anyway, I started using cocaine on July eighth, 1988—July ninth, 1988 rather. That's what kicked it off, period. I was off to the races ever since. Two months after that, that's when I knew, right then, I was an addict and didn't want to help myself. Every piece of money I got my hands on, I tried to get me a piece of cocaine. Like two months after that, by September of 1988, I was at my peak. That's when I started tricking. That's when I started shoplifting. Doing anything or every-thing to get some cocaine. During the week I would average 'bout seven hundred dollars a week. Either by tricking, shoplifting or welfare or going to school. So I say I averaged seven hundred dollars a week. The first of the month, SHewWWWWWWW! I had three friends that got their SSI checks, disability checks. I was always a smooth talker, espe-cially on cocaine. All you had to do was to say a couple words to them. I had all three of them one day in a hotel. Just us four. Each one of them had at least five hundred dollars' worth. So that's what, fifteen hundred dollars? I didn't have to have a dime. I was like the runner. I would go get five packages for them. Tell them it's more than it was supposed to have been. So I would keep that pocket money, okay. By the time their money is gone, I would have at least five hundred dollars in my pocket. By just flipping like that or taking out.

I didn't always trick. I tricked somebody else too. You know what I'm saying? Say it's a guy that I always wanted to have, okay, to have sex with. They never give me the time of day. But if I had some cocaine, he was mine. For either that night or that day or somehow. And then when I finally had them. . . . You know, I was so busy looking at that pipe, I didn't even want them. You know what I'm saying?

There were these other guys, but I wasn't really sexually involved with them. I just wanted to be with them, okay. I may have played with their penis a little bit. I might have had went oral with it a little bit, maybe injected in me for a couple of minutes, but it wasn't really whereas you're having sex together, because like I say, I was so busy looking at that cocaine and that pipe. And I knew I had money in my pocket or they had money in their pocket. I wanted to get high.

About twenty percent of my money came from hustling. In September of 1988 I started tricking and shoplifting. I started taking clothes here and there. Stuff like that. I would go to a mall, usually in Melrose. I also went to a couple of spots downtown, stuff like that. Nothing really big. I never really was a big shoplifter. But I have shoplift. I made about two hundred dollars like at a couple stops.

Most of my money came from welfare and friends. Back then I was getting ninety-seven fifty from welfare plus I would get sixty-seven dollars for food stamps every two weeks. I sell my little bit of jewelry I had. I also started school the week after I arrived back in Jefferson. I got my first voucher check for four hundred dollars a week after that. So school every week was a hundred dollars, and then two months before I graduated it was two hundred dollars. So that was my habit right there.

Back then my habit was about seven hundred dollars a week. That's through my will and that included the free stuff I would get from my friend. So when I was really getting on I would usually be up about seven o'clock in the morning and just find somebody that's getting they check or whatever or I knew somebody that was getting their check. You know, I would go in the hit house I knew. I always knew somebody in there getting high. All I had to do was just sit there. On one block I got high on, it was about seven hit houses on that block and each hit house everybody was known. Everybody knew China. Especially if they didn't have a pipe. 'Cause I kept a pipe with me. Two, three of them at a time. So it wasn't no problem. You're not gonna use my pipe and not give me nothing. You know what I'm saying? Also, I knew drug dealers that I could go and get 'caine from. Didn't have to do nothing for it or whatever. You know, it was according to how you treat people when you get your money or you treat people when you get high.

I spent a lot of my day just walking. Walking either to the bank or the hit houses or walking 'round, you know. Just walking. I would be out of the shelter at seven o'clock. Just be out, period, until like quarter to eleven or whenever I got in there because I knew the guards. So that wasn't no problem. I would be getting high all that time and then in the afternoon I would be getting high.

I wouldn't eat that much. I may sometimes go back to the shelter at five o'clock to eat. Sometimes. It's according if I didn't get high or not but if I was getting high there wasn't no food on my mind at all. I lost a lot of weight. I'm five feet, five inches and I'm wearing a size thirty-two pant now. I was down to a twenty-eight, twenty-sevens, okay, and that was back then. I could squeeze into a twenty-six. So I lost a lot of weight.

Well, I think I started using drugs because of Tito's death. But I'm not going to blame it on that. Because I really just wanted to, period. I really just wanted to. I liked the cocaine high when I was smoking on that boat.

I liked the high it gave me that night and there on in. Nothing like that first hit. That first hit is a powerhouse, okay. I never thought about becoming a dope fend. I didn't care if I could control it or not. I had that attitude which I just didn't care. When I was getting high, I just didn't care. I was saying, "Fuck it!" That's what I was saying.

I kept using 'cause I wanted to. I liked the high. I really wanted to keep using. It made me feel good. It made me feel like I was on clouds, no care in the world. I could have ten dollars in my pocket, knowing I got a hundred. But I finally said, "Hey, I can't!" It was bringing me down. And I couldn't . . . I didn't like myself anymore. I mean, it's a shame that it took all that time for me to realize that but. . .

And when I remember them crack houses. . . . They all horrible. They all operate the same way. House person at the door when you come in. You either give them a caps if you're gonna smoke a lot of caps or give them a dollar or something. They all dirty, smelly, but you don't pay that no mind when you're an addict. People sitting there smoking and they look horrible. Dirty scarves on in their hair. I'm talking about the women. The men were horrible. They were dirty, whatever. It's worse now because they more dirtier, more horrible-looking people in there. It's a lot of smoking, getting high, trifling people coming in and out of crack houses. I done seen people schitzing in crack houses. Feeling for something they don't have. Feeling on their clothes and things for something they don't have. That's a schitz! I done seen people fighting over the shit. I done seen somebody get stabbed, and truthfully, they just kept on smoking. It's as simple as that. Just don't bring the cops to their house, you know.

Yeah, I saw somebody get stabbed once. He owed the drug dealer money. Drug dealer came in there. "Where's my money?" He didn't have it. Drug dealer stabbed him, pulled the knife out, wiped it off, and walked out. And we still sat there and hit. I don't know what happened to the guy who got stabbed. He was just laying there. All I wanted to do was finish my shit and get the hell out of there. But I was gonna finish my two caps that I had sitting there. I knew that before I went anywhere. The high told me not to leave. The high just told me not to.

Once I saw this bitch, her period was on . . . took her nasty-ass, trifling-ass period pad off and threw them behind this refrigerator. I snapped! I bust that pipe and everything. She was the woman of the house, but I bust that pipe and everything and left out. It was so horrible, and she smelled any fucking way. Yeah, that was the most unusual thing I ever seen.

So a crack house is a trifling place to go. First of all it's abandoned. There are no light in it, candles all over the house, broken-out window, shit like that. You have to constantly watch your back, 'cause like I said, you're in a crack house, okay. Like I just told you the guy got stabbed. That could happened to anybody. But that cocaine will tell you it's not going to happen to you. Don't worry about it. Just like I told you I had a little bit of cocaine inside that pipe and I had two caps sitting in front of me. I seen this man get stabbed and I just looked and turned my head. Hoping that it wouldn't happen to me.

But I learned my lesson by using crack cocaine. I really learned my lesson. I'm not going to say I'm never going to do it again, but I'm take it day by day not to do it again. And pray to my higher power that He will keep me off that bullshit. 'Cause it's horrible. It's a horrible experience I experience in my life. It's as simple as that. It's horrible.

Cocaine can control anybody, anybody. That shit is a mess. It really is. I love my family to death. Today, I love them to death, but if one of them was to die today or tomorrow, I know I don't have to use cocaine as an excuse to get high because they died today. May he rest in peace, if Tito was to come back alive and die again I know I do not have to go to cocaine to use it as no excuse. Just sitting here talking about it is making me sick. It's forty-seven days I been clean today, okay, that I haven't been near a drug dealer. I haven't been in a bar. I haven't been to a Jamaican to cop me some joints, okay. So sitting here talking about this is really making me sick because I know what I've been through. I know what I did, you know. Crack cocaine is not for anybody, at all. It's not even for rich white man to do, and got all the money he can possibly want to spend on this bullshit. It's not even good for him. 'Cause it will bring him rock bottom. I miss all my material things I had. All of them. That I gave up for that bullshit.

I knew I hit bottom when I left Matt and went back to that shelter, this year. That's when I knew. Simple as that. That's when I knew. He was still using and I wanted to stop using. I was fed up. I was tired of being tired. I was tired of looking tired. I was just tired. Simple as that. I was just tired.

I wanted to stop completely, not calming down, but stop completely. I mean, I knew if I would calm it down, I ain't gonna do nothing but build it back up again. Ain't no way a person can say that they'll slow down on smoking cocaine. 'Cause you can never slow down off that shit. Never. Ain't no way you're gonna go into a hit house with two hundred dollars in your pocket, just take out forty and get sixteen caps—no, eight caps, yeah, and get eight caps—and save the one hundred and sixty dollars you got in your pocket you're gonna keep and go home with. Ain't no way in the world. 'Cause one is never enough. One is too many and a thousand is never enough. If I didn't have crack I might use joint or maybe drink a little bit. But when I was smoking I wanted more. It wasn't a point where China was too amped up where she wanted to come down, because I didn't.

You know, when I were tricking with the guards, I knew I was selling myself to get that shit. I saw it that way. I knew it was, but like I said I just didn't care. I wanted that cocaine. Today I don't have to do that. I can get money from a man and don't have to do a damn thing with him unless I want to. See, I knew when they reached in their pocket and pulled that twenty dollar bill out or left two twenty dollar bills out, I knew I had to give them something for that, either my mouth or my rectum. At the time I didn't think about myself and what this was doing to me. But it did. Now I thinks about that—how dirty and cheap I felt when I did what I did, but at the time I didn't care. All I know is that I'm gonna get this money. I used to rush them to get they shit off. When I had oral sex, I did it so hard and so roughly that they couldn't help but to . . . do it like that in an instance. So I could hurry up and get that drug in my system. I had to have it. I had to have it. I didn't feel no kinds of feelings at all when I did what I did but I do feel them now. Now, I feel hurt. I feel cheap. But I'm not gonna dwell on it 'cause I knew that was not me doing what I did. That cocaine had me doing that shit. It really did. So I'm not going to dwell on it or beat myself up over it. I'm gonna better myself over it.

I can't really have anything against dealers. Because they didn't hold a gun to my head to use this shit. The only person I blame is myself. Don't get me wrong. I wish they would catch every drug dealer in this city and all over. I wish they would catch every single one of them and lock them the fuck up. Because it's not only me they're hurting. They're hurting this young generation also. Walking around here looking like zombies. Have you seen any of them lately? Fourteen, fifteen years old walking around here looking like zombies, okay. So like I said, they didn't hold no gun to my head to get me on that shit. I chose to. I put the gun to my head, not them. I screwed up myself and just didn't even know it. That's how I feel about it.

I don't think they should legalize drugs. Not any. It's killing people. It's killing us all, especially the black generation. I came across a couple of whities during my addiction. I worked a couple of them for their money but it's killing all of us. Simple as that. Drugs is killing us all. Thank God, I do have good health. Thank God, I didn't get AIDS through my addiction or the HIV virus. It is a good God. I'm strongly trying to find my way back to Him. Not back to Him but into Him again. Like I was.

Before I got into drugs, work was important 'cause I loveded material things. Right now work isn't important because I'm trying to find myself again. I don't want no more headaches. No more worriations. Not right now anyway. Eventually, yes, I will have to find a job to maintain my life all over again. But right now I'm not worried about working.

It's all about honesty today. That's the kind of program I'm in today. Because it's so many gay people out here that been experiencing the things I'm telling you and not coming forth and telling somebody. Which they should, okay. It's a fucked-up thing when you come from a halfway decent background, always got what you wanted as a child, stole things just to be stealing them, okay—didn't have to—and to then get on cocaine and fuck up your life and not tell somebody. But it's beautiful to recover off cocaine. It's a beautiful thing. I'm telling you. It is. Right now, my goal is to stay on this recovery road. Make my meetings, get a sponsor, talk about the tragic times I had with cocaine but also talk about the good times I am gonna have. Stay in a positive relationship. No getting high whatsoever at all. Work on getting my own apartment. A job first of course. Work on getting my own apartment and I want a car this time around. I do want a car and hopefully, by the grace of God, I'll go back to school. It's a lot of things, a lot of goals that I can see clearly now. I can walk out this door and actually hear the birds and see trees. I don't see darkness. I don't see a pipe right there in my face, okay, and it feels good. It really do. I can look in my mirror today and say I love you. It feels good. But like I just told you. If anybody ever want to know about a person experiencing with cocaine, ask China, she'll tell you. You'll see it in her face, you'll hear it in her voice. It ain't shit. It ain't shit and if you doing it because the crowd is doing it, you gonna fuck yourself up. I'm telling you. I was one of the lucky ones. I didn't do it because the crowd was doing it. I did it because I wanted to do it. Do you know what I'm saying? Bottom line, cocaine ain't shit. It will take everything away from you. Everything!

*"I was in quicksand, and I found
a branch to hold on and pulled
myself out of it."*

Detra

I know some people say that drugs allow people to cope with their problems. Not cope, but escape from them. It's not a coping situation 'cause you don't cope with your problems when you're high. You just postpone them until after you're sober up. So really it's just a way of trying to escape, but it's just like, you know, it's just like they just waiting there for you when you wake up. When I get high, right, I'm able to play those roles better because of it. So when I'm with those customers I can get into the role model better. But I'm still trying to figure out why I continue to use drugs. The time when I was in the hospital for five months was about the only time I've stopped using drugs for a long period of time. I've signed up for treatment, but I never went. Well, I do have a habit, and from what I hear, these programs take so long to get in. You still have to shoot up while you're put on a waiting list. I do want to stop, 'cause it's getting to the point where the stuff is really garbage. I'm getting tired. I am getting tired.

My street name is Detra. When my mother's mad at me or something like that she calls me by my real name. When she feels like playing with me, she calls me Detra. I'm thirty years old. My mother is fifty-five now, and my father died when he was thirty. I guess I was around nine or ten when he was shot.

He worked at one of those there meat storage, cold storage freezers, up there on Seventh Street under the bridge, Hering, Seventh and Pendleton. We used to live at Twenty-third and Hering. King Street was having a gang fight, a gang war with Coaltown, the Barnfield Street gang. My father was coming from work, walking up Hering, and he caught a stray bullet. They caught the fellow and they prosecuted him and all that. My mother made sure of that 'cause she went to court, you know. Made sure that he got punished. I don't think he did life or anything like that, but he did go to jail.

When he died I didn't cry. I was more concerned about my mom and how she was taking it. My mother refused to bury him in the tie, the traditional, because she said he was young, you know. She didn't want to dress him like that. Well, he had a black silk suit with a white turtleneck and a medallion with a fist on it, which represents strength. And me and my brother we wore black silk suits and white turtlenecks, and my two sisters wore pleated skirts with the black vest and white turtlenecks, you know. And my mom didn't want all these phony relatives that only comes up, she said, "They only come out when someone is dying." So she didn't want all that. So we didn't have the usual thing at the house, you know, when the family comes. She didn't want all the relatives calling, getting into her business about insurance, you know. My mother is very, very . . . she just didn't believe in all that because they were phony. And then after the funeral she told me and my brother, "Y'all go out and have fun with your friends. I don't want y'all 'round the house moping and stuff about Dad." So I wound up, you know, going out with my friends, hanging out with them. And then I also think she wanted to be alone, you know, because a couple of night after, I used to hear her crying late at night when everybody was asleep. 'Cause it was like, I think, about seventeen years they, you know, were married.

I remember him. Although I'm closer with my mother than I was with my father, he was very . . . he was very good. My brother resembles him more than I do, but, you know, I never forget when I was little, some fellow, some boy had hit me and I wouldn't hit him back. And my father gave me this ring and told me that it was magic. And he told me, whenever I don't hit someone back, the ring would get tighter and tighter, and I had believed that for a long time, you know.

I remember little things about him. Like we would ask to go to the movies. So we had this vestibule. He said, "If y'all can get past me," talking about me and my brother, if we could pass him we could go to the movies. So we rush on, climb over him, and stuff. So I remember good times with my father.

I also remember one time I had hooky school with a friend, a neighbor, and that's the first time he ever beat me, you know. I had . . . my father made me apologize to Mom for hooking school. I also remember a couple of times when we lived at Twenty-third and Hering. In this shed kitchen, I found a syringe, and I said, "Mom, what's this?" And she wouldn't tell me, and she just took it away from me. But after I got older, I start figuring out things on my own. I don't know whether it was a habit or he just did it sometimes. I do know that he did use heroin.

When I got older my mother told me my father was incarcerated for shoplifting. He used to boost. I used to always tell people he was in the service, you know. He used drugs, right, and he used to boost. My mom said he was considered one of the best boosters. Him and . . . and we used to call this fellow Uncle. His name is Artie Franklin and we called him Uncle, right, but he wasn't our real uncle. And him and my father was boosting. My mom said that they were like one of the best dressers in the world, best boosters in Jefferson. So I image that that's why he was in the penitentiary.

His death wasn't a big turning point in my life though. 'Cause like I said he wasn't there when we were growing up, you know, and my mom is the thing in my life, you know. She was the power player, you know, to me, like the head matrix. She was the matriarch, head matriarch. Yeah. She still is, you know. What she say goes. Like, we're grown and my brother, my sister have had . . . but she call on that phone and say something, you know, or if she found out that one of us was doing something wrong or stupid, she still is that head. She tells us to do something, we'll do it, you know.

I was also close to my father's mother. Her name was Caroline, Caroline Jones. When I was young, I couldn't say Caroline. So I used to say Cary. So that was her name. Everybody called her Cary, you know. And she say, "Whose baby are you?" I'll say, "Cary's." She used to work at this here restaurant, Clark's Restaurant at Seventeenth and Dover. It was a restaurant and it was a bar in the back, right. I think her and the Jewish fellow who owned . . . I think they were messing around, you know. She was there for years and years.

Anyway, I would come in there and eat free and all that stuff, and there was a movie over across the street, which is now a church. But up next to the restaurant, well, that used to be a movie next to there, and the owner let me and my brother come in free on Saturdays, and then at lunchtime we could go over my grandmother's and eat lunch and then come back into the movies when she was working and stuff. So anyway, yeah, she was . . . I guess by me being the first born, you know, I was very tight. . . . That affected me, that affected me when she died immensely.

She died before my father. So I guess I was around eight or so, like that. When my mom told me about it, I ran all the way from our house, right, all the way up to Seventeenth Street, 'cause she lived on Seventeenth and Cumberland, over top a beauty shop, and I ran there by myself early in the morning. And my father was there already, and we started crying. I kept saying that she wasn't dead. I went to the funeral. I heard them whispering about whether or not to let me go or not 'cause they knew how tight I was with her. But they wound up letting me go. And so when I saw her, right, I kept saying she didn't look like her. I kept saying, "That's not Cary, that's not Cary." I start crying and I blacked out, and they took me out the funeral home and stuff like that. I didn't go to the cemetery. My mother wouldn't let me go.

She was going with this fellow, a ex-prisoner or whatever. Anyway, after they broke up, I was told she started messing with a young guy that lived around in the neighborhood, a young black guy. I never known him. I never saw him. But she used to keep . . . she got paid under the table. Anyway, she kept jars of quarters and dimes in them big pickle jars they used to have. She used to have jars of them under her bed, quarters, nickels, dimes, and stuff like that. When she wanted to give me change she tell me to go up under there. Anyway, the day they found her, they found the door broken open and they found her laying on the floor naked, right. And all her money was gone, you know, and they were saying something about this fellow she was seeing, you know, that he was up there or something. Anyway, it was never proved and no one ever saw him, so I don't know what the case was. I don't think it was not foul play. I think they were fighting or there was an argument or something and it might have started something and he might have panic or something like that. I don't think like him attacking her or strangling or something. I don't think that happened in foul play.

My grandmother used to drink a lot. After she got off of work she go back there in the bar and she would drink. And then it was the speakeasy, Miss Brown across the street from her, and she used to hang in there all the time, you know. So she had cirrhosis of the liver, you know.

I remember having a dream after her death. I don't know if everybody have a dream like that, but when my sister passed away, my niece had a similar dream. Well, my grandmother kept saying, "Come on," you know. She was telling me to come on, right, and I kept saying, "No, no." And then my mother woke me up, and let me sleep in the bed with her that particular night.

Yeah, I also had a sister to die. The sister that I stay with now is the youngest one. I had another sister that was older than her. Betty was into drugs, and she died. She had an artificial heart valve. They say that was from the coke that had eaten her heart valve or something. Then she had a stroke.

I'm the oldest, but she was the oldest girl, you know. She was twenty-seven, I think, when she died. She died three years ago. She had a different father, and was conceived when my father was incarcerated. Her father useded drugs. I think. He is in jail, and he's doing life now. His name was William Jones. He was known as one of those old gangster guy, stickups and all that stuff. Anyway, he doing life. My mom told us that. Redbone . . . light-skin people always thought they were cute and stuff like that. . . . And she died, but I loved her to death. So there's four of us, two girls and I have a brother.

Betty was the only one who wasn't one of my father's kids, but my father loved her to death. He used to call her Betty with the tangerine belly. Make little rhymes and stuff. And she loved him to death, you know. She was very affected at the funeral. Crying and screaming and stuff, you know. That's when she found out that he wasn't her real father. I had already figured that out, you know.

I was closest to my mother 'cause like I would help her watch the kids and stuff. When she was carrying Coco, that the youngest girl, right, I was doing things like washing dishes, helping her clean up, washing clothes and stuff like that. My brother was outside playing baseball, hanging out with the fellows. I didn't mind at all. I was 'bout nine year old then, someplace around there.

My father came back home to live with us during my preschool age. Like I say, we lived in the projects then. And it was a knock on—I'll never forget this one—it was a knock on the door, and I answered the door. And he said, "Is your mother home?" So I said, "Yeah." But I knew who he was, you know. I don't know how, but I knew who he was. And I jumped up in him arms. And I started asking him, "Is you gonna stay?" I asked him if he was gonna stay. He said, "You have to ask your mommy," you know, but he wound up staying with us. I think that's when he came home. Yeah, he came home from jail then. We lived in the projects, Walter Anderson projects, and when he came home we moved out of there and we moved to an apartment at Thirtieth and Barnfield. Then when my sister, my younger sister was born, we got a house at Twenty-third and Hering. So they were going to tear down those houses and make a schoolyard. So that when we had to move, and we moved to Twenty-sixth and Barr. That's where everything start happening. All my . . . what would you called them . . . my turning spots in my life.

So, okay, on Twenty-sixth Street, I remember my father he had quit his job for a better, doing the same kind of work, but for the government. And him and my mom went shopping and he bought the new, new outfit, jumper—you know, whatever they were, those one-piece sets, you know all that. Then he was laid off. Okay. After that he start heavy into the drugs. He left my mom for this woman, named Paulette. She was into drugs, you know. And then that's . . . that was it. That didn't last too long because he died.

This is bringing up thoughts that I remember, but I'm trying to put them in the sequence that it happened. So the order might be a little messed up here. I think my father lived up . . . okay, let me put it like this. He was with us when we moved there to the new house. He was messing with this girl, this Paulette, but he was still coming to the house. See what I'm saying? And later on I found out they were doing drugs together. And then when he got shot coming from work, right . . . my mother, my mom hated her, Paulette, you know. And we didn't talk about it too much. She didn't want to talk about her.

But after that, right, she had to support us. . . . She didn't work. My mom didn't work but she knew how to . . . she taught us this, how to do checks. She always told us, always have a checking account because you never know when your electric or something like that. . . . That way, even if you don't have the money in the account, you can write them a check, and that gives you enough time to get the money together, you know. She used to tell us little secrets, little hints and stuff like that. She used to do checks for furniture, air conditioners, things like that, and sell them.

She'll open a checking account, right. Okay. Like say she get a hundred dollars to open a checking account, then she'll go to Pennyman's, that was a furniture place, Silo, and buy a bedroom set or whatever. Write a check out for it. They'll send it out and then she'll write the check out for it.

So she ordered it over the phone and they ask credit or charge. And she say cash, you know. So they send it out, and she'll write a check out for it, and then she'll sell it to somebody that wanted it. Like her friends might say, "I want a living room set" or "I want an air conditioner," and she'll order it through the phone, over the phone. And they'll bring it out, and she'll write a check out for it and then she'll sell it to the people. The company would send her threatening letters about the check. First, they would tell her that the check bounce. So send a money order or, you know, cash, whatever. Then they'll say that they're gonna put it in the hands of a detective servicing thing. Then they'll send a couple of letters, and then after awhile they'll stop, 'cause eventually I guess their insurance pays for all of that, you know. And that was the end of that, but this is how she made her money.

She did it for quite awhile, you know. A couple of times she got caught, right, and they would give her like a year's probation with restitution or something like that. I'm not sure how old I was when she started doing the checks. I don't know exactly. I'm quite sure she was doing these checks for quite awhile, but when I knowed about it . . . it had to be when I was in junior high school, Boyer Junior High. Eighth grade, so I guess that's what? . . . fourteen . . . thirteen, fourteen . . . when I was in the eighth grade. I was in high school, John F. Kennedy, when she stopped. I was in the eleventh grade. So she did it for about three or four years.

I remember one time she order a ring. A cocktail ring, I'll never forget it, seventeen diamonds in it, right. And it was brought out by United Postal Service, so that federal stuff. You know, mail fraud, whatever. And she had it under "Cynthia Rice," and after she got the ring, she wore it for awhile. Then when times got tight she sold it. About three or four years after that, the federal people came out and asked for Cynthia Rice. She knew what it was about, right. So she said no Cynthia Rice live here, right. So they asked her to write the name Cynthia Rice twenty times on this paper. They're trying to see if her signature was the same. But she always do it differently. So I guess they never had a case because they never came back out on that, you know.

She also did this thing with credit cards. Somebody would bring her a credit card and she would use them or whatever. She had connections where if the credit card was too old this person would buy all old credit cards. Ship them over to the West Coast, and for each old credit card you get fifty dollars for it. She had that kind of connection.

I also remember a time when the police came and confiscated some things from the house that she had got from a check. They knew . . . like an air conditioner and a stereo, right, which they had the serial number of and she wasn't home that day. To keep from us being embarrassed around the neighborhood, he just act like he was coming, you know, taking it to get it repaired.

They confiscated it, you know, then after that she stopped, you know. She stopped the little hustling. She start getting widow's compensation, you know. She had to fight for that a long time. Then when she finally got . . . she got a large, very large check, you know. She stayed with me for awhile. She stayed with my brother for awhile, right, and then she got a little house down there in Kendall, down on Sycamore Street, near DePaul, DePaul College. That's where she's at now.

It was real hard for my mom then, you know. 'Cause I think the best times of my life I remember is when we lived on Twenty-sixth Street and we had a nice house. It was hooked up so nice. I was really proud of it, you know. I used to sit outside with the stereo blasting and door open so people could walk by and look inside, you know. And during that time is when I realized that there were other people like me—gay, you know—because before that I was always by myself. I was in junior high school when I found out there were other people like me. My first friend, you know, that was gay, I met him junior high school. We were in the eighth grade.

I always knew I was different from the fellows. I had a lot of friends that were females that I hung around with, playing rope and stuff, but I was very . . . I couldn't play the men's sports very well like baseball and all of that stuff. And . . . I always liked looking at fellows. I didn't know why. I just liked looking at them.

I didn't know nothing about sexual intercourse or nothing like that until I was forced upon, you know. And that happened before we moved to Twenty-sixth Street. I guess ten or eleven or something like that. There was a recreation center down the street from us. Athletic recreation center on Twenty-fourth and Hering, and in the evening, between six o'clock and ten o'clock, I used to go over there for arts and craft and drama classes. And the older fellows used to go over there to play basketball in the gym. And it was this guy, I'll never forget him, his name was Timmy. He was dark-skinned with a scar down one side of his face, and I guess he was about nineteen, eighteen or nineteen. And I was always afraid of him 'cause he . . . when it was time for the place to close up he would stare at me, and it made me nervous. And one night he waited outside for me, and he told me to walk him through the playground, right. And so, being scared of him, I walked him through the playground. And he . . . stopped me and told me that I had to give up something. At the time I was thinking, I thought he was talking about money or something. And I told him that I didn't have no money. So he said you have to give up something, and he patted me on my butt. I still didn't know what he was talking about, but I was scared to death. And then he grabbed me by my collar and took me down in the boy's bathroom. The boy's bathroom was situated where there was these steps that goes down underground, right, and he ripped my jean open and laid me down. And when he entered me, the hollering, because it was real painful, so he put his hands over my mouth, and then he did his little thing, right. When I got home I didn't tell nobody, but I took a bath. I was bleeding. I took a Band-Aid, put it across my butt, you know.

But then, whenever I ran into him, he used to catch me, you know. Like I may have to go to the store for my mom or something and I would run into him and he would catch me and take me somewhere, like in an old house or something, and have sexual intercourse with me. Then I would get an ass whooping for taking so long at the store, but I still didn't tell.

One day, he had caught me and he took me into this alley, and this is the first time I had ever had oral sex. He made me go down on him. But I rather have done that than the sexual intercourse because it was like real painful, but he made me stop and he wanted to have sex. So I said I know a place where . . . I said I know an old house where there was some mattresses in there. So he said, "Okay, let's go." So we were walking down Farmer Street, and I was walking ahead of him real fast, right. So he told me to wait up, and I started running and I ran and turned the corner and I screamed, and it was a police parked on the corner and they jumped up, jumped out the car, and they grabbed him. I kept running. I didn't see him anymore until I got older. Until we lived on Twenty-sixth Street. Come to find out, right, he was on parole or something, and he had violated it, and he had to go back and do years.

It was funny how I met him again. Yeah. Years later. My sister, oldest sister, Betty, told me she had met a new fellow, and he was taking her to the movies. So she was upstairs getting dressed and this fellow knocked on the door and I opened the door, and it was him, years later, right. So I said . . . you know, I was flabbergasted. So I said, "You don't remember me do you?" So he said, "No." I said, "You don't remember the little boy that you used to fuck in the playground years ago." And then he smiled, "Oh, yeah! How you doing?" Like that, right. So I said, "Alright." He said, "Is Betty here?" I said, "No, she's not here." But she was upstairs getting dressed. So he left. He said, "Tell her I'll be back later." So I said—no, by then me and my sister were real tight, and she knew about my homosexuality—so I said, I said, "Your friend," I said, "he's the one," you know, I ran the whole story to her. The whole bit about what happen, where I met him from. So when he came back to pick her up, right, she smacked him and told him don't come back to see her no more. So that was the end of that, you know.

As far as being raped, I thought about it. I didn't like it at all because it was painful, right. But I didn't harbor on it, you know. It was just . . . when he did it, okay, I didn't like it, but like it didn't . . . it didn't traumatize me or nothing like that. I was just too young and immature to feel that he robbed me of something. As far as now, I don't . . . as far as me thinking that he done took something from me or like kept me from experiencing women or something like that. No. It was a turning point though.

When he raped me, right, like I said, I didn't know nothing about sex or nothing like that. So therefore I . . . I really didn't know, you know, I just didn't know anything. All I knew that he went in me, and it hurt very badly, and I didn't like it at all. So that's all I feel about it. I didn't see it as sex. I just saw it as something violent and something painful. It was just something terrorizing, you know. I was scared, it was painful, it was uncomfortable, and I didn't like it. I just put it out my mind until it happened again. Until the next time it happens, you know.

I had told my sister after . . . let me see . . . okay, after I learned about homosexuality and stuff, and I was more comfortable about it and everything, I started telling my sister about things, you know, about gays and fellows especially. I had two shoeboxes full of letters from different fellows, alright. It was mainly like writing fellows in the penitentiary that wanted to meet and write to somebody and I used to let her read them, you know. These fellows never saw me except for pictures I sent. But they would write things like, "I want you to be my queen" and all—you know the lines that they give—and she was just flabbergasted that these fellows, you know—they sent pictures, gorgeous fellows— she was just flabbergasted that these fellows would feel this way about another fellow. So I was explaining to her, right. I said there are a lot of fellows that mess around with gays. She didn't believe it.

So there were a few fellows they used to come and see her, and one of them was . . . one's name was Doc, right. So I brought it to the attention that he wanted to have sex with me. She didn't believe me. So we made this little setup thing. I said, when he comes over, I said, you just go upstairs and hide behind the dresser and I'll prove it to you. So she went upstairs and he was over there, and I said, "She'll be right back," you know. So he was waiting for her. So I was playing my Diana Ross records, and we had a big mirror in the dining room and I used to pantomime. I would be up there dancing and all that stuff. So I could see that he was getting aroused, right. So he told me that I had a big butt, and he liked to get into it. So I said, "Ain't nobody here right now," you know like that. So he said, "Where are we going, in the cellar?" I said, "No, we'll go upstairs in my room." So I took him upstairs in my room. My sister is behind my dresser now, right. And he was pulling his pants down and everything, and she came from behind the dresser. I said, "See, Betty, I told you." Well, he wanted to beat my butt, you know he wanted to kill me. And, you know, she cussed him out, right. So after he left, out of humiliation and stuff, I told her, "Listen there are a lot of fellows that like men and women." I said, "They may not tell, you know, say it in front, you know, bring it out, but most of them are like werewolves, they come out when the moon is full," you know. "They like doing their thing at night." So after that she started understanding men, and you know when men . . . so when the fellows were talking about faggot this and faggot that she always was, "Don't hand me that shit because you probably fucking one too." You know, shit like that.

But at nine or ten I felt very strange about being gay. Like I said, I knew I was different than the fellows even earlier than that, you know. I always found myself being by myself. When I did try to play baseball or something with the fellows, right, they always wound up chasing me out the game because I couldn't hit the ball or I couldn't put the ball in the basket. There is one game I used to play called five-ten-ring-out where they had teams, and one team catch the other team and put them in this little block, and when your team members have to run and say "five-ten-ring-out" to free his member out of there. Now, that game they loved me in because I knew how to run real fast. And like my whole teammate be captured, right, and I'll be the only one that could save them and get them all out. So that was the only game they really wanted me to be in, you know. But the sports, no. It was nothing happening on the sports, you know.

I found myself day dreaming and alone a lot. When I got to Boyer Junior High School. . . . First of all, Richard Cobb, right, went up to the eighth grade when I was going. I was in the seventh when they changed it, and so they transferred those that was going to the eighth to junior high school. So I was in Boyer Junior High School and I met a friend there. My mom use to call us Mutt and Jeff. His nickname was Dinky. And we used to hang around a lot. Okay. We never said anything about, "Hi, I am gay and I'm . . ." you know, nothing like that. But we just knew that we was alike, and we just hung together a lot. And then I notice that for awhile he wasn't coming to school with no lunch money. So I asked him why he wasn't coming to school with no lunch money. He said that this person was taking his lunch money, you know. So now this is my best friend. I said, "Who is it? After school you show me who it is." Now, I was no big tough, you know, but I wanted to know what was going on. So he took me around . . . after school we went around Baker Street, and this person, named Eddie, was the one taking Dinky's money. Now, he wound up being gay. He was gay too, right. So wind up all three of us wound up being real tight, you know. Sitting on the steps, playing records, 'round Eddie house. He was raised by his grand-mother on Baker Street. And we be drinking sodas, sitting out there. And then that's how I started meeting other gays 'cause then Eddie introduced me to Barry and then Jesse—they were brothers and they both was gay and they lived down the street further, you know. So now I'm starting to meet other people like me, you know.

When we moved on Twenty-sixth Street, that was the first time I did it on my own, right, with this fellow that lived on Harper Street. You know how kids, you know, call each other's mothers' names and stuff like that. So that's how that one started. We were calling each other—his name was Nicky—and we were calling each other mother names. So he said, "Oh, shut up before I come up there and fuck you," right. I said, "Yeah, you come out here and try it." So that's how that one happened.

He came outside and we went in this here old backyard and I let him screw me. And, okay, this was our little secret. We were doing this for about a year. Just me and him. Now, I was elevenish, I think between eleven and twelve, around there, between eleven and thirteen. Yeah, I had just started meeting Dinky, you know. So yeah, junior high school.

Junior high school was like the turning point when I start experienc-ing new thing, find out that there was other people like me, having sex with Nicky, and I was enjoying it. And the fellows, okay . . . the gang in neighborhood was called Twenty-sixth and Pine gang, and . . . and they knew I was gay. They always called me "faggot," "little sissy," or something like that, you know. And they were big bullies and things. But this one named Duke, they called Duke, he caught me coming out of Nicky's house late one night. So he asked me what I was doing in Nicky's house. So I told him that Nicky wanted some records that I had and I brought them over there. But he didn't believe it, and he told me to come over, to be at his house tomorrow morning before school or he was going to fuck me up. His mother go to work early in the morning, and he lived on McCormick Street, right behind my backyard. So I was around there and he was looking out the window, make sure he seen me coming, and I came in and we started having sex on the sofa.

So somebody in the wet cement in the alley—the grown men was doing something to the wall—and somebody had put on there my name and Nicky's, you know. And this, you know, took me out, that my name was up here with Nicky. You know how they do like with Yvonne and Ron and put a heart shape. Well, they had my name and Nicky's up there, right. So I said, "Oh, my God, somebody know." You know. So I took a stick and tried to scrape it out. So then I had stop dealing with Nicky. Duke and I was having sex once in awhile.

Now, most of the fellows in the gang, right, I had sex with one time or another. But in the daytime it was faggot this and faggot that in front of their girlfriends, you know. Until one day I just got angry about it. I said . . . 'cause they all was trying to hide it from each other, you know. And they all had dealt with me one time or another. So I told them in front of their girlfriends. I told them that "y'all call me faggot this and faggot that in front of y'all little girlfriends," right—which the girls were friends of mines, you know—I said, "but are you telling them that y'all fucking me at nighttime?" you know. And then, the girls, you know, were laughing and calling them this and that, you know. The boys wanted to whoop my ass, but I was gone in the dust, you know. I said that, and then I fled.

And then my mom had told me about when it came to fighting, because she always believed the fight, whether you win or not, you know, she said, all you have to do is just showing that you will fight, and they will leave you alone. I was sitting on the water ice stand and Nicky's brother came up to me. Showing off in front of the fellows—and just steady punching me in my chest, right. I picked up a milk bottle and crashed him in the head and we started fighting. But after that I had no trouble with none of them as far as physical abuse was concerned. And some of them, you know, they still wanted to have sex. Even after I had exposed them, you know. And this went on and on.

Then we found out about downtown. This is where all the gays hang, up on Badger Street. This used to be between Thirteenth and City Hall on the other side of Main, right. It used to be a Fox movie and this little street called Badger Street and this famous seafood place called Patterson's plus the gay bars, but the older gays, you know, would hang in these bar. We couldn't get in, but we used to hang up there and by hanging up there we meet others our age and that was gay. We all hung together. The police used to chase us from one side to another. Be about fifteen or twenty of us, you know, just acting crazy and sissying down Main Street and stuff.

So then we start hanging downtown. Now, the fellows up Twenty-sixth Street told me and Kenny, the queen that lived up there, that we were neighborhood faggots and that they didn't want us out the neighborhood anymore. You know, one of those thing. We didn't pay it no mind, but we still hung downtown and stuff. By hanging downtown we start experiencing new things, sexually and every other kind. I mean we was just exposed to so much stuff.

Oh, yeah, this remind me. Like up Twenty-sixth Street when the fellows used to say, "Play with this," I used to wonder why they want me to do that, you know, play with their thing, to masturbate. I didn't know nothing about that. And I had never had an orgasm at that point. Until one day I had took . . . one evening I was taking a bath and it just crossed my mind about these fellows and how they used to tell me to play. So I was . . . I said, "Let me see." So I was doing it myself. But my arm got tired and I stopped, right, and then another night I said I'm gonna continue till something happen. So I kept doing it, doing it, then I start feeling weak and jittery and then the sperm came out. I just looked at it and rubbed it, you know. Then it got in the habit where I was doing it every night, and my mom, she used to say, "What you taking so long in the bathroom for? What are you doing, playing with yourself? Come on out that bathroom." Well, that's how I learned about the jerk-off situation, masturbation.

Downtown, I start learning other . . . foreplay. I start learning that there are fellows that really falls in love with other fellows and not just one for screw in the butts. I learned that there was a variety of different types of varieties of homosexual, you know. Drag queens, you can consider all types. I learned this by being downtown, you know. That's when I got my first boyfriend.

So I was fifteen when I had my first boyfriend and I met him downtown. He was from North Jefferson. He was from Vair Street and they called him Mookie, right. Now, Eddie . . . me, Eddie, and Dinky, we're still hanging out, right, but me and Eddie we started getting more close now because we used to run away from home together. Like if I had a argument with my mom and stuff, I'll call Eddie. "I'm packing. I'm leaving." Everything might be kosher at Eddie's house, but because I'm leaving, he gonna leave too. So there we are downtown together hanging. So that's when I met Floyd—Mookie. He had ran away from home, and his cousin, well, his supposed been cousin, Scott, they were together. So I was hooked up with Mookie, and Eddie was hooked up with Scott, and we would hang together. Early in the morning when the milkman bring the milk out, we get the milk, and the bread man bring the bread out, we get the bread. And then you go to Corley Square or out in the park and sit and play around, you know. Up in the bus terminal, when Greyhound was on Fifteenth Street, you put . . . I forgot . . . fifty cent or something and you could take a shower, alright. So Mookie and Scott taught us how to climb over it to take a shower. And they taught us how to go into Blair's in the basement, in the bargain basement, and put on a pair pants underneath our old pants and things like that. So we were changing clothes and throwing away our old clothes and taking them down and taking a shower. We used to steal little rings, you know, to make ourselves look ritzy and stuff.

Well, you know, when I ran away, first of all, I call them minirunaways, because there were no more than like two or three days or something like that. I guess I did it about four times. 'Cause like sometimes Eddie would have a argument and I do not feel like running away from home, you know. I didn't feel like it, everything's alright. But we had this little pact, so I got up and left, you know. I'll come back about two days later, starving, hungry, and then I'll go back to school. Then after awhile, she just . . . you know, there was no curfew for me no more. I could go out and come back in the morning and stuff like that. So that eliminated the running away situation because I could hang out, you know. You know, this is like on the weekend, you know. She definitely wanted me to go to school. So on the weekend, like on Fridays, I can go out, go to the parties, and I can come home on Saturday morning without being in trouble. So it was peaches and cream.

My mother got involved in a relationship with this guy, Jeff, when my father died. It was a drug relationship. He was on drugs and he got my mom to use drugs. She started using heroin. And he was one of those . . . he wasn't as educated as my mom was, you know. And she taught him about the checks and things like that, you know. So but he never looked the part as far as going to stores. He just didn't look that part. He lookeded suspicious. He was illiterate too. So my mom did that.

They got along with each other alright, you know. It was the drug that they had in common. But there were plenty of verbal fights over things like him, you know, not giving her the proper amount of drugs or something like that. Or him going off somewhere getting high without her—you know, drugs. I call them drug arguments.

He didn't assume any responsibility in the household as far as telling us what to do and things like that. My mom wouldn't allow that. He didn't work or help out either. Like if he made some money he would give my mom some money like that, but as far as going grocery shopping or buying us clothes. Uh-uh! It was just that my mother felt that by him not being, you know, our father or anything and nothing more than her boyfriend or a companion that he had no right to be.

When she got involved with him she didn't decrease the time she spent with the family. It was just altered. You know what I mean? You know like, since they were doing, you know, their little hustle and things, right. . . . Okay, my brother was outside playing with his friends or doing what he was doing, I was watching the girls, you know, or cooking breakfast or fixing lunch for them or something like that, you know, and. . . . So like I said, I was sitting and had my music playing—I was into my music a whole lot. So I don't know if the rest of my sisters and brothers knew it or not. I did. That she was starting to get high, you know. I don't know if they just didn't want to know it or. . . . Well, I know my two sisters might have been ignorant towards the fact. I don't know if my brother just decided to ignore it, but I knew what was going on.

Before he came in our lives I was trying to find myself, you know. Trying to find out why I was different. But as far as my relationship with my mother before she met him, my mother and me were very tight. She was like who I looked up to. In fact, when I started dragging, alright, I imitated her a lot, you know. Back to when I was little, I just remember certain little things like when she would take me and my brother somewhere and the fellows on the trash truck would whistle at her and stuff. I used to feel so proud about that. She had sexy legs, and she had this sex mole on the back of her leg and she would wear her heels and her jet black stocking. And she used to work at this after hours club called the Elite Lounge. And in the evening, she said, "How this look? Should I wear this or should I wear . . ." I said, "No, wear the orange one with the shingling," you know, "with your black heels." I would help her get dressed, you know. Things like that. So I be standing there watching her get dressed and things. So that's how I entered life, when I start dragging.

So anyway, back to Jeff, now. Before he came on the scene everything was peaches and cream, okay. My sisters and brothers . . . my brother, we didn't have too much to say about it one way or the other. But my sister, Betty, right, the one that passed away, she was very vocal, as far as how she disapproved of him. I always felt that my mother loved me. She was . . . in fact, she was so worried, you know. She never expressed it but I could see . . . I mean she never said anything, but I could see the expression on her face, right. Whereas, she was a little more worried about me accepting him than she did the rest of the kids. So I put her more at ease when I told her, I said, "Look, although I don't really care for him but if you're happy, then I'm happy. Long as he don't hurt you or anything." That was like a relief for her.

After he came on the scene, she relied on me as far taking care, you know, my sisters and them, and you know while she went out and did her little hustling stuff with him. And then they would go upstairs. Back then, she used to have the front room, and me and my brother had the back room. When he came on the scene we switched around. She took the back room and we took the front room. So when they came from their little hustle or whatever, you know, they used to cop and then they go. . . . I knew they had something 'cause they go straight on upstairs and close the back room door, lock it, and do their little thing back there. I be downstairs, playing music and cooking and all that stuff, right. And she may holler downstairs, "Oh, what did you cook? Did you cook what I told you cook?" And I said, "Yeah, I cooked that." You know, blasé, blasé, you know.

I guess she was in that relationship for about a year, maybe a couple of months less than a year. Then she had to do all that cleaning up by herself, as far as getting clean. She tried to stop using heroin after he left, right, because she always thought by her being a mother and older that she didn't look right going copping from these young people, you know, and stuff like that. So she never liked going on her own to cop. He did all the copping, but by him not being on the scene anymore, you know, I guess she had to, you know, but I guess it was so uncomfortable for her, she wound up getting on a program, and then she's the type where she don't like people to tell her what to do, you know things like that. So she wound up getting off the program, getting the meth out of her system on her own, and then that was that.

But she hit rock bottom, you know. She lost the house, and all that stuff. After he went back to jail for the violation and the robbery and stuff, she got caught, you know, doing her little check thing and stuff like that.

Alright, shit, I'm trying to get these ages. . . . I start dipping and dabbing with drugs, using heroin at around sixteen. This was the time when I start going downtown and everything. I told you this is the turning point, you know. I was introduced to it. But like I said, me and Eddie, Mookie and Scott, right, we were always together. Even when I was back home with my mom, right. I would still go downtown, or me and Mookie talk on the phone for hours. You know, we'll listen to this record, playing records to each other over the phone. We met older people, older fellows, some were gay and some weren't. And this particular one had some heroin and gave us some to snort. We were over their place. They had a little place up in North Jefferson. We were over there and we started snorting, you know. They lived over top a pawn shop, right up here. And we start snorting and stuff like that, right. So that is how I got into it.

Let me see, that was around sixteen. My mom start getting sloppy as far as her hustling was concerned, and start getting caught and stuff. They gave her probation and pay restitution. She . . . they cut the electric off, things like this. I was in twelfth grade, and it was graduation time, right. I didn't want to go to all that, you know, because I knew my mom didn't have the money for the . . . you know, to get the new outfit and stuff for the prom and all that. And then I really didn't want to go no prom anyway, you know, 'cause I wasn't interested in no girls. So in a way she was relieved. 'Cause I said, "Mommy, I don't want to go through all that," you know. I say, "I'm not going to no prom." During this time the bills are stacking up. She was trying to cop on her own but was very uncomfortable about it. She was getting on a program to get off the heroin. The only one that really needed the watching out was the baby, you know. She was like maybe nine, you know, Coco. I graduated, and that when I really start getting into the drug, right.

My mother was struggling. Trying to keep the house, and trying to, trying. . . . You know I think she was trying to put things back like it was before Jeff came into the scene. I used to call it the Fall of the Roman Empire, you know. That was my little thing. Everything was peaches and cream, and then a barbarian came in and destroyed it. And I think she was trying to get things back to that way, because she talked about it a lot. You know, how things used to be.

Alright, I was doing my little thing with the high. My mom was trying to clean herself up. She didn't know I was messing around. When my brother graduation came up, right, the girl he took to the prom was pregnant, and her family talked him into marrying her. You know marriage and all that stuff. And, you know, I told my brother. I said, "Well, because she's pregnant that don't mean you have to marry her, especially if you don't care for her that much to marry her." Right? My mom was telling him, "Do what you want . . . don't be pressured to answer if you don't want to." I kept saying, "Where y'all gonna live?" I said, "You know the situation with Mom and all of that, and her problems." He wound up getting a job. He got a house down on Llewellyn Street, right. That's down near Remington and Oldham. So that's where him and his wife was at, okay.

By this time my mother lost the place. It was like a empty shell. My little sister, she was like mainly staying up my grandmother, which lived on Porter and Dover. Betty was in North Jefferson with her man. Now, all this time we didn't know she was messing around with drugs, right. He turned her on to drugs. And so it was like me and Mom in this shell. This shell that used to be our house.

There was nothing in there. The furniture was gone. The electric was off. We had candlelight. Eventually the water was cut off, because of the checks she wrote, and they wouldn't accept any more. Her pride is just too-too, you know. I wasn't gonna let her stay there by herself. We start washing in alcohol, you know. She said, "That's good for you anyway," washing in alcohol. She always had some kind of saying for doing what she was doing. I used to come in with money. She never asked me where I got it from, but I think she knew. I was working on the street. I used to get dressed over somebody's house, or go in the gasoline bathroom. Put on my makeup and stuff. Before I go home, I just take it off. All this happened after I graduated from high school.

I always hate talking about my mother using heroin. Like I said, I looked up to her so much, you know. I could see the hurt in her. I could see the hurt, the humiliation. But I wouldn't let her know how hurt I was about that situation. I told her if it makes you happy, when it was concerning him, if she's happy, then I'm happy, you know.

I was hurting terribly. I was embarrassed that she was using. I was also embarrassed that she was with someone like that, you know. A lot of people knew what he was into. Whereas, with my father, I don't think . . . I'm almost positive that he used much more discretion. This one didn't care, and then the fact that my friends' families and stuff in the neighborhood start knowing. And that was embarrassing. That the neighborhood starting, you know . . . the house that I used to be proud and keep the door open, I didn't do that anymore. So all these things that was hurting me, I kept it in. Wondering if other kids go through that—are there any kids my age going through that type of situation with their parents? Making excuses, you know, okay, like when Dinky and Eddie . . . I had stopped my company from coming over. Once in awhile when one of them did come over, and if something wasn't normal or something was gone, I used to make excuses for it or something like that. Before, I used to let them come in and we sit and play records, but after that, we either sit on the steps or we'd go out in the park or to the playground or something.

I think she started selling the furniture because she didn't want to take too many chances, you know, as far as the police and stuff like that, and being caught, you know, but still at the same time she had this habit to support. So I think that was why. I was happy when she got on the program. Also, she was miserable. She did not like the idea that she had to see a certain person, and talk to them about things that she normally deal with herself, you know. The fact that she would be punished, like she didn't get her meth if she didn't show up at her appointment or something like that. She didn't like that at all. That was real, real hard, and she stopped going. She started going to her doctor, getting something to sleep at night and stuff like that. With the medication, the pills and stuff that help her sleep, she managed to get the meth out of her system without being real uncomfortable. And now, I think that's another reason why she's not interested or hadn't been interested in being with another person because of that. Now that she done built up everything, got a nice porch house and all that stuff, and her grandchildren. I don't think she wants to take that chance any more.

It was horrible. It was really horrible. There were no light, no water. There was nothing downstairs. Even the carpet off the floor was gone. We stayed, me and her, stayed in that place in the dark, laying on a mat . . . a mattress. We went over my grandmother's and to the restaurants, and things like that. We lived like that for about eight months. Before it started getting real cold, and then she went to live with my brother. I either lived in a hotel, with a friend, or whatever. That went on for about four or five month before I got my own place on Fourteenth and Hering. So I always, you know, I made sure I had enough money to cop, get a hotel room for the night, you know, something to eat. Then, I had made a real big sting, and I went and got an efficiency apartment.

The sting was for seventeen hundred dollars. He . . . I met him up the Christine Club. He spent fifty to go out with me, right. So when somebody spend that much money, you know, well, he got some money. So when he was paying for my drinks he opened his wallet and I seen this big roll. So okay, so we got in his car. I usually like to take care of business in a car, because it's cramped and it's close together. Whereas, in a hotel he may take his pants off and put it way over on the other side of the room. We went near the Art Museum, and I had his pants down, and. . . . Well, before, he called hisself being slick. He paid me the fifty dollar bill, and he took his wallet out and put it on the floor between the door and his seat, right. And I was giving him a blow job, and I had reached my hand up under the seat and felt the wallet. So while I was taking care of business, I went into the wallet, took the money out, and stuffed it up under my wig. Okay, so now, you know, money makes noise, so I start making loud sounds like I was enjoying it, you know. Then after I took all the money, I put the wallet back. So after we got finished he put his pants up, and he was driving me to. . . . He said, "Where do you want to go?" So I said, "Take me High Street, High and Church." He was driving me to High and Church, and I was hoping that he didn't go for his wallet and check it, you know. But I seen him reach down. He just reached down there to feel, to see if his wallet was still down there, and that's all. So he let me off at High and Church, and I got a taxi and I fled.

And then when I was in the taxi, I just bent down and reached in my wig, and I seen all these fifties and hundred dollar bills, right. First, I went back to my hotel room, because I had to cop and didn't want to carry all that money with me up to Walter Anderson. So I took out the amount that I was going to cop with. Then I went back and took off. Then I thought, I said, now I'm going to get me a place, you know. I always give my mom some money when I make a nice sting. Always. For me, that's good luck for me. And then when I told her how much it was, she was so worried that I was gonna get robbed up there either copping or some dude was going to charm me out of it. I said, "Mom,

you know better than that, because you done taught me about fellows."
I found an apartment at Fourteenth and Hering. I called it the suburban
part of the ghetto, because it was right across the street from Zion
Tabernacle, and that one whole block was lined with pretty trees and
stone brick house and stuff. So I found a place there, and it was a
month's security. I gave him that and two months in advance. I started
buying little things for the place, plus keep my habit up.

So this period, the Decline of the Roman Empire, lasted for several
years. So from around fourteen. . . . Alright, it started from the time Jeff
came on the scene, and gradually it deteriorated. Like I said, I was giving
her money, and she never asked me where I got it from, because if she
knew she would have told me to discontinue it. I knew that she needed
a little money, and then I had my habit. I couldn't stop anyway.

This was a very difficult time for me. I was with this fellow who was
a dealer, right. I met him at a club, Club Christine, and he appealed to
me, right. That was supposed to only be a one-night thing, but after that
he used to come out looking for me. We started seeing each other and
we started having sex. After I got turned on to the drug situation, he was
more my druggie than my man. Before then I didn't know anything
about the drug situation, you know, until we actually hooked up. I knew
he kept a lot of money, you know, but he told me he worked. Then,
when we did get tight enough, he told me about his business.

First, he was just a sex thing, and then he kept on insisting on me
getting high with him and then one day I tried it and I start liking it.
Then we start . . . I guess you would call it hooking up, or whatever, but
this was . . . my reason for it was because I had started doing it regularly,
you know. Whenever I asked for it he would give it to me, and I started
doing it regularly because I like the high. You know, after awhile when I
first realized I had a habit I thought I had a cold. He said, "Detra, you got
a fucking habit, you don't have no cold." You know, I think if I would
have continued thinking that I had a cold, I would have just left it as
having a cold, you know. But since he told me I had a habit this added on
to it, and I just started doing more and more.

I was seventeen when I started and it took me I guess about six
months, eight months to develop a habit. Heroin was the first drug I
ever used. Before that I would like drink, you know, have a drink or

something. But heroin was the first, heroin was the first. He shot me up. That first high was . . . it's something you can't explain. It something you've never felt before, especially if it's your first time. It's something that made me feel so relaxed and peaceful and contented. It like a state of mind it has you in. You're floating and there are no problems, you know.

He kept getting on my nerves about trying it, you know. He kept just getting on my nerves about it. So I said, "Okay, what the hell." I said, "Come on, because you're getting on my nerves keep asking me this and I keep telling you no." So he gave me a little bit and I liked it, you know.

And then this was about maybe fifteen cc's or something like that. That's a little bit. He was doing like ninety, you know, or something like that. And anyway, and then what he was putting in there for himself, fifteen, I was like out of it, and then after awhile it started getting . . . after awhile I started getting used to it and I wasn't feeling the fifteen and I started wanting more, then he started grinning, and he said, "Oh, I got you now." Which he did 'cause then it got the point whereas whenever he wanted me, you know. I think that was his purpose of getting me hooked, to control me.

In the beginning I thought I would be able to say, "No, I don't want any," and be able to sit up there and let him do it while I just drink a soda or something, but it wasn't like that. Every time he got off, I wanted to get off. I started feeling my stomach turning, and my glands, you know, saliva in my mouth, and so I'll break down and ask him for some. I'll say, "Where's mine?" or something like that.

I finally learned to hit myself. Well, by watching him do it, after he got busted I had no alternative but to try it myself. The first time I did, I did it 'cause I had a mark where he used to always hit me. So I went in that same spot and that's where I got the hit at. After awhile, right, it started getting more and more difficult trying a find a place to hit. But that's when it wind up where I started hitting in my leg, because it was starting to get so difficult to find a vein in my arm. I've only shot up in my arms and in my legs.

I've seen people go outrageous places that I would never use. You know, like in their groin. I've seen one queen, two of them, they went in their penis. They would make it semi-hard. It gives me chills to the bone. They would make it semi-hard where that vein would pop up and then they'll hit. Bonetta, right, she had a miss one time and an abscess and after it healed up it was a hole in so deep you can take the edge of an eraser and stick into that hole. In her penis. Oh! I had seen them take off in this vein here in their forehead. I used to call them Frankenstein. 'Cause they be standing there nodding with this needle still stuck in them. I say, "Child, why don't you take that out your head." And they in the kitchen like this, nodding with this needle sticking out their head talking about "Boot it again, boot it again." I say, "Oh my God!"

I was in a relationship with that dealer for about a year. Maybe a year and two months, something like that, before he got busted. I had a really big habit and no way to support it. I was forced to make the transition. I just, you know, I walked out there, you know, where everybody, where the girls hustled at, and got me a trick. It was like that. It was no planning or no. . . . I just knew that I was sick. I knew that, you know, certain spots where they make money at, where girls and stuff make money at, and I went up there. I turned my trick and I copped, and I sat there and got me a hit, and that was the beginning of the ballgame.

Anyway, my mom, when she was staying with me, right, she found out that . . . I knew that she already knew, you know, she had to know that I was using drugs, but I wasn't feeling good, and she had some money and I asked her for some. And she asked me what it was for. So I told her that I wasn't feeling good. Then she said—she knew what it was, but she wanted to take me through this, you know—so she said, "What's wrong with you? You need to go to the doctor's?" I said, "No, Mom, I just don't feel good. Can I borrow some money?" She said, "What do you need the money for?" You know, taking me through them. . . . So I just told her that I had a habit, right. She said, "I was waiting for when you gonna finally tell," you know. Then she told me, you know, that I needed to get my ass on a program. So I kept telling her that I would, I would, but I didn't get on no program. Then eventually the money came in for her widow's benefit thing. This was after years and years and years of fighting it in court. Then, that's when she got the house down there.

My mother believed in God, you know, but she used to say, "God is in your heart." You know, things like that, you know. She does things, you know, like if she . . . like for example I was in the hospital and she used to write down things like, "God help him get better," and things like that and then put it in her Bible, you know. That's her way of asking God for help.

My mother used to tell me things too. I guess by me being the oldest, she used to tell me her problems, you know. It made me feel grown up. And by my mother not shielding me that way, shielding me, and not lying or sweetening or covering it up, right, I was more prepared for certain things. Well, I think if she had me in a more protective role, things like that, I might not been prepared for . . . I wouldn't know how to deal with it. You know what I'm saying? I . . . okay, like for Dinky and them, okay . . . Dinky was the youngest. His mother died at birth. His father raised them. So his brothers and sisters always protected him, you know. Lied to him about life and all that stuff. So when, okay, when he realized his homosexuality and was out there, he was very naive, you know. Was believing everything a fellow would tell him and stuff, you know. Whereas, my mom used to tell me, "Niggers talk a lot of shit." She used to always say, "Always get your own," you know. "It's nothing like your own." These little things I remembered and, you know, that's how I feel about it now. She said . . . she used to say, "You'll get more from a stranger than you do from your own family." Whereas, like asking my brother, my sister when she was alive, for something, I would get it faster from a stranger than from them. So the little things that my mom told me wound up being true.

So I learned that independence is very important. Having your own, trying not to rely on people for things that you need. If you're in a relationship, try not to be the vulnerable one in the relationship. Other words, try not to be the one that's overwhelmed, you know. Some relationships one person may be more involved than the other person. I feel as though the relationship that I was in, right, I . . . they were always more consumed in me than I was in them. My mom feels as though you have more of a power position that way, you know. And like . . . and I found out that to be true. 'Cause I've seen some of my friends where they were the one that was more obsessed and they were like treated like dogs, you know.

I rather not be in any relationship. Which I've found much more relaxing anyway, not being in a relationship at all. Not having feeling, not being in love with a person, because even being in love with a person, you know, it's like pleasurable and painful at the same time. You can't get enough of them, you know, and when they're not there you want them to be there. I rather just go to sleep without having all of that on my mind, you know. So when I find . . . lately like if I find a person and they're trying to get me in a relationship, I usually just backs off. I tell them I just don't . . . that's just not in the cards for me now, you know. I've done experience that and I'm just not ready for that again.

Respect was an important thing for my mother. She said . . . she used to always say, "If you give respect, you get respect." She said, "Demand respect, especially if you give it," you know. She also talked about keeping yourself clean. She used to tell us, the first thing a person look at is your head and your feet. If you got runned over shoes or something like that, she used to always . . . you know, the first thing a person look at is your head and your feet. And things like, always keep clean under-wear on you, you never know when you're going to the hospital.

When she found out about with my homosexuality, she told me about douches, taking a douche, you know. She used to tell me if you knew how to talk you can get what you want, you know, by talking and never have to give it up—having sex for it, you know. That went a long way with me, even when I'm out there tricking, right. A man might ask me, "Do you swallow come, or golden showers? Do you like being beat?" right. Okay, say what they want to hear, then when you get that money do what you want to do, you know. And if you know how to talk properly and know what to say out your mouth, you're able to go 'head and get that money without doing what you don't want to do. I learned that from her.

I used to always think that I was the, you know, favorite, but I guess it wasn't the fact that I was the favorite, but that I was the oldest. So therefore, she, like I said, she confided in me more because I was the oldest. I personally think, now, that I'm the favorite, because we've been through so much together that she hadn't been with the rest of the kids. And that's one of the reason why I'm a little more closer with her. My brother, right, he remind me so much of my father, but he's very independent, but he's very gimme, gimme, gimme. He'll take, take. But see there's one thing that my mother have that I didn't get from her. I'm a little more emotional than she is, you know. A little more . . . I don't like to use the word "humane," sensitive than she is. Whereas, she used to say like being in love with somebody or something like that . . . she used to say, "Love is in your ass." I guess this was after Jeff's experience, the Jeff Era, I used to call it, when she was with Jeff. She used to say, "Love is in your ass." She said, "When you feel it, you go 'head and get your rocks off and that's it."

When it comes to relationships and being in love and falling in love and all that stuff, well, I still believe in it. I used to feel that when two people love each other, they sacrifice for each other, you know. To me that was love. She say, "That's bullshit."

She had a whole different little varieties of ways to discipline from not watching television to cutting off allowances, not able to go to certain places we had plans on going, or staying in your room, different things. It have to be something very, very, very bad for me to get a beating. I've been beaten for hooking school. I didn't do too much stealing when I was coming up, but mainly what I got it was for hooking school. Oh, if we lied on an adult, you know.

She would use a belt. The most serious beating I ever got was the one my father gave me, and that was for . . . that time I told you I hooky school with somebody. Yeah. By him being so heavy handed, and he was using his hand, and it was hurting so bad, I had welts, and I had peed everywhere, you know. Then he made me stay in my room, and then, when I asked to come out three days later, I had to apologize to my mom for "hookying" school, you know.

She was very clean. She believes in that, and she said, she used to always say, the kitchen, the bathroom, a person can tell your house from the kitchen and your bathroom. Definitely keep them clean, you know. Even after Jeff, the place still stayed clean, you know, because she got in her thing, it didn't stop her cleanliness or nothing like that.

Before she got in her bag she did all the cooking. I used to cook sometimes. Like I said, she had asthma or when she was sick, I used to cook for the kids. When she started using drugs, right, I cooked quite often.

She was also particular about the way I dressed and how I looked.

Even when I start dragging she was very particular about how I looked. Like when she was staying with me, right, and I would get dressed, she was around and she always made sure that I didn't look like no whore or anything. You know, wearing stuff up my ass. I'm still that way when I'm dressed. Dresses just above the knee, nothing all the way up here. Mucho colors, you know, things like that, conservative basis. You know, because of her values about how a person should look, right, it made me able today I'm able to go into like different hotels without being spotted as being a prostitute or something. A lot of my customers like that because they can go in a place, a public place with me, and they may see black and white but they wouldn't see man with a prostitute or something like that.

I don't go out with black men financially. First of all, they don't have the money, like the white man. Second of all, a black man takes a longer time to come, to reach a climax, than a white man, and time is money, you know. Then, most black men think they're so slick. They want all this. This want this and that, and take forever for them to reach a climax, and then when they do, they try—girls get a lot of bad experience—they try to take their money back and all that. I find that white men treat black women much better, and they reach a climax like that, you know. They don't take you through a lot of changes and they spend more money. So I deal with white men. But for my personal pleasure, black men.

In the beginning my mother was concerned about the kinds of people I hung out with . . . with Dinky and then about them being gay. . . . When I started hanging out with them she had an idea that I was gay, but she just didn't want to accept it, you know. I remember she told me a long time ago when I was real young, right. My uncle told her that I was gonna grow up and be a little sissy, and she smacked him, you know. So I guess my relatives saw things that she didn't see or ignored in me.

I think for my uncles and them I think it was one of those old superstitious things whereas if a boy wasn't real macho and stuff he'll grow up to be a sissy. I think it was one of those things, you know. But the fact is that when I was babysitting and my mother wasn't home and stuff, I used to try her dresses and heels on. This was when everybody else was asleep, try the dresses and heels on and stuff.

My mother discovered I was gay when I was at. . . . The older queens had a selling party down in Erie. Me and Mookie, Eddie and Scott, we went to the party, right. I had this little short wig. Somebody gave it to me, but I can't remember now. And I had that on with a little eyebrow pencil and Eddie had his own with a little eyebrow pencil. Somebody must've called the police or something, and the police came and raided the place and locked the older ones up for corrupting the morals of a minor. So us four sitting up in the cell scared to death, right. And then they had to call our parents. So first Eddie's parent . . . oh no, first Scott's parents came, right, and they told him that he was at this freak party. So you could hear the echo, the belt, the strap, you know, echoing in the hallway and he hollering. So I was scared to death. So Mookie was talking about "Don't worry, I'm not gonna let nothing happen to you." I'm saying to myself, "Now what is he gonna do?" So then Eddie's grandmother came, right, but she didn't beat her or nothing. She treated him—when you get back home he was gonna get an ass whooping. Then my mom came, right, and they told her, "Yeah, your son was at a freak party, you know." I had took the wig off already, but I forgot the eye shit that I had on there. She said, "What is this shit you got on your face?" She smeared it all over my face, right, and then took her pocketbook and just bashed me upside the head and we went home, and she made me sit there and tell her about this party. To me that's worse than a ass whooping. When they actually make you sit there in front of them, "Don't look that way! I'm talking to you. Don't . . ." You know, one of those thing and will make you go through details, details, you know. So that's what she made me do.

So she was concerned about the people I hung out with. She thought Dinky and Eddie was corrupting me into being a sissy. She didn't never call them faggots. She used to call them asses. "Keep them asses out my house" or "Stay aways from those asses." Things like that. But after awhile, when she start understanding about homosexuality, right, then she start accepting it, and then that's when she was telling me about respect and giving respect and getting respect and things like that, and never let nobody use, never do nothing that you don't want to do.

So by the time I was around sixteen she had accepted the fact that I was gay. As for my brother, he didn't care one way or the other. We never had a fight in our whole life as children. Never had a fight, you know. He just did his little thing and I did mine. I remember one time, I was downtown. I had this phony ID card to get into the bars, and I was downtown, me and Eddie. And him and his friend was up there and they were with these two older, older queens. They were school teachers, right. And I was shocked to see them. They were trying to get in the bar. So he called me over there and asked me for my ID, right. I said, "What you doing?" He said, "Just give me the ID." It was a gay bar so I gave him the ID, right, and then we went in the bathroom and he told me that "these two dudes was gonna give me and my homey some money." They wound up going to East Jefferson with them, to their house, right. He never told me about if they did any sex, but when he came he said they got drunk. The two gays got drunk and fell out, fell to sleep, but before they fell out to sleep, they said help yourselves, and they wound up stealing their color TV and their component set and their money. But that's the first and last time I ever heard of him being associated with some gays.

My oldest sister knew, right, Betty . . . well, when she first found out, she didn't accept it all, you know. We got into horrible fights, but then when she got used to it, we became very tight. She . . . it was this club. This was when the gangs started turning to clubs, right, and it was this girl club called the Pretty Girls, and they only picked the very best girls and only the popular girls to be in it, right. She was picked and she was so excited about it. So I told her that I knew some shop where she could get clothes and don't have to worry about somebody else having it. It's one of a kind, like by being downtown, I knew about the boutique shop, Samantha's, Unique. So she was so excited. I took her up there. My mom gave her money to get a dress or something. I took her up. Help her pick one out, and then I stole one. You know, that way she would have two, you know. I taught her how to put false eyelashes on, eyeshadow, and things like that. I had learned a lot of stuff from *Vogue* and *Bazaar* magazine that I used to steal. I used to put them up on the dresser and watch and imitate when I was by myself.

Betty was arrested for misuse of credit cards. She was over in one of those malls in Somerset County. Her and this fellow, and the credit card, you know . . . she had used the credit card the day before, someplace else, and got over with it. And she took the chance to use it the next day, and it showed up as being, you know, as being a hot card. One of the fellows that hooked her up was a pickpocket. He would go on the buses, you know, with the newspaper bit, and all that. Okay, so the money, you know . . . they'll split the money up, because she'll be with him, like camouflage, and then she'll use the credit card.

When we were growing up my brother and sisters were very close and very protective of each other. For example, my sister Betty, in the neighborhood, one of the fellows had . . . she was around the corner or something . . . and one of the fellows had said something pertaining to me . . . excuse the expression, fucked me in an old house. It was a lie, but anyway, she went off, you know, pitching a bitch and everything and ran in the house and got a butcher's knife. And so I'm asking her what's wrong, and she's telling me, so I have my jeans on and a pajama top. So I'm running after her and my mom running after me, and the dog running after her. So we all wind up around the corner, right. So the dude had a gun, and me and him was at it, and my mom kept saying, "Please don't shoot him, don't shoot him." I kept saying, "Shoot, motherfucker! Shoot, motherfucker!" He pulled the trigger and it misfired or it didn't fire, and it was this here chair frame in the trash. I picked it up and just started beating him in the head. And there were some other fellows from the Twenty-sixth and Dover gang. They were there and they all start running. Me and Betty were chasing them across Twenty-eighth Street with the butcher's knife and the police came and then we wind up going home. But that's an example of how tight we were.

During the time that I grew up, at that particular time, right, it was gangs in my neighborhood. That was the main problem in the city. Like I said, Twenty-sixth and Dover gang was home right there at Eighteenth and Barr. As far as drug selling and stuff, that was really, you know. . . . So really the only real crime was trying to keep the gangs in order. And the shootings and stuff like that.

Well, like I said, the block I lived in is where they hung at. As far as they're fighting and ganging, they always went different areas to do their gang fighting and stuff. Like I guess you would call where I lived at home base, and when they start fighting and stuff they would go wherever, you know. They may fight the Sheikhs or Coaltown. So they'll go down to their turf and do the fighting and then come back home and hang out.

Some of the fellows in the gang I was sexually involved with—about half of them—and the other half wanted to. Just didn't have the nerve to pursue it. Then when I got older I ran into some which they had went to jail and had got educated. As I call it as far as sexual, homosexuality is concerned. Came out, ran into me, and they were into a whole different ballgame, you know, as far as, you know, just anal sex. They learned a whole lot of other things when they were in jail. And when they came home, I maybe ran into one or two and we, you know . . . they offered, "Let's go get high," or something like that. And then we wind up having sex, and they come out with their little bags of tricks, you know. And these nigger . . . and these were the same ones that was faggot this, faggot that, you know.

Yeah, usually when a fellow says he's been in the penitentiary or just came home from the penitentiary, ninety-nine percent of the time when it comes to homosexuality they done a whole lot on both sides. My mom call it "pancakes," "making pancakes." They could have been, okay, the man in the relationship, right, but at the same time, they let their woman, the queen, screw them, you know, to make sure she reach a climax. In other words, interested in making sure that she is satisfied sexually. On the other hand, if any fellows should try it, they would knock their block off.

As for me, well, okay, after I had that fight with Nicky's brother, right, I was like accepted in the neighborhood. I was just, you know, gay, and like I said the other couple of gays that moved in our neighborhood, like we were considered Twenty-sixth and Dover's gays and nobody else's. Like they had their women, you know, Twenty-sixth and Dover women, and they had their Twenty-sixth and Dover gays. At the time, you know, at the time, they used the word "joint." You know, "You're my joint," you know. They didn't use "girlfriend," 'cause we weren't no girls, you know. So therefore, it was like we were Twenty-sixth and Dover joints, you know.

And like I said, when we start hanging in town and not in the neighborhood anymore, they start getting upset about this. So if we were gonna screw anybody, we were gonna have sex with people on

Twenty-sixth and Dover and we weren't supposed to be going down-town picking up people and having sex. Or going to some other gang or something like that. We were supposed to be the gay girls of Twenty-sixth and Dover.

These fellows still considered theyself a man, you know. Not a gay man. I doubt if they even thought about the situation as being bisexual, you know. I image they just thought that they were heterosexuals and no more. They had they girlfriends and stuff, and as far as them having sex with us, it didn't count. So therefore they didn't considered them-selves as homosexual, nor a bisexual. Just a heterosexual that had, you know, that had sex with a gay person when they weren't able to have sex with their girls. There were a couple of them that was more . . . more involved with the sexual play with homosexual. I don't know if it was because they had been to reformatories, and done that in reforma-tories and stuff, but I noticed that there were a few of them that would get . . . really get down. I mean, throwing the tongue in our mouth and sucking on the chest, and the love making and the whole bit. Where most of them were like put the grease in, just go 'head and jam you, you know, "I want to bust a nut." But there were some that really wanted, that was really passionate with it, you know. But they were all trying to hide it from each other. That was kind of comical, you know. You know, this whole group of fellow, and they all trying to be macho, macho.

There were a couple, right, that I later on in years found out were gay. That they wanted a homosexual affair more than they wanted a heterosexual affair. This is the way that I rationalize. They were in reformatories, like a Juvenile Detention Center, and that's where it started from, you know, as far as having homosexual . . . hooking up with a homosexual. And then when they got on the street although they had their girlfriends they missed that homosexual affair. So therefore when they ran into one of us and they got with us, they always took me somewhere where we could be comfortable. They insist on getting buck naked. Where most of them they just want you to pull your pants down and touch your nose. But these want you to get naked, and they want to make passionate love. Those I considered as bisexual, you know, be-cause of the women they also . . . the girls they also hung with in life. As

I got older and ran into some of them later, some of them were actually hooked up with other queens, you know.

But it wasn't hard or difficult for me to live in that neighborhood. No, it wasn't. It wasn't difficult at all. In fact, you know like I said it was time when I would hang on the corner with them. With the girls, with the fellows, you know. So like I said after awhile it was like just accepted, you know.

When I start going into town, right, okay, and start meeting different queens and stuff, I started wearing tighter jeans, you know. I start wearing tops that looked more feminine. Things like that. I had my hair permed, curled. We use to call them Greek boy curls, you know. They just little circles all over. Like the Greeks had curly hair. A little mascara, lightly mascara, little things like that. I wore the same kinds of things to school, but very lightly. Not where it's so noticeable, but very lightly.

When we were in junior high school and it was time to go to high school, and you had to choose. You had three choices, you put your top, number one is the one you really want to go to, then number two, then number three. Dinky talked me into putting down John F. Kennedy. I didn't know that John F. Kennedy was an all boy school at the time, right. So I put down John F. Kennedy. "Let's go to John F. Kennedy." "Okay, let's go to John F. Kennedy." So that first day we gets there and meet in the auditorium, and I say, "Dinky," I say, "ain't nothing but boys in here." She said, "Yes, child, that's why I picked this . . ." I said, "What!" You know, I went off on her. I said, "Child, why didn't you tell me this was an all boy school?" I would have never went to no all boy's school, you know. And so I said, "What am I going to do now?" So I was thinking about getting transferred, right, but I said, "I'll try it out."

I was so nervous being in this classroom with all boys. 'Cause most people can look at me and tell that I'm gay, you know. Especially then, I was so feminine, with high cheekbones and all that. So I just used to be real quiet and stuff, you know. I remember one day we were in gym, and they have you sit on your little spot, your designated spots, right. And it was this queen that I knew and they had went to Kennedy like a few years, before I got in there, and they came back to visit the teachers. Well, this child had on these tight belt hipsters hanging off her hips, hair sprayed silver, you know to a point like Diana Ross, and makeup on, and she come to visit, to say hi to the gym teacher. And she seen me sitting there, and said, "Hi. How you doing?" I said, "Oh, Lord!" So all the fellows looking at me, right. I said, "Oh, my God!" I was embarrassed and nervous because my clothes is in this locker room—you got to take showers, you know. Now, I've been exposed, you know.

So anyway, I managed to get through there. Most of the queens that I was, you know, hanging out with in J. F. Kennedy, we were in the choir, you know, because we made the choir and we were library aides. And so the queens that wasn't in our little clique used to catch hell from the fellows, beat up, and everything, you know. But the ones that was in our little clique, the fellows didn't bother with, you know. They may say faggot this, but they didn't do nothing physical.

And so some of the fellows like from Tenth and Bank gang. . . . It was these two twins, Jamie and Joe, they were from Tenth and Bank and they likeded me and Kenny. And Kenny was the one that lived up the street from me, Bradford Street. And they wanted us to spend the weekend. That was impossible for us to spend the weekend with them, you know. They used to come into the library or cut class and come in the library so that they could see our little drag pictures—you know, pictures of us in drag and stuff—and listen to stories we used to tell, you know, about things.

I remember the last day of school, we had said we were really going to sock it to them. We were gonna come there with the hipster hanging off and the chain belts and the mascara. It was about eight of us, right. The only one who came to school the last day was me and Dinky. And we had hipsters hanging off our hips and mascara, and we were the only ones in there with all these fellows. I said, "Oh, my God." And we had to take our books back to each classroom, and so these fellows were following me from class to class. So I ran into this classroom that wasn't my classroom. I thought it might have been a teacher in there, but it was a classroom full of fellows and no teacher. So one fellow said, "Give me a cigarette," right. So I was just giving out cigarettes just so they could leave me alone. Then I seen Dinky easing by with a bunch of dudes behind him. So I hollered, "Dinky, Dinky." So they turned around and seen Dinky and start following Dinky. I haul ass down the steps to get out the school. And then here come Dinky running out school, right.

And we were talking about . . . we were saying they were judy bitches. They did not even come to school, you know. This was the last day of the tenth grade.

When we were running around and stuff there was a lot of finger popping, but I wouldn't say we were real flamers, but we did our little share, you know. Like . . . like another one, Jeff, who came into our school in the middle of the term. Now, she was with the older queens, although she was our age, right. So she would like come from school straight from hustling off of High Street, you know. With the short wig on, mascara, and stuff, but she'll have jeans on with fishnet stocking and penny loafer. So they stayed after her ass. They, you know, . . . they came to a point where she had a taxi waiting for her after school because the fellows were just harassing her too terribly, you know. 'Cause then she wasn't in her little clique.

It took a lot of strength . . . gut to be out then. It took, yeah, it took a whole lot to be yourself and enjoy yourself. With the bashing and the fear. I guess I was able to do it because the particular group of gays that I was hanging with all felt the same way. You see what I saying? And so we did as we felt, you know. I guess if I hung with the type that was so . . . that were insecure with their homosexuality, I probably would have been the same way. But I didn't hang with those guys who were in the closet. I was hanging with those that expressed theirself, and the ones who enjoyed theirself, and that's why I was like that too.

I dealt . . . well, I dealt with the situation as it arised. Like, for example, the name calling. Sometimes, like we'll run into a fellow that would . . . especially, it was somebody that we knew that was calling us names, you know. And we knew for a fact that they were hypocrite or that have done things with other queens, we expose them. Right there on the spot in front of their mother, whoever, because we felt like if they had enough gall to, you know, to do this to us, knowing that they are in this too, then what they get is what they deserve. Whereas, all they would have to do is just don't say nothing to us, and leave us alone, then they wouldn't risk that, you know. And then fellow that we didn't know, right, and was name calling and stuff, then we'll tell them, I say, "Yeah" . . . we say something like, "Well, yeah, y'all like . . . you're like this in the daytime, but at nighttime you're up on High Street trying to find some queen to screw," and that shuts them up, you know.

The violence situation, right, when it comes to violence, is usually in gangs. It's never one fellow who's trying to fight. They always get their heart pumped up when there is a bunch of them. When it's a bunch of them and only one gay person, you know, and therefore you have deal with that accordingly, and get out their way. Don't stand and fight a bunch of people, a gang of dudes.

In school we didn't have too much trouble with all of that. Our little clique didn't anyway, because . . . because most of the fellows liked us. I mean, some of them like us sexually but not just sex. Just liked us because we were funny. We kept them . . . we kept them laughing and stuff. There was this feather factory in town and when the balls come up, we'll go up to this feather factory during our lunch break and steal us some ostrich feathers or what chicken coop feathers or whatever we need for our gowns and stuff. And take them back to school and put them in our locker. So during between classes, right, you may see one of us on the third floor with ostrich feather walking down. . . . And the fellows be falling out. So they liked us.

I didn't get into any fights into high school. In junior high school I did. In the locker room, after gym, after the showers. I hated taking showers. They used to hang in the showers waiting for us to come through so that they could ground on our butt or . . . you know. I hated showers, but one fellow happened to call me a faggot and one word led to another, and he swung and hit me. He had one of those belts with the big buckles on it, and I took it away from him, and beat him with it. Well, for a queen to beat up a fellow, you know, that's a no-no. So his homey wanted to jump into it, but the fellows wouldn't let him 'cause they said it was a fair fight. And the dude took his belt buckle and I didn't have anything, and I still beat his butt, so. And then when the other fellows see something like that, you get a little respect.

I like the guys I hung out with because they were like me, you know. I always thought that I was the only one in the world that was different, you know. I became more demonstrative because I hung with them. You know . . . it's not that I thought that the way homosexuals were about, it's just that, that's the way I was feeling on the inside, and by meeting these guys, I had the opportunity to express the way I wanted to always, you know, the way I felt, feminine. Before then I had to suppress it because I never seen anybody . . . no other fellows act like that. But then I met a group of fellow who felt the same way and was expressing it, right. And this is how I started. It was something within me.

I had thought about sex change, but—you know, it ran across my mind—but as for me to actually change my sex, no. I have a moral and religious hangup about that, you know. I mean, I was born like this. This is the way my mother brought me in the world, a male. As far as me being a homosexual, that was part of the deal. You know what I'm saying? And I could not, I would not be comfortable laying up there getting cut up and everything to be a woman when that's not me. You know what I'm saying?

Like I remember a fellow in the bar. He had told me that—he was commenting on my attractiveness, right—and he was saying that God knew what he was doing. He said, "Because if you had been all man," then I would have been too much, as far as being with the women, and he said, "if you would have been all female," I would have been too much. So to equal it out, He made me gay, you know. I never forgot that.

I wanted to be a fashion designer when I was younger. Then I wanted to be a model. Now I want to be a sociologist. I think young people that are realizing that they're different need so much help. I don't think it's really out there for them. Because they committing suicide. They're getting into drugs. They're not able to talk to their families. And to have somebody that can just come and talk to you means a whole lot. I had to go through that alone until I found a group of people that were like me. If they knew . . . if there some kind of thing they had hooked up in the schools, right, not only homosexual, anybody that felt different, can come and talk to you, I think that would cut down the suicide rate among kids.

My mother knows I'm doing what I want to do. I'm not hiding. I'm not disowned by my family. You know what I'm saying? It's so many that I know has been completely disowned from their families. No communication whatsoever. I'm myself, and I'm blessed being myself, you know. That's a whole lot being gay, you know, 'cause some people go through so much being homosexual.

But I have secrets too, things I haven't told her about my life. Things like I almost got killed by a trick. I almost got strangled to death. You know, I think that would really frizzle her hair. He was a white guy who was in his thirties. He was a big, strong guy. He wasn't nice-looking, but talked very nice, talked very nice. I guess he was some kind of psycho nut thang, you know. And I had went out with him, and I didn't know. . . . I turned around and there a dog in the back of the car and I didn't know it. And then when I turned back around, he had his hands around my throat and he was squeezing me. And he was talking about how beautiful it was, and he was just squeezing me, and I blacked out. When I came to he was still squeezing, and I guess you get that last little extra strength and I went for his eyes with my fingernails, and I dug into his eyes and he grab them and I jumped out the car, and I left my pocketbook and my heels in there. And he said, "Here, come back and get your pocketbook, come back and get your pocketbook." And I was just running down the street trying to breathe, you know.

I never wished I was different, not to be gay. Because I always felt that if it was meant for me to be, it would be, you know. So there was a reason for me to be gay. Oh, I love children, and I would like to have children if there was some other kind of way to have. . . . That's why I think I consider my nieces and them my kids, because I don't have my own, and I'm so attached to them, you know.

However, I have not always been comfortable being gay. I have not. There was a time when I wanted to die. I think about committing suicide. This is why I had said something—remember I had said about the kids, it would eliminate a whole lot of suicides if there was somebody—because I had tried it.

I tried to commit suicide. It wasn't nothing that something somebody did or it was something that was in me. I couldn't find any help. I didn't know what was the problem. . . . Like I said I knew there was something different about me. I didn't know who to go to. I thought there was no one to go to, and during that time there was no one to go to. I didn't think my mother would understand it. I thought she would even be upset, you know. In other words, I had everything to the extreme. I felt like I was the only one in the world that was different, because I never know anyone else, you know. And it wasn't for the fact that I met Dinky in junior high school, I might have tried to commit suicide again, you know. By finding that one other person that's like that, maybe it was two in the world.

I tried to take a razor blade and cut my wrist. I was home alone. It didn't work. I was just sitting up there bleeding. So then I just rinsed cold water and wrapped it up, you know. It just didn't happen fast enough. I had wrapped it up, and before my mother came home I took the rag off it and put a Band-Aid there, and she never asked me what happened. I guess she never noticed it. I had a long polo shirt on.

I was I guess around twelve, thirteen. Something like that. I had been in a lot pain. And the rape only complicated it, you know. I can't even put this in words. Before the rape, right, I felt to where I knew I was different. I think I'd known that from time one, that I was different. I knew I was different. By me not knowing what it was, and knowing that there was nobody like that in the world, and then by him raping me, I thought by me being that insignificant, where I'm the only one in the world like that, that's why it was done, you know. I thought he raped me because I was the only one in the world like that. Words like self-esteem and all that. I didn't know about those words. I just know what I felt.

I think the rape confirmed that. Subconsciously, I think so. Yeah, that I wasn't important, you know. I was obsolete. I could be what . . . anything could be done to me. It didn't make no difference, you know, because I was the only thing like that in the world.

I still haven't told my mom about it. I told Dinky, and Dinky told me about when he got raped. He got . . . he was . . . yeah. By his brother's close friend, you know. He lived in the high-rise projects on Barnfield Street. And the fellow took him to the twelfth floor, which is vacant, and that's where he raped him, and then threaten that he would kill him if he told it or not. He was around the same age as I was when he got raped.

We aren't the only ones either. I know one where his older brother raped him and his brother let his friends rape him because he was gay. By his brother's been older—his brother being older—he knew he was gay. He use to call him "little sissy" and all that stuff, and he screwed him and he let his two buddies screw him.

It's not uncommon at all, and I found most of it happening when they were very young. In the eyes of these people you're very immaterial. That these little pieces of immaterial things you can do what you want to do to them.

I would summarize my early years before I got on my own by saying. . . . Well, that's kind of hard. Okay, the fact that it was very difficult but I feels as though I was in quicksand and I found a branch to hold on and pull myself out of it. Now, my drug situation is a different story. I wish I was strong enough. . . . In that regard I wish I was like my mom, where she pulled herself out of it. I still find myself very weak when it comes to drugs. I think the only way that I really will be able to come out of the drugs if I stopped dragging. Because if I stopped dragging, then the hustling would stop. The hustling stop, then the easy money would stop, you know. I would have to find other means, like working, to make money. I know people that work cherish their money more and therefore makes it last longer. Whereas, if I mess up three or four hundred dollars a night, it's no big things because I can get some more tomorrow night. You know what I'm saying?

The dragging, the sex, and the drugs are related, but I don't think I'm addicted to the sex. It's not sex. It's not sex, not to me. To me it's more like acting, acting, and illusion. You know, the fact that I'm a male and I can. . . . I guess that's the power play in it. I'm a male and I can make another male fantasies come true. Things that he always fantasized, I can bring them to life. When I'm high, I feel like, what's that "Fantasy Island," I can say and do things to make men lust for me like Cleopatra. I gets into a fantasy world like that, you know. I have made men get on their knees, you know, and they loved it. I have beat them. All types of things. I had a couple of men who were willing to leave their families for me. Although some queens will feel as though that's really grand, me, I think you would have nothing but bad luck if you would have a man leave his family and children for you and you're gay. I think you will end up with bad luck because of the kids, you know.

Yeah, the fact that I can dress up and look different anytime I want to with different makeup, eye shadow, different color hair, different outfits.

I remember when I first hit the streets and I started coming downtown I was dressed up, right. I was wearing a white see-through dress. I had a pair of heels. . . . Now, I'm tall. With heels on I'm even taller. I'm about six foot, three inches, and with a heel like this on, and it had a gold plate in the back and strapped around the ankle, hair blowing in the wind like a commercial. And I was walking across High Street and one car hit the other car. I thought it was fantastic, because they were staring at me. One time I was waiting for a light, and I heard them whisper, "That's a model." And I was just strutting, you know.

When men meet me they don't suspect that I'm a man. Not unless I want them to. As tall as I am, not unless I want them to. I had men they said they wanted to go out, right, and they wanted to know where they could find a drag queen. Well, I said I'm a drag queen. "No, you're not." You know, and because they see the breast and stuff, you know. "But I am a drag queen."

I can alter the voice. Most of the times I don't be so conscious about my voice, because when I start talking to a trick, I guess it's conditioned and I can go 'head and talk and they just don't, you know, notice it whatever. Or they might be so interested in me they don't notice it.

I know a lot of gays that compromise your feelings to where they want to be and play this role, macho, to be accepted and still wind up not being happy because they're not being theyselves. Then say they go out to a gay bar, then they have to watch to make sure nobody run into them they know or something like that. And to live their whole life like that. I have enough esteem in myself where I don't worry about things like that. I feel like my family accepts me like I am. As long as they accept me, I can deal with the rest.

I was eighteen when I finally got on my own. You know, I made a big sting, and I had a friend, another friend of my mine, named Sunni, we decided to get an apartment to share. I think I lived with Sunni for about ten months. Now, we never had an apartment before. We didn't have no reference, not all that. But we managed to run into Randall Smith Real Estate on High Street and they had in the window a list of apartments. So we just went in there and inquired about them. And we wrote out the application, you know, and put some false information as far as jobs is concerned, and gave him a deposit and then we came back and they told us that we got the apartment. It was on Thirteenth and Dover, second floor back. It was like an efficiency, you know. It had a kitchen, a bath. It had one big one and then a smaller room connected in the back. So that's where me and Sunni's first apartment was.

Let me see. That's when I started getting on hormones, and . . . start branching out. That's when I started dragging on a regular basis. You know, an everyday situation—day and evening. I started hustling more. I started using more drugs. I start meeting a different class of queens. These were hustling queens that were more into just hustling and making money for their habits, clipping and things of that sort. I start going up to a different club, called the Bolero Club, because a lot of the Italian drag queens hung at.

It was gay club, and a lot of Italian that were into different crimes and different gang crimes, you know. Some of them I think was associated in the Mafia, the North Jefferson Mafia. One time I was approached when I was up there at the Bolero Club, I was approached by this Italian and he asked me if I was interested in getting into this group, whereas they send you to different cities, like some part of the year it's good in one city, and in another part of the year it's good in another city. So wherever, whenever it's good they send you to, you know, a certain city, whether it's Miami, wherever, San Francisco. They want me to do prostitution. But the thing is that they set you up with clients. You don't go on the street. They put you in an apartment. They give you an allowance to buy clothes and stuff, and they set you up with different clients. These were more like influential people, you know. Like . . . I don't know if I should or able to say names or stuff. Anyway, he was telling me about this, that I would get an allowance, money for clothes, and set me up in an apartment. Okay, all that sound exciting and stuff. And I was getting ready to say "yeah" without even thinking. Then he told me about the fact that it was a lifetime thing. Then it clicked to me that this was organized crime, you know, the Mafia bit. So I . . . instead of me freaking out about it, I said, "Let me think about it and I'll let you know when I come back tomorrow night." I didn't come back up that next night. Anyway my breast start coming out then and I start getting really feminine. My body start getting real feminine, and it was like exciting because the fellow start being more into me—emotionally where their feeling start getting involved whereas it wasn't just they wanted to screw me and that was it. They wanted to hook up and stuff like that. By me being young and, you know, all that was exciting, when two fellows were ready to fight over you and stuff like that.

Anyway, we let other queens stay at the apartment. Like by it not being their apartment, they didn't care. They just start doing everything. Breaking into other people's apartment in the building, bringing in other fellows that was destructive and everything. So I wound up just leaving. I left Sunni there and I just left, you know. Start staying at hotels, you know. I pay by the day. I go out hustling, make money to cop, and pay my hotel room. Things like that, you know. Then, let me see. I lived over Somerset County for awhile, over in Bedford.

I decided to start taking hormone therapy because the fact. . . . Like I said, I start meeting a new batch of queens, and they were looking fabulous, you know, breast and bodies and stuff. And they were telling us, the younger ones that they adopted as their daughters, they adopted us as their daughters and nieces and things like that. So they were telling us, we had to go . . . what doctors we had to go to see. There was one in East Jefferson, one in South Jefferson . . . two in South Jefferson, and the fact that the only thing we needed at that time was our medical card from welfare to get what we needed. The doctor that I had, he was giving me Hylutin and Delestrogen and TACE—seventy-two milligrams TACE that I took one a day, right.

I stayed on hormones for about five years—on and off. I started around eighteen. And I would go regularly for awhile and then I would stop, and then I'll go again for another month. You get your shots every two weeks. The pills you take every day. So I may go regularly for two months and then I may stop for awhile and then I may go again, you know, like that.

My old friends, right, they were inexperienced and didn't know anything. Just realizing that they were gay, you know. And we were just sissying up and down the neighborhood and downtown and stuff. Okay, when me and Sunni got the apartment and we start getting heavier into drugs and then we start meeting the older queens, you know, that were into all this . . . while we were still in school—that been in it for years.

And so all that there little sissiness and that little playing, they been stopped that, years ago.

I met the old queens from hustling in certain areas where they would be at, going up to the clubs where they would be at, going to cop at different places and then going someplace else to take off, and where they would be at. And by us running into each other so regularly, then they would adopt one of us like for their daughter or things like that. The older queens, right . . . we had a little family. My play mother, her name was Kathleen. She took me as a daughter because I was tall and dark-skin like she was, and she taught me how to go into pockets, the trick as far as clipping is concerned. She taught me all that. She taught me about dealing with bullshit fellow, you know, who come on you with lines, not to believe them. Things like that. Kathleen had three sisters—so they were my aunts, you know. Came to a point where you have a grandmother—like, I mean the real older queens like Miss Flossie and all. They were like your grandmother and stuff. They were much older than even Ebony and them. My play mother was about maybe thirteen, fourteen years older than I am. That would have put her in her late twenties, maybe thirties.

These were all black queens. Now there are a couple of white queens, right, who liked the blacks more than they liked the whites. In other words, there were a couple of white queens that had black hus-bands. They knew their way around black neighborhoods, and were known in the black neighborhoods where blacks wouldn't bother them. They hung with the black queens, you know, so they actually consid-ered theyselves like black, you know. So there were a couple of them. There only two of them.

From these queens I learned how to make your money without all the sex, you know. A lot of the girls, real girls, and a lot of the queens that were out there hustling, they turned trick for trick. In other words, have sex with this trick and that one. Each one they would have sex with. Then that wasn't the game. That wasn't how it was supposed to be. They taught us how to get one trick and make your money for the whole night. And that involved dipping in their pockets and going in their wallets and stuff like that. Nothing violent, you know, because

they were feminine too and very ultra-fem. So all that mugging somebody was just out the question. But learning how to rob somebody with
finesse. You know, to dip. To go in a person's wallet. To take their
wallet out their pocket, take the money out the wallet, put the wallet
back in the pocket, and button it back up. So when he pulls his pants and
he feels that his wallet is still back there, he think everything is cool
because his button is . . . but he don't realize the money is gone until he's
home or whatever.

You'll go out with them. You know, like they pick like . . . Kathleen.
A trick will pull up and she'll say I have my daughter with me and she'll
a virgin, you know. This arouses a lot of white men, you know. This is
her first time and I'm teaching her, you know. So quite naturally he
wants me in there too because I'm innocent—first time and all that.
She'll be taking care of as far as clipping, you know. I may be doing
something like letting him suck on my breast or something like that.
Some kind of diversion so he wouldn't paying her too much attention
as far as what she's doing. And I'll be at the same time watching and
seeing what she do, so that when the next time, I'm doing, and she'll be
with me.

So the first time, me and Kathleen . . . the first time Kathleen took me
out, you know, she went through the routine about me being her
daughter and all that. Okay, she wound up getting a hundred and
seventy-five dollars from him and then we took a taxi. We went up to
this house. This is where most of the queen went at anyway. This sex
change, she had a house. She also sold drugs, and a lot of the older
queens like my play mother and all them, they stayed there. So us . . . the
younger one . . . we would come over and cop and get high there and sit
around and talk. So anyway, we took a taxi and went there. We copped,
you know, we took off, and she said, "Now, did you pay attention?" You
know. She asked me did I notice how she did such and such a thing, or
noticed how she took the wallet out or noticed how she made noise so
he wouldn't hear the money crunching like that. So then when we go
back out, you know, that same evening because we done spent that
money up getting high, and then we go back out. I'll pull the trick over
this time, and explain to him that this is my first time and my mother is
with me and you know and this is exciting to the man, to the trick, you

know. So then I was real nervous, you know the first time out, I was very nervous to point that I was shaking, right. And Kathleen noticed it. So she stopped me and told me, "Let me suck on this a little bit," and then she sucked till I got myself together. Then she put me back on him again, right, and then I wound up doing it.

And then we fled around the corner and we got a taxi. And I had got like two hundred and ten dollars. We split it in half, you know, because we were already high. We split it in half. And then we went up to the club and we had a couple of drink and then we met another trick at the club, and I took care of that one too. And we had him take us close to the house. So therefore we clipped him close to the house. So we didn't have that far to flee when we left. It was for about three hundred something, in that area, and I split it in half with her, and then we went in the house and we got high and we stayed in.

And then, you know, she'll come in and she say, "Alright, my daughter has graduated." You know, she'll tell the rest of the group. My daughter is graduating, you know. And see, they had this little clique, this little club, the inexperienced queens like me want to get in so bad, but you had to make a sting for a thousand or more, you know. And although I had made that sting when I got the place, it didn't count because I wasn't in the family then. But when I did make my big sting, when I made another big sting and it was in the thousands, then I was in the "VIP Club," they called it.

It was prestige. It was the fact that they all stuck together. Whereas, for example, if I came over and I was sick, right, one of them would have enough money to get me on. They didn't see one of their club members sick. They took care of their own, you know, in that little batch. Anyone that wasn't in it, she'll say, "Child, you nothing but a non-strip." She say, "Wait till you make your thousand and get into the VIP, then I can see what I can do for you." You know, one of those things like that. So that's how that went on.

Those relationship are still going on. It's not . . . it's not as close or as regular as it used to be, 'cause now I'm out on my own and stuff. But like I may call her or we may have dinner together or may go out. Something like that. It's like visiting your mom, you know.

See, one thing that my play mom felt as though there was no room for was romance, you know. As far as hooking with a fellow, you know, being with one fellow. She thought that was immaterial, you know. "If you wanted," she said, "after you made your money, and all that stuff, and if you wanted to be with somebody for that particular evening then you go here," you know. And that's it. But as far as actually setting up house with somebody, which I did at one time.

You know, I met a fellow and moved over Somerset County with him, right over in Bedford. This took me away the family-hood, you know, the family and stuff. You know I was still hustling, right, and with him, okay. I was around twenty, twenty-one when I met Curt. He was the same age. He had a job as a taxi driver, but he was in an accident. So he was getting workmen's compensation, okay. So I was doing most of the hustling, right. He knew I was working.

He was getting high too, you know. His thing was burglary. He'll go up Sussex County area, Maple Hill, where he was originally from, and do burglaries and bring things back and sell and stuff like that. And, you know, we stayed together, and got high together, and stuff. He was ducking the police, which I didn't know. And when he had got busted one time he had this back time he had to do, and he wanted me to wait for him and all that. You know, you say you will, but I didn't. I just went on and went back to Jefferson and continued. I went back to my old routine. I was with him for about three years.

I moved to Fourteenth and Hering, and that's when my mother came to live with me. She lived with me for about seven months, about six or seven months. And then that when her money came through and she got that house. I stayed there for . . . I stayed there for about another year, and then . . . I was having trouble with the landlord, you know.

For some reason he found out that I was gay, a homosexual. He was really nasty, as far as homosexuals were concerned. He would turn my water off from the basement. Things of that sort. The electric off. Things that he wasn't supposed to do, that was illegal, he would do anyway. In the beginning he thought I was a woman. I don't know how he . . . anyway, he was an African, he was from Africa, so he was going through a lot of changes. So I had to go to court, but by me being out hustling that night, you know, and I'm getting high, I was supposed to be in court at nine o'clock that morning and I didn't wake up till twelve.

By me not being in court, he won the court case. I was being evicted. So my things, my furniture and stuff, I got somebody to move down to my mom's house, and then I went to a hotel again, and then, you know, I stay there.

I started staying in hotels again, and I did that for about six months. Okay, the house where I told you my play mom and all's at, this was down South Jefferson, and like I said, the person that owned the house was a sex change that sold drugs. Now, I could have stayed there. In fact, there was a couple of time that I stayed there. Like on the weekend and stuff, but I just couldn't live in there because it was so many and I wasn't used to it, you know. There were so many queens staying there in the house, and . . . and I was used to my privacy, and then thing that was going on, I just couldn't get in the swing of it. I just couldn't get to the fact that I was with a bunch queens, in this one area. So like I said I may spend the night there or spend the weekend and then I would leave, you know.

After awhile I had met a fellow, a prison guard, a white prison guard, and he put me in an apartment at High and Wicomico, right. And I stayed . . . that's where I stayed at until the operation. Until I had the operation on my leg. I was twenty-six, twenty-seven, around there when I had that operation. By me being in the hospital so long, he couldn't keep the rent up, you know. He had his own family. He lived in the Southwest. I had lost the place. That when my lifestyle started changing, after the operation and stuff.

Yeah, I was in the hospital. I had an operation on this leg from using drugs. This is when I started doing speedballs, cooking dope together, and I had a miss, and it turned to an abscess on the inside and it infected this leg and they told me they were gonna have to amputate it, you know, because I couldn't go to no hospital because I had this habit and I had to keep it going, you know.

So I was still hustling. When it was start hurting real bad, right, I knew it was an abscess. Okay, when I first missed it, I didn't feel my drugs at all, you know. But I thought it might have went what we used to call garbage veins or something. You know, certain times a person may get a hit and don't feel none of the high at all. We say, well, you done hit in one of those garbage veins. Something like that. But that next day, this leg was extremely painful, you know, then I realized that I had missed the day before. And I didn't go take care of it, but I was still walking on it in high heels and all the weight when you wear high heels, and. . . .

See, usually when you miss you take Keflex, antibiotics, to help, you know, take that away—the infection away—and I wasn't taking any, you know. And then it had got so bad where I couldn't stand it anymore. This whole leg was just like this, swollen up. So they said they had to get it out. So I thought they talking about lancing it, you know, but it was the suctioning machine. They gave me a . . . they numbed me from the waist down, alright. . . . I wished they would have put me to sleep, but they numbed me from the waist down, and this was in the operating room, you know. I had never been to the hospital before, nothing like that, and my mom, before I went into the operating room, I was already scared, but she was crying, you know. I said, "Mom, don't cry, because you're gonna make me cry." You know, and they took me in, and the anesthesia and all that stuff, and this machine that they used to drain all that stuff it also damaged some of the muscles from here down, some of the muscles, the nerves, the ligaments, right. They cut it on both sides.

They had to cut me. Yeah, and they kept it open, right. The nurses said they never seen anything like it. They kept it open to where you could see the bone, right, and they took gauze and stuck up their finger and stuck it in there, and they had to do this . . . remove it every day. So they were giving me morphine, you know. The doctor said "as needed." So I took advantage of that too. I was in pain every five minutes, you know. I told my mom when I be on the phone, I say, "Okay, mom, I got to . . . I'll call you later. It's cop time, you know. It's time for me go and cop." And then when I called her back, she say, "Oh, you must gone seen the cop man." I said, "Yeah," you know, then I sit on the phone and talk to her. But I stayed in the hospital five months.

When the doctor told me that they were going to amputate it, and that I could still lead a normal life with an artificial leg, I use to joke around. I said, "Well, how can I lead . . . how can I wear spike heels with an artificial leg?" right. I had the doctors and nurses laughing, but inside I scared to death, you know. Then after the doctor came and told me that, a priest came in right behind him, and asked did I want him to pray for me. I said, "Yes," and then he gave me this booklet, Matthew, called the rock. You know, the Book of Matthew. And I read the whole thing. The next day, the doctor came in to examine my leg and he said it was some kind of miracle or something, because he was getting ready, getting me ready for this amputation. But he said it was healing from the inside out, you know, and then he felt as though the amputation wasn't needed. And then they were talking about a skin graft. I know they take skin from one part and put it on another, and then I said, "Oh, my God, they gonna take the skin from my behind and put down there." I said, "I wonder how my butt gonna look," you know. But then when we got done in the operating room they didn't do that. They wound up putting stitches in there instead. Then he told me that I would have to use a walker to learn to walk. I did use it for a little while, but then afterward he said that I would have to walk with a cane for the rest of my life. So I was determined not to. My vanity, you know. So he was amazed that I didn't, you know.

This was . . . this was about . . . about five years ago. I was around twenty-four, twenty-five. So then, after he was wrong about that, you know, about the fact of me walking using a cane, then he said I was gonna have a severe limp. Well, my vanity again wouldn't allow me to walk with a severe limp, you know. Vanity can be a strong thing, you know. So I do have a slight limp. It shows up more like when I get real high, you know, and then I have a tendency to limp, you know. So now he said I would have swelling for the rest of my life because of the main artery being destroyed during the operation and the blood have to go through the smaller veins and arteries. So therefore my ankle will swell up, you know, if I stand on it a lot or do a lot of walking. Well, that is still true.

Because of the operation, right, a lot of things I cut down on. Whereas, before the operation I was like twenty-four hours getting high. Whereas now, I may get high, then I'll go home. I don't party or go to the clubs like I used too. Before the operation, I stayed in drag twenty-four hours, whereas now, I only go in drag for business, and then I'll come out of drag.

I felt as though if I would kept the pace that I was going, I probably would be dead by now. I was in such a fast pace, in a fast lane. The large amount of money, the heavy lifestyle, the heavy drug using, this was twenty-four hours every day. Whereas now, I'm . . . like I'm with my sister's now. So therefore, and by her having younger kids there, I don't get high at home. I go up South Jefferson and then I come home. I don't stay in drag all the time. I get in drag for business. My adoptive family, I see them when I go and cop or something like that, but I don't hang out with them as much as I used to.

I always wanted to be in a relationship. I don't know if I . . . I just thought that was the ultimate me, being in love with somebody, and somebody in love with me and we setting house up, you know, and things like that. I'm cooking, and coming from work, you know. The time that I was with Curt, it was nice. He had his moment where he could get violent, and he was, you know, like possessive and jealous. But I considered that . . . attractive, you know. The fact that he felt that way about me to the point whereas he was jealous if he would come in the bar or something over there on Mentnor Avenue. He came in the bar and he seen somebody buying me a drink or something, I would see it in his eyes how upset he would be. And I may make a grin, you know, and that would burn him up 'cause he thought I was making a joke of him or something. But it was just the fact that I thought it was so attractive that he was jealous in that way.

My mother and Kathleen thought that a intimate relationship was just a distraction from accumulating your security. Like getting involved emotionally with a man and setting up house and stuff eventually will only lead to a downfall, to a point where they take from you more than they give or contribute, you know. By me being an old romantic, I thought it was nice being with somebody and sharing with somebody.

He was the only one that I would consider as my lover. There have been other fellows in my life, but I didn't have the time for them, and they didn't . . . I didn't have the feeling for them to make time for them. I did it to have the drugs and the money, you know, and they were like third, they would come in third, whereas when I met Curt, it was different. My feelings for him—I was attracted to him and vice versa.

I met him because a friend of mine told me that money was good over in Bedford, right. She used to live over in Bedford. So one particular night we went over there, and there was this here delicatessen where all the fellow and the queens, everybody that hung on the stroll used to go in this here place that stayed open all night. So she took me in there, and by me being a new face, the fellows was asking who I was and all that stuff. So I get a little nervous when there's a whole lot of fellows around me. And I had this dress on with all the back out, you know, and saw all these strange hands on my back. So anyway this fellow came in, right, with hazel-brown eyes, tall, brown skin, and, you know, he was like looking into my face and I was looking like into his and it seemed like there was not nobody else in the place. And he asked her who I was, because he knew her, and she introduced us. So I said, "Why don't you invite him over Jefferson when we get finished making some money," right. So she invited him, but he knew that I asked.

So about five minutes later I had got a number and he had four one hundred dollar bills. I was taking care of business with him for thirty dollars, and I always had a habit of feeling up under the seat to see if there was any knives or gun, and I felt this money, and I put it up in my panties. So when we got finished, he reached and check, right, and he said, "Now, you better give my money back." I said, "What money? You're not getting this money back that I took care of business for." He said, "Naw, I'm taking about my four one hundred dollar bills you took." Well, my heart went like this. So then I got out the car like I lived right there. I said, "Bob!" I just hollered up, I didn't know who these people were. I said, "Bob! Bob! This man trying to get his money back!" Anyway, he zoomed off. So I ready to go now, you know. I've made this little money. I'm ready to go back to Jefferson to cop. And so we didn't see him, so we walking back towards the Rapid Transit, and then this fellow running up hollering, "Betty! Betty!" And it was him. So he went over to Jefferson with us. And we went back to the hotel, and we got high, and everything. So she had to sleep on the floor because him and me was in the bed, you know. Usually, I have a habit of checking and seeing what going in me, seeing what the size is and stuff, but this time I was high, and I didn't check and I didn't check, and he was like abnormally large, right, and he was just working me overtime to the point where when we got finished I was . . . he had screwed all my drugs out of me. I was sick as a dog, you know, and I had to cop again. Anyway, from that day on, we were together from that first day for the whole three years. And that's how that happened.

He became a priority to the point where I cut my communications with my adopted family and stuff, and moved over to a place where I've never been, which was Bedford, in Somerset County. So here I was over here in a new city. A new batch of queens that hated me, hated my guts. They remind me of some football players who trying to be women, you know. They had habits, but they didn't know how to clip. So that messed with them, and then I was dealing with somebody that they had wanted. To the point whereas they would get him high just for him to hang around them. And then when I came on the scene, I just took that away from them.

Now, my ideal partner is someone that is emotionally involved with me equally as I am with them. Someone who wants to build something together for the future, you know. Someone that was involved enough in me to actually want me to get off the drugs and will go through certain changes to help me get off the drugs—like being my backbone. As far as saying, "Well, Detra, listen, I want you to stop this hustling and I'm going to help you do it," you know. "I'm gonna be there for you even when the times are rough," you know. So therefore, we can build something together, without the drugs between us.

But nowadays lot of fellows that one time in the past I thought would be good investments for the future got themselves involved with this smoking, which I consider the worst high in the world. I tried crack one time and it was disgusting to me, you know. I was with a fellow and that's when I tried it. It was disgusting. I have seen so many fellows that had a lot going for them that are now homeless, downtown selling themselves for a tote, not even for a nickel cap, but for a tote, you know. They're willing to do anything sexually for it, and, oh, it just takes me away.

Like with the heroin, right, you can have a shot and it will hold you, but with this crack, it makes you . . . you never get enough. When you take a tote it makes you think of ways to get more. To the point where you don't care how you look, you know. Where you don't want food, you don't want to eat or anything. With the heroin addicts, at least most of them did care about their appearance and the type of hustling that they were doing like checks or things that had to deal with the public. They had to dress and look accordingly. So therefore, you know . . . but this crack is the worsest thing I've ever seen as far as getting high is concerned, and to me it affects women even worse. To the point where they don't wash, they smell horribly. Down where I cop at, one particular evening I had seen two girls, right, and this one fellow, and they went into the alley. And they were giving him a blow job, taking turns, and he was smoking this pipe and they kept begging him for a tote. He was saying, "Wait. Just go on and finish doing what you're doing." Oh, it was just ridiculous.

Anyway, I used to think that I would be the one cooking and thing like that, and he'd be coming home with the paycheck. Now, I would want one whereas we both wake up in the morning and I'm fixing breakfast so we both can go out to work. He either drop me off—we got one little car and he drop me off at work and pick me up, you know, and we come home together. In other words we're both working to achieve what we want. So to me that's a little more attractive.

But for me right now, I don't see that in the cards as far as me being in a relationship because of my habit. I don't want to get in a relationship with another addict, you know. I've been the route before. I don't want to go through that again. It seem to me to be very rare, very difficult, rare for me to find someone that's willing to go through all these changes to help me get off the drugs. So therefore I only see me at one point trying to get myself off the drugs, getting myself together, getting my own spot, and then getting involved.

See, this dragging situation I feel like this. Dragging is only temporary. I mean . . . I can't see myself sixty-five years old and still dragging. Either you stop dragging or you get a sex change. Now, I'm not for no sex change. So like eventually I intend to stop dragging, you know. Being like I am now, you know. Whereas, I consider myself still feminine, but, you know, I can buy things that are like uni-sex. So eventually I know that I will stop the heel and the dresses and stuff. But this is when I will also stop the hustling and the drugs. So therefore, if I do meet somebody, it would be somebody that would want me like I am now.

I never been with a homosexual before. See what I'm saying? I have been with—the type of thing where there's two homosexual and one choosing to play one role, the top role, one . . . well, I never had no homosexual relationship like that. I never dealt with another homosexual.

Curt was straight. Well, when I came into the scene he became bisexual. He dealt with a homosexual at one time, not in a relationship but just a sexual thing—one-night thing. But I'm really the first homosexual he ever dealt with as far as living and setting up house with. See what I'm saying? I just can't see myself with another homosexual. In other words, with another gay man who has played a variety of different roles in other relationships other than the man role.

I cannot see myself being involved with that type of person, because of my femininity. In order for me to be in a relationship with another man I would have to have a man that's either straight or bisexual or a straight man who finds me attractive or interesting enough to get in a relationship with me. So those are the only type of men I'm used to. Those are the only type of men I'm interested in. I have been . . . been to the bar where, you know, where gay men hang, and they hook up with each other, and sometimes I sit there and wonder and who is the masculine, who's the husband, who's the wife, things like that. And I just don't . . . I know what I am. So therefore, as far as me changing up— I want to be the husband this day, and the next day I want to be . . . —that's not my thing.

That's part of his character, that aggression that men usually have in a sexual thing with a woman. Now, I don't mind taking initiative, but when it come to a part when he grabbing the grease jar more than I am. . . . The next thing he want to wear my heels, you know. You know what I'm saying? Or like in our relationship I may run into some of his friends from the past that gonna come up with, "He was my wife." Then my feeling would have to be really, really be into him to ignore a whole lot of that. There can't be two fems.

Like Curt . . . first, his physical attractiveness. He was tall, and he had hazel-brown eyes. He was a sexy, masculine evilness about him that turned me on. He was truly the dominating one in the relationship. To the point where he took no shit, in control completely. And if you were his woman, you were his woman, you know, and at one point, they used to call us Siamese twins, because you would never see one without the other. Like in the daytime, when he used to go and play pool with all these fellows. And I would be the only one in there with all these fellows to the point where they got used to it, and they respected me because they know he would kill a brick over me, you know.

Then, when he wasn't doing his burglaries, he was out there with me, protecting me. One time I was with three white fellows, and I had clipped all three of them. I took care of one business, clipped him, took care, clipped him, clipped. . . . I was afraid that they were going to find their money missing before I got back to the spot, right. They wanted me to go to a hotel with them in Mansfield. Now, Mansfield was a little town that was whitish and didn't like blacks. One of those little tips. So I said, "Let me go tell my old man that I won't be home"—I'm gonna spend the night at the hotel, you know. So they drove me back to the spot where Curt was at, and I got out the car. I said, "Listen, I done robbed all three of them and they want me to go to a Mansfield hotel." So he told me to go on home. So I turned the corner and went on home, but then I could hear then arguing, you know. He was saying, "No, my woman is not going to no Mansfield hotel and all that stuff." Anyway, I don't know if they found, before they left. . . . No, he told me, when he came back to the house, he was out of breath 'cause he had ran, cut through some alleys and stuff, they had found their money missing, you know. And so they were on his shit in the car, you know. They had drove off and then I guess they found their money missing and started backing up on him and he was cutting through these alleys. So anyway when he wasn't doing his burglaries he was out there watching me.

After that relationship I didn't want to get into no more relationships like that 'cause it took a whole lot out of me, you know, emotionally. Especially when they locked him up for something that happened, some kind of violation that he . . . that he never told me about. Anyway, that's when I went back to Jefferson and I got back into my other routine.

Well, I didn't lose touch. . . . I mean when he came home he came looking for me. He came over here to Jefferson and we were together, you know, that day and that night we went to bed and stuff. But I told him that I, you know . . . I wasn't interested in getting back into that. Because I just like the idea of me being free, and I just didn't want to go through all that again.

It's a little more accepted than it was then, you know. A drag queen doesn't have to go through as much changes as they used to go through. A drag queen now that are working in Blair's, J. C. Penney, you know, where their employers know that they are gay . . . and stuff, you know and accepting that, but awhile ago that was ridiculous. If you didn't play the part and get away with playing the part of the female then you wouldn't get that job. Or if they found out you would get fired. Whereas, now, you know, they know that this person is a drag queen and they can still hold on to the job. So it done changed a whole lot.

It was much more dangerous when I first started out. Okay, now, I know there have been groups of blacks that would beat up queens and stuff, but, okay, every time I ran into it, it was never no violent thing. It was a sexual thing. Where, for example, if me and a friend of mine, Sidney, we be together or something and we run into four or five dudes. They didn't want to beat us up, they wanted to screw us. You know what I'm saying? So those were kind of situations I would run into and would have to try to get out of without it turning violent. Where there's a group of fellow that wanted to have sex, you know, and there is too many of them. Therefore, I have to figure a way of getting out of this situation without it turning violent and they ready to jump on me.

So in the early days it was like it was much more of a question of being raped than being beaten up. So today you're much more likely to be bashed. Well, you know that's what they say. They say there is more gay bashing now, but I haven't ran across it. This gay-bashing thing I heard mainly on television, you know, but the ones that I see involved are white gays. I don't see the black gays on TV being, you know, seeing that they being gay bashed.

Well, you know being gay in the city now it still has its certain amount of ignorance, you know, as far as the straight people and the prejudice, but I think it just a little bit better than it was before, you know. Whereas now, you know, there a lot of gays that are being accepted by straight co-workers and things like that, and have lunch with them, and things like that. Whereas before it wasn't like that, but on the same hand there's still a certain amount of prejudice and ignorance too, especially with the AIDS situation.

You know, the most unusual thing somebody ever asked me to do was this here fellow with a beard and everything that wanted me to dress him in drag. This is a macho, bearded . . . and then go out with me downtown. I mean, like he had a blond beard and everything, and I put on the blue shadow. . . . Now, see, I didn't know he wanted to go out with me, and I had this blue eye shadow on and he had this red lipstick and this here black fishnet stocking and black heels. He was bowlegged like a cowboy, and all this here blond hairy legs, right, and he had this here tight skirt and this here white blouse that he was going to bust out of any minute. And he want to go out. After I had dressed him, right, he wanted to go with me in town.

This was no sex. This was dressing and being with me, right. So he gave me the money for dressing him, and then he was going to give me seventy-five dollars to go with him in town. So this was another one where I couldn't get real close to dip. So I said "Okay," because I wanted the extra seventy-five dollars, but when we got outside, right, and we got towards High Street, I left him there. I said, "Wait a minute. I got to go tinkle." I had to piss. I went through the alley and out the other way, and caught a taxi, because he wasn't . . . it was bad enough walking up to High Street, right. And everybody was dying and all, you know. They were all on the street falling out. I said, "Oh, God!"

And this was his regular thing. This is what he liked doing. I asked him why he won't shave it off. He said his wife won't let him. He was married and everything. He wasn't no gay guy. He wasn't gay. He just like wearing women's clothes and dressing up in women's things and he wasn't allowed to do it in his house. He would carry stuff in his trunk, and then he would meet me and I would take him and I would dress him, but this particular night he also wanted to go out with me downtown, and stuff.

Up to the clubs! To the gay bars! Dressed like that looking like a nut. The police would have locked both of us up. Oh, yeah. And I had the face makeup on him right, and it was all on his beard. This face makeup was all on his beard, and stuff. It was a mess. It was really a mess. But he felt so real, you know.

*"Only a pro know how to do
something like that.
Only a pro."*

Keisha

When I was growing up, I was close to my mother. Because she was the only one I always was around. 'Cause, she was . . . I mean, my mother's a very nice person. She's very sweet. She'd give you anything in the world. Anything. She was just heart. You know what I mean? She was down to earth, you know.

My father, he didn't approve of me being gay and he knew I was gay. I knew he knew I was gay, but he was trying to make the man part, and I wasn't going for that, you see.

We used to travel back and forth from Dorado, Florida. That's right off of Seagra. And my pop he would work on the farm, you know, and start doing labor work like far as picking oranges. And my mother would stay home and I would go to school and my brother would go to school.

They met in New York. My mother was in college and my father was working at a Greek restaurant that she went to. They met and they liked one another, so they got married. My mother was born in Maryland—Westerville, Maryland—and my father was born in Dorado, Florida.

My father, he had me, my brother, and that was it. See, I got other sisters and brothers also, but she got them by somebody else. They lived with my grandmother up here. My mother and my father, they just had me and my brother, my baby brother. I'm twenty-five . . . twenty-six.

He's twenty-two. . . . Well, I'm the oldest of him, but I got an older brother older than me.

And we was like on the road mainly, back and forth. When we leave from Florida, when the crop get bad, then we go upstate New York. That's in Cannon, New York. And we would pick apples up there, Delicious apples, gold, yellow. And when we leave from there when the crops, you know, died down we would come back to Jefferson.

We would stay in one place just until the crop is out. That would be like all summer long—the crop was in was oranges—from June all the way up until I'll say about October. That's when it start getting the cool front in Florida. And then we would leave from there and spend the rest of it, from October to all the way until I'll say 'bout March, we would be upstate New York. Then from March we would be down here, from March until June, we here in Jefferson. We'd take the train from New York, come to Jefferson, stayed in Jefferson at my sister's house, and then from Jefferson we would go back on the Amtrak back down to Florida. There never was like a settled point, you know, just like always following the crop.

It was fun. I thought it was fun. Traveling and meeting different people, and stuff like that. It wasn't a bad experience or nothing like that, but you just, you know, you get to know different people. It wasn't just black people doing this, it was Jamaicans, Spanish, you know, white . . . but I say it was more blacks, you know. I got to knowing different people, but what I didn't like about it was I got comfortable with some of the people, like friends, you know, neighbors and stuff, and then I got to leave them and meet new neighbors and I didn't like that too much.

See, my mother was a registered nurse. See, everywhere she traveled, she would change her job plans to go on up here, see. When she was in Cannon, New York, she changed her job over and so she was working a different part of New York. She was working in Rochester and he was in Cannon. She would come up on the weekends and see us. In Florida she worked in the hospital down there. I forgot the name of the hospital, but she worked in there.

My mother was taking care of me in Florida as an infant and my father worked in the mills that they have down there. Then when I was five we went on the road. We didn't go to the same place in Florida, but you went to different places. We didn't work for the same person because this man named Chris that my father knew always told my father what orchard that he can work at.

And the people we worked with, we knew them. My father always was the bookkeeper, and the bookkeeper keeps how much money that you make, see. And by him being the bookkeeper and everything, they know they can't take advantage of him 'cause he already know how much money he made, see. And he make sure nobody take advantage of nobody on that campus, because he kept track of how many bins each family had. As far as foodwise and stuff like that, everybody chipped in, but you can keep it in your own campus, but you can also take it out and cook it in the kitchen.

We stayed, like . . . wait, how I'm gonna put this? . . . They had like people that have a speakeasy, okay. And the man that had the speakeas-ies, right, had a trailer on his land and we would live in that trailer. So we mainly lived in some man named Skelton's trailer. We lived in his trailer. And we stayed there all up till October. Then we'd leave from there and go upstate New York. When we lived upstate New York, we lived in a cottage, like, on the land, and it was like everybody had their little section of houses, but we all eat together in the same kitchen.

I worked in the fields on the weekend. My brother was just growing up. He would just come out in the field, but he couldn't work and, you know, like my father would go up on the ladder and pick the top. I would have to grind the tree. That means go around and pick the bottom of the tree. When I got a little older . . . like thirteen . . . I was in the tree. And the ladders is tall that you carrying. The ladders is . . . you know them ladders that they be having painting with? That's the type of ladders that we be carrying.

It wouldn't take me that long to fill a sack 'cause I'm used to it. It ain't take me no more than twenty minutes. We had five rows, me and my father. Just the two of us. Then it's some people from . . . where our row stop it's five more people, you know, in they row. So, it's like 'bout thirty or forty people in the whole field. But the land is big, with all the orchards and stuff there. So it's 'bout that many people.

When we got up in the morning, we would go to one orchard, and we would work in that field that day. And we worked in that orchard till it was clean. See, it's so big. You see so many orange trees you get tired of them. You get tired . . . you get tired of them . . . I got tired of them, my mother got tired of them. We worked all day long. We would start at six in the morning, and we'll finish 'bout five. We'd have our lunch. It's up to you how long you want your lunch to be, see. You can sit there for a hour. Some people just ate a sandwich and still picking oranges, see. It's just up to you. Same way in New York, the entire whole winter. Every year same orchard up until the age of I'll say fifteen.

The money was good. At that time my father was making eight dollars a bin. That means you got a long row, long row to yourself, see. You got like I'd say about five rows to yourself. That whole row I'd say last us about two weeks, then we'll pick the other row, and that's the other two weeks all way down. So we made pretty good money. Our bin are bigger than this table. It's twice the size, but it's deep. And it got two hooks where the tractor come and lift it up and dump the apples on top of the truck. The oranges is the same way. But the oranges is more higher than the apples, 'cause oranges sell quicker than the apples. At that time they was getting like twelve dollars a bin.

We went to school. You know, we went to Cannon Junior High in New York. When we was in Florida, right, we went to Haldeman High. I wouldn't start school there. I would start school upstate New York in October. But see, in Florida when I did started school, I was always a month 'header than the kids upstate, because Florida you learn quicker, see. Like upstate New York—that's like a country, I learn quicker than the kids in the city, see. When I got here they went through the books I done went through already upstate New York or in Florida and they was just getting to the books here, see. I wasn't never really behind, I was always ahead—it was just mainly ahead of kids here in the city, see.

Well, I was doing this from six until the age of sixteen we was on the road. We was just traveling like from upstate New York back down to Jefferson, then Florida. Then my mother and my father separated. My mother got tired of running from one state to another state picking apples and oranges. She just wanted to settle down in one spot. But see, by him so used to that and that was part of his life, she didn't want me and my brother to be like half growing up here, get used to one part of the state, then get another part of the state, you know, we just know about the roads. . . . I mean, we don't have no friends or access to our other family or nothing like that. So she left him, and we came up here to Jefferson. And my older sister, which I didn't even know I had an older sister—see, my mother didn't never sit down and, you know, explain it to us 'cause we so much on the road—but when I came up here, I lived with my older sister.

When I was growing up I was afraid of the dark. You can't see nothing. I ain't wanna walk in the dark. I could see things in the dark. Yeah. I was born with a veil on my face. So I can see things that's moving that ain't supposed to be there. I get scared of that.

Like my grandmother for example. I was close to my grandmother. She was nice. She was a school teacher, in Westerville, Maryland. And my mother went and got her and brought her up here, 'cause they had her in a nursing home. I was living in East Jefferson then with my mother. My grandmother died when I was seventeen. After she died, I went to church after she died. I got my hair cut and everything. I wore a man's suit. Carried the Bible all the time, you know. Because . . . oh, long story. . . . It's just so hard to experience something that . . . something happen to you. You the only person that . . . that you know. . . .

Okay, when she died, right, the experience that I went through after she died I didn't know it was supposed to change me or what, you know. Just like some people don't believe in spiritual things, like ghosts and stuff like that . . . which I never did, but the experience that I went through, with her spirit. . . .

Well, she died, right. Okay, and I was gay—you know, dressing in women's clothes. Right after she died, okay, I wore her clothes. See what I'm saying? And I would hit the street with her clothes on, in high heels and everything. And go out prostituting. And so one day, after we came back from my grandmother's funeral, and everything, from Westerville, Maryland, we came up here, and I walked my little nephew to the bathroom, wasn't nobody in the house. When I walked him to the bathroom, they all camed in while I was upstairs. My grandmother couldn't use the bathroom. So my mother put my grandmother's potties up in the back room. Like a closet . . . it was big enough for a room, but it was more like a closet, you know. So she put it back there. I went and propped the door open, you know. I opened up the door and just, something just went through me, you know. So I don't know, it's just like a . . . something like push you . . . like a hard wind that come push you. It was like that. And the experience I went through with that. It was . . . scared. I mean . . . it was scared, you hear me. It was scary, you know. I don't think a human being on earth could ever want to go through nothing like that.

It wasn't the seeing, it was the feeling. It's like when somebody take control of your mind, and you aware of this person taking control of your mind. See, that's what I'm saying. My sister-in-law told me. She said when I came down them steps I was up off my feet. She don't know what threw me or what. My hair was sticking straight up in the air and everything. And when I came down the bottom of the steps, I hurt my ankle. And I ran over to my sister-in-law, and I couldn't get off her. She was pregnant. I could not get hold, I mean, let go that woman, you hear what I'm saying? And when I finally let go of her, I just started crying. I mean, I just started crying, couldn't stop crying. I cried for a whole week. And I was so scared, right. I went over my sister house . . . I stays over there . . . I couldn't sleep, I would holler for the Lord.

I was feeling guilt. I was feeling guilt, 'cause I had took something from my grandmother when she was on her deathbed. I had took money from underneath of her when she was. . . . I didn't know she was on her deathbed. I took about three hundred 'n something from her. And then I went to this preacher at Pendleton Avenue, Ninth and Pendleton. I went to that church, and he told me that I was repenting my soul, see. And I didn't know what repenting meant until he explained to me what I had done. Then I didn't want to hear that, 'cause I'm gay and I'm like, "Wait a minute. What's going on here?" And I ranned away. I went to New York. I caught the train and went to New York. I couldn't stand clubs. You know how a person die and they leave their scent behind them. Everywhere I went her scent was there. And the only person who smell it would be me, see. And like I was losing my mind, you know.

When I came back to Jefferson from New York, my mom took me over to this place where they keep people like that, you know, something wrong with them and something like that upstairs. And the man, he couldn't find out what was wrong with me, you know. I would always think I see her hair falling, I mean stuff like that. Like pieces of her hair. She had long gray hair, you know. Like you see hair like floating down, like that. And the only person that would see it was me.

And when I got over that, Lord knows, when I got over that, I didn't wanna stay in that house or nothing. It took me about a month, 'bout a month, and then we moved. My mother moved out of that house, and when she moved out of that house, we moved down to Twentieth and Barnfield. Moved over there.

Before that though, I cut all my hair off. Stopped wearing women's clothes and everything. I started going to church. I went to church through that whole time. I stopped prostituting and stuff . . . everything. I would just walk the street. I couldn't sleep. I would walk the street all night long, I mean, all night long. Certain spots I would think I'd see her there. I'd be running. Late at night and I'm running, you know.

At some point I went to sleep and I woked up I was like . . . didn't feel nervous, didn't feel jittery, or nothing. I wanted to know what I was doing. It's just like if a person just snapped and come back, see. I didn't know what was going on with me. When I came back I said, "Mom, where my clothes at?" She said, "You bought all boy clothes." "What you mean I bought all boy clothes?" And I mean, it just took me out, you know.

So in upstate New York it was just my father and my brother and me. My mother was working in Rochester. My father he was, you know, nice and everything. He would look out because we was children, you know. And he always give my brother more 'cause he knew I was gay, you know.

I realized that he knew I was gay from the moment this man named Glenn, this Indian guy, came in my cottage and asked for my father's sack and my father was working. And my father got off work, was coming home, to get something, right. He'd seen Glenn then. I was giving Glenn the sack. And he said, "What you doing, man?" And I didn't know Glenn was gay. Glenn likeded little boys. And I didn't know that. "What you think you doing?" and, you know, starts going on with Glenn. Told him to get the fuck out.

And then he told me . . . sat down and told me then. And you know he said, "I know something ain't right about you. You my son and I know my son." He said, "I know that you might be . . . you don't know the word of 'sissy' or 'fag' or whatever," he said, "but I know that, you know, you like different, other things." Now, he sat down and explained to me. He said, "I'm a man. I like your mother, see. You wouldn't like the same thing I like," you know.

Then right then and there it came to me, and then I just came out and told him. I told him I likeded boys. And he said, "Well, it's not the right thing, and I don't approve of it, you know, but you my child, and if I can't break you, I don't want to be around." So I said, "Okay. I just tell my mother when I see her." I felt hurt, you know, 'cause he was my father. I felt hurt and everything. Little touched there. You know, I cried, you know. I was twelve. And then I just said, "I don't care." I told him my mom would look out for me.

My sister told my mother that I was going to be gay too. And my mother said, "Oh no, that boy ain't gonna be gay." She said, "Yes, that boy is gonna be gay." My mother couldn't deal with it. It was hard for her. She could deal with the point that I was gay, but she couldn't deal with the point of why I was dressing in women's clothes.

But she don't know right now today what my father said to me. Uh-uh. She don't know. And I didn't talk to my mother 'bout me being gay till I was seventeen. 'Cause up till seventeen I was still doing boys' clothes. I was dressing half and half. Girls' shoes, boys' pants, girl blouses. Like that.

When my parents split up, my mother dated this man named Wayne. I don't know how she really met Wayne. I didn't like him. I didn't like Wayne because he didn't like me because I was gay. He has a brother that is gay, but he didn't like me. And so Wayne was big and black and selfish. Only person he wanted 'round him was my brother, my baby brother, and my mother. They's the only ones he wanted there. He didn't want me there. So I didn't care. But he would help out a lot. He helped my mother out a lot. He was a contractor worker. He would fix like screen doors, you know, put cement like in the yard, cement the basement floor, stuff like that.

I would take stuff from him. I would take his money from him, 'cause I know he ain't like me. He would get drunk and I'd take his money from him. Then I took his pistol from him and sold it. I took his shotgun from him and sold it. I just didn't like the man. 'Cause he ain't like me.

He lived with us, but when they wanted to have they little . . . whatever . . . they still would go to a hotel, and leave me and my brother there with some money, you know, and food. Or either they would deliver pizza, stuff like that, you know, that we would want. When they gone I was responsible for everything. Making sure my brother don't get in no trouble, make sure he alright. I was like seventeen or eighteen then. But see, I just didn't care. I didn't care they went to a hotel or not, 'cause I still was going out, see.

I realized I was gay at the age of eleven. I realized that with my first girlfriend. I tried having a girlfriend and she wanted to kiss me. I told her, "No." And she said, "Why?" I said, "Uh-uh." And she said, "What's wrong with you?" I said, "I don't know." And then we used to talk and laugh and stuff like that, and then I told her, I said, "You just don't attract my attention." I said, "You just don't do nothing for me." I just told her . . . I said, "Look, I don't know . . . I don't know what's going on, but I don't like you." That's what I told her, just like that.

I was in New York, upstate New York. We was on a school bus when I told her this, and she ain't cry or nothing. We was kids. Just laughed it off and stuff. But it was this boy that I hung around with that I would just look at. Other words like lust. And he was cute. I was eleven, he was eleven. And I mean, at that age that would just turn me on. That's when I realized I was gay. But I kept it hidden. I didn't say I was gay or nothing like that—back then they used "sissy"—I said to myself that I know I like one boy.

Certain things I wouldn't do . . . what boys would do, like as far as play football, basketball, and stuff like that. They'd say, "Ah, you ain't nothing but a little sissy." Like that. I was feminine. Other words, I was like more clean. I always like stuff like stay clean more . . . everything got to be perfect, you know. I was like that 'bout myself.

Any little thing somebody'd do, I would be offended from it. I cried about different kinds of things. I cried about things that people would do to me. Sometimes kids made fun of me. Because they was like, "I don't know 'bout you, man." You know, stuff like that, you know. They ain't just said little things underneath they breath, you know. Do little smart stuff like I would get up, go sharpen my pencil, they would knock my books over, you know, stuff like that. I always was alone, you know. Always took a long walk, or something. Then I was like I can't talk to nobody, I don't know how they gonna react, you know. Then I would sit down and cry about it, you know.

My parents got along fine. They would kiss one another. And look at TV with one another on the couch, and stuff like that. My mother be laying on his lap, stuff like that. They had a real nice relationship with one another. Sometimes they would fight, words fights. See they was always the type that'd word fighting, and if they would fist fight we would never knew about them. Like "Damn it. I'm tired of this shit," stuff like that.

My parents wasn't strict. When my mother would beat us, he would get mad, and if he hit us, she would get mad. They always asked questions, you know, stuff like that. It was like somebody always seen us doing something and she would just talk to us, see. It wasn't only them eyes looking at us, it was like neighbors' eyes and up the road eyes looking at us. 'Cause, see, in Florida, everybody knows everybody. It's a little town, you know.

They tried to give us the best guidance that they knew of, you know. Knowing when to play, when not to play. Knowing when to, you know, do certain things, as far as like react to certain things that somebody might say to you. Think before you react, you know. As far as my mother was concerned, people supposed to live a understanding life. She say when there is no understanding there is no reason why somebody should live with another person. From my mother I learned the values of being honest. And being honest with yourself. And don't hide nothing, 'cause that means you're hiding from yourself. And try to keep myself up no matter what type of things I go through. Keep my hygiene and everything, no matter what I go through. That was very important around her.

My father . . . well really, he was more on the verge of the man supposed to take charge of everything, you know. The woman 'posed to stay in the kitchen, and the man supposed to just come home from work and the woman supposed to do certain things. He was just concerned about you growing up being this man, and I didn't want to hear that. And always have money in your pocket. That's the only value I learned from him.

My brother, it was a close relationship 'cause I was raising him. He was underneath of me. He didn't notice I was gay, 'cause he so busy running in the street, acting so much like a little boy. And as he got older, then he realized I was gay, but he's not gay. He was bad and spoiled and always whining. That's how he was.

When my mother was in Rochester I did all the cleaning, and I cook. Yeah, my mother taught me off and on how to cook when we was in New York. When we was in Florida my mother did all the cooking. She was always home, you know. See, my mother workeded at night, and then she would get a car and come over. She would be there like six-thirty, quarter to seven, something like that. 'Cause when she would be waking us up, she still in her uniform. And then she would go to bed.

My father cooked on the grill mainly on holidays, but he would come in and cook some things too. I didn't really had to cook for my father, but I cook, I clean, I wash dishes, and I was vacuuming her little rug, you know. I would do like a woman work, you know. And then when he would come in from work the house would be so sparkling and clean. He couldn't take it. No, he ain't like it, 'cause he saying it ain't like what a man would do. It's like what a woman would do.

And he was mainly strict on me how to dress and everything. Because he knew I was gay. And he thought no boy don't 'posed to have this—like say if I would have my shirt open, and no T-shirt underneath of it—no boy don't 'posed to be walking 'round here like that. Or if I had tight jeans on, "No boy of mines gonna be walking 'round with tight jeans like that." And stuff like that. And I would just look at him.

The first time I had sex was in the bathroom in school. In Cannon, New York. I went in the bathroom to go to the bathroom, but I seen him in the bathroom pissing. And he turned around and shook his dick at me. He was like, "Come here." And I looked at his dick and I was like, "Uh-huh. I know what he got on his mind" to myself. I went over there to him, and he was like, "What you into?" I was like, "What you mean 'what I'm into'?" And he was like, "Oh, I know you gay." I said, "What you mean how you know?" I mean, he say, "I know you a sissy." I was

like, "How you know I'm a sissy?" He said, "I can look and tell you." I
said, "No you can't." Like that, right. So he was like this, "Here. Feel
that." And I felt his dick. And I just was like this, "What's up?" I was like,
"Well, what's up with you?" Not "What's up with you," but back then I
would say, "Well, what you want me to do?" And he was like, "Well, I
want . . ." I guess he was like "I want you to suck this dick" or whatever.

I ain't have no friends till I was fourteen. My first one, I met him up
in Cannon, New York, in school. He used to come from where he lived
at over to our campus, and hang out with me and I would tell him, you
know, "Come on. Help me, you know, pick some apples" or something
like that. He was a white kid. So he didn't mind, you know. And then we
would be playing . . . like running, tapping each other, or whatever. We
would just play. We would just walk together somewhere, you know.
Start skipping water with rocks. Stuff like that, you know.

The next time I had a friend was in Dorado, Florida. I was on the
same age. This was some boy. He was sixteen. His family . . . they was
working, but they would work like on the mills. And they would just
stay down there. They wouldn't travel. And I used to go over his house
and see him. We used to sit and look at TV. Wait until his family leave,
you know. And I would get in his pants. He was black. He was gorgeous.
Built.

The first time I got in his pants I asked him. I said, "Well, I like you
and I want some of that." I mean, I just said, "I like you," and he knew
right then and there, you know. Then I started drinking beer. That was
the first time I ever drunk beer. And I got high with him. We got high in
the orange field, and I just start playing with him. Laughing and stuff.
Like laughing and touch him at the same time. Touch him on his chest,
you know. Just laughing. Then I touched him down there when I
laughed the last time. And then he was like, "Oh, you like this?" I was
like, "Yeah." He was like, "Well you . . ." I was like, "Uh-huh." And he
was like, "Oh. You wanna see it?" I said, "Sure." And when he whipped
it out I looked and I start rubbing it got hard. And that was the first time
I ever had a man that went up in me. And it hurted. I told him, "Wait a
minute, honey. You gotta take it easy." I told him that. And he took it
easy. And it still hurted. I . . . . "Just take it out. Just take it out." And he
was like, "Come on, come on. It ain't gonna hurt you that bad." He said,

"Don't worry 'bout it." I said, "Okay, come on. We'll try it again." We went back to . . . it's like a bar, not a bar, but they call it the Red Lion Lounge. Went to the Red Lion Lounge, he got some more beer. And I got drunk. And I ain't feel no pain after that.

Um, the first time. . . . Oh, God, it was alright. After I got over them pains going through me, I seened him, I say 'bout a week later, at a store. And he was like this, "Why didn't you come over?" I told him I would have to relax. I told him my head was spinning the next day. It wasn't that. I knew what it was. And he was like, "You wanna get high?" And I was like, "No, I don't want no more beer." He was like, "Come on." He wanted me again, and I told him no. I had to watch my little baby brother. So that Saturday was coming up and then we got together then. We went back out there. But we ain't do nothing. We just got high. He just grind and stuff like that. So we start . . . we start talking 'bout different things. What we gonna to do when we grow up. Little child fantasies, you know, stuff like that.

That was my steady one. He was dating girls, but we was still seeing one another. He get tired of the girls. He get tired of them 'cause he have more fun with me, see. Certain things girls can't do what another boy can do. Like I mean a girl might wanna, you know, they wanna be romanced. He might wanna just go jogging or running off somewhere, or walking the road or something. Certain girls don't wanna do all that. They don't wanna get they shoes messed up and all that. And by me in sneakers and everything. . . . Then I'm looking like a boy and he looking like a boy, so, I mean, people didn't notice us or nothing.

I was in love with him. I don't know how he felt 'bout me. I didn't care. I just liked what I seen. I went with him till about sixteen, and then that's when my mom decided to come up here. I was so evil 'cause I left that man down there. I was mad. Ooh, I was mad. She's like, "What's wrong with you?" I was like, "Nothing."

I started prostituting at the age of thirteen. This was in Cannon, New York. But see I was working the road, on the side of the road, late at night. It's dark out there. I would get up late at night, sneak out the door, say I'm going to the outhouse, and go walk the road. And cars go past by. One or two. Late at night, three or four. And I would drive them down to the field. And then I would charge them. . . . I didn't know what

I would charge them. I just would charge them money. Some of them would give me like ten dollars. Some of them would give me twenty. But I didn't know what to charge. I would give them oral sex. That's all I would give them was oral sex.

Because I wanted money, see. I was on a allowance budget, see. My father put me on a budget, like allowance. And I wanted money, 'cause certain things I like, pretzels at the end of school, certain outfits I likeded, and he wasn't going for it. So I made my own money that way.

See, I felt as though at that time when my father when he said that I was gay, at the age of thirteen, I felt as though I might as well get ready to know how to get my own. So I would just walk the road. Car would pull over. . . . Guy would say, "Come here. What you doing out at this time of night?" I would tell him, "Nothing." He would say, "Well, how old are you?" I would lie about my age. I would say, "Well, I'm seventeen," or eighteen, or something like that. And he would say, "How far you going down?" I would tell him, "Well, I'm just going down to my friend's house at the next lightpole." Then he would say, "Well, get in. I give you a lift." Then I would just sit there and talk to him, you know. Then one thing would lead to another.

I would say, "Look, I'm gay." I wouldn't say I was gay, I would say I'm funny. And he'd say, "So what you mean you funny?" And I would, like, hand motion, like that. And that's all. . . . "Well, what do you do?" "I give blow jobs." At the time I didn't say blow job. I say, "Well, I suck your dick." And then he would say, "Well, I don't know." I would say it was okay. Then he would say, "Well, what, you just doing it for nothing?" I would say, "No. I'll do it for whatever you can give me." And that's how it went.

Half the time they would be like, "Well, you just get out right here." See, I don't know if they were straight or not. I would think it was because . . . I think it was because that they were straight. I really do. Then again, I really think because half of them was grown they could know a child when they see a child. The other half just didn't care.

The next thing was, I'd come back . . . I'd sneak back in the cottage after I finished that so I can get up and go to school in the morning. Then I would hide my money underneath my mattress. I would wait till the weekends really, 'cause when I first did it, I did it during the school hours. I was tired. Then when I got used . . . you know, as far as having myself . . . going out there, I'd say, "Oh, I'll wait till Friday." That way I could sleep all day. And I would just, you know, wash up and everything and get my money and go to school. That's how I bought friends while I was up there. 'Cause every time they see me I always had money.

But the first time, my intention was to go out to take a walk. And when the man pulled over, see, I just was talking to him. Not knowing I'm starting to prostitute. See, I didn't know about that till I came to Jefferson. But when I first went out there and the first one did give me money, that made the idea to my mind. I told him I was funny and everything. He gave me twenty-five dollars.

I told him I was funny because . . . I mean, I don't know this man, and he don't know me. He think I'm a little boy. So I just told him I was gay. 'Cause I felt scared. 'Cause like I mean . . . I'm thirteen years old, okay. And I went out there on the road, and a man pulled over. And I mean I felt scared. 'Cause I'm in the car with this white billhilly man, twice as bigger than me, you know.

When I left the house, I was scared more than anything when I got out the cottage, how dark it was, okay. I wanted this outfit, and I walked out to think. Should I ask my father for the money or not? Then I started walking. Thinking. This the first time I ever did it—first time I walked out of the house at night—and I was thinking should I ask him, shouldn't I ask him? You know you talking to yourself. You walking down the road, you know. Then I'm like, "Fuck it," you know. I would be cussing at that age, you know. I used to smoke cigarettes at that age. At thirteen. I was sneaking smoking.

I'm, you know, talking and everything to myself and then the man just pulled over. I seen him coming, but I was getting out his way, 'cause I'm in the road. He stopped, and he asked me what I was out there that late for. I told him I was going to my friend's house up there. My eyes was big. I was scared though, you know.

He just say, "Get in." And I . . . I hesitated to get in. I just got on in anyway. And then the man was like talking to me, and then I was talking to him. He said, "Well, hi. Hi there." I said, "How you doing?" He said, "Are you going down?" I said, "Sure." He said, "How far you going down?" "I'm going down to my friend's house to the next lightpole." I wasn't really going there. I just told him I was going there. But my intention in the back of my mind was that I would need some money. But I was trying to figure out how I would get me some money. But I didn't know how I was gonna get any. 'Cause I wanted this outfit I seen. But see, by me meeting this man, I didn't know this man was gonna give me any money. I didn't come out and say. "Hi, how you doing. You want a blow job for twenty-five dollars?" I didn't come out and just say that. And I be like, "Well, look, I'm getting out right here and, you know, I'm a little gay and everything, you know. And my father's and them are back there." Then he said, "Okay," you know. "I don't got nothing to do," you know. And . . . the man really approacheded me, you know. The man really approacheded me.

He started rubbing on my legs, after I told him I was gay. And then one thing led to another, see. When he start rubbing on my legs and wanted to rub on my thang. And I was reaching and wanted to see what he had down there too, you know. And then I said, "Well, I wish I could get this outfit, you know." See, it's all coming back to me now. And then he said, "Well, you don't have no money?" I said, "No." And then he said, "Here. I want you to do this for me." So that's how that went.

He wanted me to taste his dick. And then he said, "Keep on tasting it. It won't gonna bite." You know, stuff like . . . and I just went on 'head and kept on and kept on, you know. And then he said, "Ah shit." Then he started jerking stuff off. Then I got out right there. I had my money but I was too far down. 'Cause I was past the light. I had to walk 'bout two miles. So I came on back in, washed my face and start doing all that and laid down. I'd say it was about one, two o'clock. I was tired. And my father asked me where I been at. And I lied and told him I was in the apple tree in the apple groves. He said, "For what?" I said, "I had to ask . . . I wanted to ask you something." He said, "What?" And I lied and told him I wanted to ask him for fifty cent for a pretzel at school.

Well, at the age of seventeen, I got tooken from my mother, from the city of Jefferson. They caught me prostituting. And the judge down there at the J.D., 1624, took me and put me in the Hewitt House. The Hewitt House was located at Conwall Avenue, Conwall and Earle. And I was still with Connie Miller, Rex James, and all them. They're like gay therapists. And I went through that program with them, up until the age of eighteen. No, I'd say about twenty, till the age of twenty. 'Cause I was going through a sex change operation. That's what I wanted to go through. That's what I wanted to be, a woman. Deborah and Patricia, they live down Laurel Hill—I stayed with them. They was my gay parents. So I stayed with them too until like after Christmas. Then I moved from them to the Hewitt House. And at that time I was going to school at Georgetown High. So I stayed there until like the age of twenty. I was there like three years, on and off for three years.

The most painful thing growing up was me going to the Juvenile Detention Center and when I got raped on Fifteenth and Cumberland. I was at the Hewitt House then. And I was out there prostituting. I went off with this dude on Fifteenth and Cumberland. That's when the houses used to be kind of empty on Fifteenth Street. And I went up in one of them old houses with this man. I don't know how old he was. He lookeded like he 'round 'bout twenty-four, twenty-five. And he just start hitting on me and everything.

He was built, like. And he snatched all my clothes. My coat, and everything off of me. And raped me. And the only thing I could do was . . . after he raped me and everything . . . I just told him he can have anything, just don't hurt me. I just said, "Please don't hurt me," you know. And he took my clothes, my shoes, and everything. I was naked. Naked! By it being a old house, I grabbed a old, dirty sheet and wrapped it 'round me and called the police and told them I been raped. And they called Hewitt House, and the counselor from Hewitt House came down to the hospital, 'cause the police took me to the hospital. I had to go through that test where they stick something up in your, you know, rectum to see if the dude left any sperm cells and stuff.

He just came up to me. I was on the corner. He was walking. And he just said, "Hi. How you doing?" I said, "I'm fine." So I asked him, "Are you dating?" He said, "Sure." I said, "Well, you got twenty-five dollars?" He said, "Sure." And I said, "Alright." And I walked up the street, up to Fifteenth and Cumberland, and he said, "Well, we can go over to this little old house right here." And then when I got in there, it was just it. He just start hitting me. Smacking me and punching and stuff, in my face, all in my back, in my chest, you know. And I told him. I said, "Look, you can have anything you want, just don't hurt me." "How much money you got in your pocket?" I had a little money in my pocket, 'bout thirty dollars and change. He took that.

And it still comes to me. But it has to come to me. I don't like talking about it. That's how I feel. Because it hurts, and I'm evil because it happened, you know. I never seen the dude again, you know. I would like to get back at him. It's like a anger type of thing, you know. If I would see him, I would kill him, you know.

But the reason why I was out there prostituting, or going through that ordeal is . . . I just thought that was the thing, you know. Most of the majority of homosexuals are out there prostituting, so I just thought that was the thing. I thought that was the exciting life. Yeah, but not knowing that I was playing Russian roulette with my life, see. And I didn't know that. I didn't know I was playing very really Russian roulette with my life.

In the first year I was in Jefferson I was sometime going to school, sometime hooking school, you know. And the days I hooky school, I would go downtown to swing out and hang out down at Jefferson Park. So I would have my little bag, and have my little outfit, my little wig and skirt and heels and makeup. Then when nighttime come, I would go prostituting. By time I'm coming in in the morning, it be like two and three o'clock in the morning. And I supposed to been in school. "Oh, Mom, I spend the night over my friend house." She was like, "Alright, don't go get in no trouble out there" and stuff like that. And then she was like, "Well, where all this makeup and stuff come from?" and all that questioning. I was like, "Mom, look. . . ." I ain't wanna hear her. She was like, "Well you better not be out there doing what I think you doing, you know."

She thought I was out there doing something I had no business doing. I don't know, 'cause she ain't never confronted me. And I ain't really care, see. She ain't never say I was out there prostituting until I got locked up for prostituting. But she didn't really know. I knew I was doing things I ain't had no business doing, but I did it behind the point I wanted to swing out with the rest of the people. I can do what I wanna do. I can go out there and meet my little boyfriend. And I can tell them what to do. 'Cause I was grown. And I was young at that time, and I felt that way.

Sometimes I listened to my parents. Not all the time. When they say "You not going out today" or "Don't go outside today," I would go out anyway. Or if they say, "Stay on the block where I can see you," I would get off the block. Even though I can say I was spoiled, okay, I can say that, but I always didn't want to listen. I always wanted to be the boss. And my mother knew it but she didn't approve of it. Then she take my keys from me. Like my door keys and stuff like that. So I would always have to knock to come in. In the summer . . . in the summertime she would leave me on the porch. 'Cause I was hard-headed. See, she got me back in her ways. I didn't care.

When I was growing up I was beaten only when I did something wrong with a belt. And then sometimes she wouldn't hit me. I'd have to do something real bad like steal something out the house and sell it if it was valuable or take some money. You see, my mom she was like—punishment. She ain't believe in hitting on her kids. 'Cause she say she don't wanna put a mark on them . . . us. So when she get fed up to here, she would beat us, but not real hard.

But she would leave the house and lock me in there. That's what my punishment was or take my allowance away from me. Send me to bed without dinner, you know. Make sure I don't get no sweets, cookies and candy and stuff like that.

So I have to take something out the house, very valuable, to get a good behind whooping. That means take off all my clothes and stand up there naked so she can whoop my behind with a belt.

She did that one time. 'Cause I stoled a crystal cat, and I sold it. I got like three hundred dollars for it. I was seventeen years old. That was just before I got locked up for prostitution too. She know I stoled it because my baby brother told her. Yeah, he told on me. And by him snitching on me . . . but she knew I did it before he even said anything. She called me upstairs and told me to go in my room and take off everything I have on. And I did it and everything. And then she came in with the belt and beating me and telling me, "Didn't I told you such and such . . . I was gonna beat your ass" and all this other shit. And after she whipped my ass, I got dressed, after I done cried, 'cause them beatings hurted. And then I stayed inside my room. Locked my door. And got my little outfits that I was gonna wear out that night. And I say, "I'm gonna make me some big money and don't never come back here." And I climbed out the window, and went down the alleyway. Dogs start barking and all that. And my mom . . . my brother say . . . I heard him when he said I was going down the alley. And she said, "I ain't worrying 'bout that boy. I'm tired of him." And I went downtown and just swinging out.

I knew I wanted to be a woman. I knew that. 'Cause I used to try on my mother outfits. Her shoes and stuff. Running 'round the house. I did that from the age of five. I got pictures of me in my mother outfits. Yeah, as a little boy. And they didn't know I was gonna be gay. They just took it as being fun, see. Little outfits. Like a little skirt or something. Too big for me. You know.

Every Sunday I had to go to church. But they had to go with me to church. If they ain't go with me to church, that suit was coming off. I didn't go. I would turn back and go home, change and put my tight jeans, and hit the streets. My mother and them made me go. I didn't really care for church too much until I went to church and I learned about God. I went to Bible school, and I feels I knew enough through that. But my mom she sat down and explained to me one day that you don't . . . you never know enough about the Man up above. And then that like put a little insight on me then I start going, you know. Then I would start getting into a little religious thing, you know. But I still was gay. That wasn't gonna stop nothing, you know.

Well, something got to be up there for us to be gay, that's the way I feel. See what I'm saying? I mean the Lord made everybody. So something He doing, you know, for . . . they may say . . . well, some people say, "You going to hell" and "Change your life over and everything." But I don't believe that. 'Cause nobody don't know where they going at. I can't say right now if I die where I'm going at. I was raised up on one person, the Lord.

The only reason why I think that way is behind the point no matter what you is, if you do something wrong, it comes back to you. It may have put a thought in your mind, "Why did I do this?" you know. But if I was doing something wrong, with that Man up above, He wouldn't be helping me out in so many different ways, you know. 'Cause I do pray to him, every night. We have a understanding.

So I was out there. I was out there 'cause I was . . . I never was in one city. See I was like in the country part. Then when I was looking at all this lights and big buildings, I wanted to see what was out there. It was exciting to me. And then I'm being gay and see other queen being gay and popping fingers and all that. And I was . . . I was wanna get into all that, you know. And I got into all that.

I was amazed how a man can look like a woman. I said, "Damn, I always wanted to be a woman too." And I got to asking questions, learning 'bout how to, you know, be a woman and everything. I taught myself, you know. It was hard teaching myself. Trust me. So I had to really study, you know.

I was fascinated by it until I got into it. When I got into it, it wasn't no more fascinating 'cause it was everyday life then. Then when I got deep into it, you know what I mean, my mind and everything got deep into it, and then I decided, I said, "Well, I guess what I really wanna be in life, a woman." Live my life like one every day.

See, when I got to Jefferson my sister took me downtown to show me around, you know. See how Metro Center, stuff like that. We had to catch the F bus, and the F bus let you off at Eleventh and Main. I can see little, you know, gay people hanging up in the club. Like standing on the side of the bar. And I was like this, "Wait a minute. Wait a minute, ducky. . . . Uh-uh . . . wait a minute. You right down my alley, honey." She was like, "Come on, boy. You don't know. . . ." I said, "Wait a minute, child. Let me just walk down this way." She was like, "Uh-uh. I know you ain't taking me down here with all of these people." She called us "thangs." Said, "I know you ain't taking me down there with these thangs." I said, "What you mean 'with these thangs'?" She said, "Well I gotta get outta here. I come down here to get . . . we come down to get a album." I was like, "Well, this where they hang out at, huh?" She was like, "Yeah. Why?" And I was like this, "I just wanted to know." Back of my mind I'm like, "Uh-huh, I'm coming down here by myself soon as we get home."

So we go 'round to Church Street and came up Tenth Street and went to this record store you go down the steps. We got our little records and stuff. I said, "I'm ready to go home." So we got home. I wanna go outside, see. And this time she liveded in the projects. She liveded at Ninth Street projects, the high-rise part. Right off of Pendleton

Avenue. So I said, "Well, I gonna go outside." She said, "Okay." So I goes down the steps and go ahead outside. Alright. Something said go downtown. You know your way now. I went upstairs, got my little pouch, I had my little change in it. I had 'bout twenty, thirty something dollars in there. So I goes downtown. Walking distance. I can walk. I said, "I'm a go straight down Ninth Street." This way the trolley come up. And I read the sign. I said, "Tenth Street is that way and Eleventh Street is this way." And my first time in Jefferson now. I said, "Wait a minute. I'm lost here. Something ain't right." So I just say, "I'm a keep on walking." I kept on walking until I got down there 'bout Church Street. And I said, "Oh, this is where . . . a lot of us right here. Uh-huh."

So I got down there, start swinging out. Then I ran into this child name Houston, Miss Houston. She dead now. She died of AIDS. I ran into Miss Houston and she was like this, "Child, this is where the clubs is at." And I went to Bouncin' Betty's. And they was like this, "Uh-uh. Get that little young child outta here. We'll go to jail." So I was like, "Uh-uh. Let me get me a ID from somewhere." So this guy gave me his ID, right, he looked older. He gave me his ID. And I flipped the ID on. Then they start saying you got to have your picture on your ID. I ain't had no . . . they just looked at me. And I was like, "Yeah, this is my age." Remember social security number and everything. So I started partying up in the club. Got drunk. I got drunk and seem like the, you know, room start spinning. I'm "Let me sit down." I sat down.

I met somebody up there. And I went to they house. They lived in Somerset County. And I end up in they bed. I was like, "Uh-uh. Take me home. Take me home. Right now." I don't know if it was a trick or not. I just know I was drunk. He was like, "Wait a minute. Wait a minute." I was like, "What you mean wait a minute, wait a minute? I'm ready to go home." He said, "Here, here go your money." I said, "What?" I said, "Well, look, take me home." I told him just take me down Eleventh Street. I find my way home. He say, "Okay." And he dropped me off. He said, "You know where you was at?" I said, "No, I don't. Where was I at?" He said, "You was in Somerset County." I said, "What in Somerset County?" And he was like, "You was far out in Somerset County." He ain't never told me where, he just said far out. I said, "Okay." So he took me to Eleventh and Main. And I walked up from Eleventh and Main all the way home. My sister said, "Boy, where you been at? I was up all night, you know, worrying about you. And you running 'round this big-ass town. I done called the cops and everything." I said, "Child, I went downtown." She said, "I knew something told me come down there. I knew your ass was down there." So I told her, I said, "Look. I am tired. I don't wanna be bothered right about now."

This child gave me her phone number. And I would call her at my sister house and she would meet me at Pendleton Avenue. She was older than I was. She was like 'round 'bout twenty. In her twenties. She was older than I was. She was out there hooking and everything. Prosti-tuting and all. Taking speed pills and meth. See, I wasn't into all of that. I was just into reefer and stuff. Reefer and beer. She was a IV user and stuff like that and I wasn't. I would be up in their house, but they would tell me that I had to leave 'cause I was too young to be up in there. This was all during that year. It was nice. I loved it. I loved it that year. From the age of sixteen all the way up I loved it. So till it got to the point where as though I just start doing heavy drugs.

Only thing I learned about them, being out there and popping fin-gers, and street life. Like certain people not to trust, know what I mean? Don't deal with that person. Don't deal with this person. That person ain't got too much sense. That person might beat you . . . you know. Different people they was pointing out. That's what I learned about them. They was being honest with me, you know. I likeded that about them too. And then they looked out for my safety, see. And I likeded that about them. I didn't learn anything from people on the streets about technique. I know how to do all that, honey, myself. I'm the teacher.

We would like, go to movies. Go out. Grub. Buy clothes. Buy clothes alike. Shoes alike, you know. We would be cutting up. Having fun. We were throwing hair and popping fingers and just sissying. Sissying is like, when you out getting you hair done, you know. Getting false nails on. Clear fingernail polish, you know. Buying clothes. Pop-ping fingers. Talking like, "Oh, Miss Thang. Child, please. Bitch, it ain't all about you." And stuff like that, you know.

And I was hooking, I was prostituting on Eleventh and Church. High heels and stuff like that. And my wig. And my bobby pins. And I just be cutting up. Have my earrings in my ear and be like this, "Hey, daddy, come here." All these was white men. That's all I date is white men. I don't date black men 'cause they full of shit. They wanna take you through it for a little bit of money. I mean, he want more than for what his money can buy. For example, he want the blow job and the rectum and the pussy. He want it all! For twenty dollars. Then he want you to keep bobbing and bobbing and my makeup sweating off.

So I only deal with whites, and that's all I deal with. Italians. Whites and Italians. I prefer both, white, Italian, Greek, you name it. Don't bring no black. He want too much for a little bit of money, and the white men are faster, most of them are fast. Yeah. But it's mainly they spend good money. "You got a condom?" That's the only thing I ask them. "You got a condom?" "Sure, baby." "Alright." Yes, honey." It just like that. All night. If a black man drive up, I be like this—"Go on, honey." Go on 'head with that." I don't wanna be bothered.

I would sleep with a black man, okay. Don't get me wrong. If the thing is right. But a white man will take care of you. A black man wanna work you to death. That means when he get up you get up, you know. Like say if he gotta go to work, you gotta get up and fix his breakfast. A white man just get up and put in a bagel in a toaster and puts cream cheese and keep on stepping. See what I'm saying? See, a black man, he want bacon and eggs. The whole works, see. And I can't go for that. Uh-uh.

And white men, they nice. You know . . . I mean, they nice. You can talk to them real sweet, you know. They getting nice money, you know. The ones I was dating they was older. I mean old. Seventy. It don't bother me. I just feel as though he wanted love and affection too. Who else would want a dried-up prune? That's what I'd be saying. I mean, be for real. He's dried up, you know. He old, wrinkled.

One time this white man he gave me all this money. I ran into him down Eleventh and Church. I was coming out the peep show. I was standing right in front of the peep show at Eleventh and Church. He just come right out there. I said, "Hi, baby." He had a suit on and everything. He say he was a lawyer. He was like 'round forty-five, with a toupee. And he took me to the Sheraton Hotel. That's when the Sheraton Hotel was downtown. And he took me up in there and wine and dine the girl.

Gave me everything I wanted. Gave me seven hundred dollars. Yes. He ordered up champagne and everything. Yeah. Had champagne on ice when I got there. No lie! I was like this, "Alright, Miss Sugar."

I whooped his ass. He wanted to be beat with a whip. That's what he went in the peep show for, but he wanted a person dressed like a woman. He had this whip, and he said, "Beat me hard. Beat me hard." After he wined and dined the girl, okay, then I whooped his ass. I did. He was coming while I was whipping him. He laid on the bed. He say, "Oh, you so pretty. You is a pretty black child." And he said, "Whip me." I mean he said, "Whip me, baby." And I hit him. You know, I didn't wanna hit the man. He said, "Hit me hard. Here go another hundred." Whack! "Here go another hundred. Hit me hard." And when I got finished that man gave me seven hundred dollars. And he was coming. He never touched himself. Never touched himself. He just like to be beat. And he came. I just grabbed . . . finished grabbing the bottle of champagne while he went in the bathroom and washed up and stuff. And sat there and drunk. He said, "You alright?" I said, "I'm fine, thanks." He said, "You know your way home?" I said, "Sure." He said, "Alright. You take care," and kissed me on the cheek. I said, "Alright. See you later." And I got to that elevator I couldn't wait to get down those steps. I was like this in the hallway, "Alright!" Wanted to snatch the wig off right then and there. My clothes was in the locker downtown.

I was only sixteen. But he didn't know. Underneath all that makeup, he thought I was a older woman. That man did not know till I got into that apartment I told him. I said "Well, honey, before we get in bed, you know I'm a man." He said, "What! I thought you was a woman." I said, "Yes, I am." He said, "Well, that's okay." I said, "Well, what you mean that's okay?" right. He said, "Well, we still can get into the thing, you know. I don't mind. That's what I really looking for anyway. That's alright."

I want my man to play the man role. The man of the house, see what I'm saying? That means do everything a man would do. Play basketball. Read books. Look at football on TV. Be nagging like a man do to a woman sometime. Make her feel, you know, like "Go on baby. I ain't worrying about it." Stuff like that. "Gimme a kiss honey," you know. I like macho. That's what I want. Macho man. You know, like bangee, butch baby. You know, like the mens that be rapping and stuff like that. Them type of mens I like. And that's bangee, street-like men. But just down to earth, fly. Some who could talk dirty to me. Not too dirty, but I'm just saying . . . I want to know I'm the one. You know, take control of the situation, not too much control, but just . . . just like a man know how far to go with a woman, right. That's how I want my man to know how far to go with me. He would be the one who would be the caretaker, the provider in the relationship. Right, that's what I'm saying. Like that. And then we be fifty-fifty.

I consider him a straight man. But if he doing me and I'm doing him, he's gay. If he's pancake, if he's flip-flopping, then he's gay. If he is not flip-flopping, then he's not gay, he bisexual or he's straight. So if he was in the relationship with me and he was having a relationship with another woman on the side, he's bisexual. If he's in a relationship with me and he's only dates me, and doesn't have a relationship with anyone else, then he's straight. If he's in a relationship with me and I do him, he does me, then he's gay. Just as much a woman as I am.

You got some mens out here that go both ways. You got some mens that like to be fucked by a man and like fucking them. You got some woman out here like to be fucked by a man and fuck a woman. Well, I had a relationship with a man and he was flip-flop. He was a man . . . well, he carry himself as a man, but I got the kitty. The kitty, right. And I think that's a beautiful relationship, 'cause he know where I'm coming from. And I'm a drag queen. I'm a transvestite. So he knew where I was coming from. So that was a really nice relationship.

I'm generally the passive one in the relationship. I would always be the one who would be on the bottom. So a man can define himself any way he wants to define himself as long as he does not flip-flop, do pancake. I play the woman role. That means I'm the boss. What I say goes. See, I'm the aggressive type. I mean, look, you want me just as bad as I want it too. And so I'm like, you know, honey, I like to be pampered. So same way he would do a woman he would have to do me if he want to get into my world. I would clean, wash his clothes, cook, make sure the linens and everything clean. Just like a woman do, you know. I expect him to work. He would be taking care of the rent. The money. The bills.

I was seventeen when my mother found out I was doing stuff. That was when I got picked up for prostitution. I got arrested when I was downtown, Eleventh and Beaumont. See, I met this man from Virginia up here, and I took him to Thirteenth and Chestnut. In the parking lot. That's when the parking lot used to be there. And I took him there and the cops drove up. And I didn't know no cops was in there, you know like spying on us or following us. And I'm in there bobbing, you know. And so by me being in there bobbing and everything, the police just shine the light, the big flashlight. It was dark. And I was like, mouth wide open still 'cause I was like shocked. And he said, "Alright, get out the car, Miss." And I get out the car. He said, "What's your name?" I gave him my real name. When I gave him my real name he said, "Oh. We got a male here. How old are you?" And I told him I was sixteen years old. When I was born and everything. They said, "You with a minor." And told him, "Don't you know how many years you can get with a minor?" They ain't take the money back. So I . . . I told them that he ain't give me no money, but he did give me some money. He gave me like forty-five dollars. And I told him that he didn't. He said, "Well you gotta go to Juvenile Detention Center. It's past your curfew and you got no reason being out here. You get locked up for prostitution. And he have to go in and we gon' press charges on him for corrupting a minor." And they took me to Juvenile Detention Center. No, they took me over to Eighteenth and Lincoln. I wanted to get outta there, but they was like, "We cannot let you go 'cause your mother have to come up and get you." My mom 'posed to came and got me and my mother didn't come and get me. So she let me stayed in the Juvenile Detention Center. And she let me stayed there and stayed there.

They took him over there too, see. But I was on one side, he was in . . . they put me in a bubble. They took him in the back. And when they put me in the bubble . . . the bubble was for the young kids . . . so they could watch them. They asked my mom, right, to come and get me. And she wouldn't come and get me. Because she said that supposed to teach me a lesson. So when I stayed in there, I stayed in there until I went to court. They told her what they caught me doing 'cause she asked them what I was charged with. They told her for prostitution. Well, she said, "Well, let him stay in there." I stayed there for three months. They took me to court, Family Court. I went to Family Court and after I went to Family Court they took me to the group home. Hewitt House. No, first I ain't go to Hewitt House. First, I went down here to this lady . . . these two ladies Deborah and Patricia. I went down there to them. They two gay parents. Lesbian couple looking for a gay child that's already gay. Like gay runaway, see. I was into that type of facility.

Oh, I got along with them beautifully. It was a black couple. Down in Laurel Hill. Down there. I got along with them real nice. I stopped hooking, and I went back conservative then. I stopped dressing in drag. I stayed with Deborah and Patricia for one year, and after I left there, I went to the Hewitt House on Conwall and Earle. I stayed there until the age of eighteen. I was sixteen years old when I got locked up in the Juvenile Detention Center. I stayed at the Hewitt House till I had turned eighteen. And when I . . . well, eighteen and a half though really. So they helped me get my apartment. And they gave me a birthday party in my apartment.

I went back into drag at the Hewitt House, but for a year I ain't go in drag. I wanted a sex change. And that's how I ran into Connie Miller. She's a transvestite therapist, counselor. And I was going for a sex change operation, through that process. So I went into drag. 'Cause I ain't feel right into boy clothes. I just didn't feel right, you know. I couldn't be me. I didn't go back into the streets at that point. When I got back into the streets, it was little later after the Hewitt House. I was in full drag then all the time. So I've been in full drag ever since I was seventeen.

That was the first time I ever been caught. I ain't like the Juvenile Detention Center. Them little young boys. I was . . . I was fighting every day. They got on my nerves. I got in fights because I was gay. I got into fights because of cigarettes. I got into fights because certain people likeded me, you know. Little childish stuff.

Certain people likeded me, and certain boys didn't like that, you know. They would start a fight with me. They would like push me or something like that. Like I'm in line or something, they would push me. And I would go off. I got into so many fights up there, you know, and then it died down 'cause some of the boys was getting shipped out, you know. They was like a bunch of young boys don't like no sissies, you know. And they would tease you, call you names. "Faggot. Sissy. You ain't nothing but a fucking freak." Stuff like that. It made me upset. That made me pissed off. It made me want to fuck something up. And that's what I did. I just tell them I'm a fuck them up. I say, "I'm a fuck you up. Watch. Keep playing. I'm a fuck you up." And they thought I was playing. But I wasn't playing. I would just call them in the cell. Tell them let's play some cards or whatever. I just fuck them up. I beat their ass. That helped . . . that helped a lot. That . . . I ain't gonna lie, that helped a lot. Because I got more respect. Then they said, "Look. Don't mess with him. Don't mess with him. He'll kick your ass."

I talked to my mother 'bout two days after I was there. She just said that, "Now, that should teach you a lesson like going out to get into any type of trouble." That's what she told me. I talked to my mother about four times. Four or five times. And then that's when they took me. I believe she signed me over to them. I asked her. But she told me the city took me away from her. But I didn't believe her, 'cause it just don't sound right. For the first time me being locked up for prostitution, the city just ain't gonna take me away from you. I think she ain't wanna be bothered. That she got tired. Fed up worrying about me. So I guess she feels that if I'm in a boarding home somewhere, that the least worry.

I told her I feel upset behind it. But she said she didn't do it. She keep denying, but I still don't believe her. I felt anger behind it. And I felt as though she did something that I wouldn't even do to my child. She didn't have to lie to me. She coulda told me the truth, you know. But I ain't that angry with her. 'Cause, I mean, I'm over it. I'm grown now. I can forgive but I can't forget.

I'm very close to her. Very close. She calls me and tell me come down there and help her with things like that, you know. Like a sister and daughter. I'll put it like that. She don't have no problem with the dragging or the gay stuff no more. She grew outta that. I see her every week. Sometimes more. I see her so much I just be, "Look, I gotta go home, take me a rest."

I quit school while I was there too. I was sixteen. I would say 'bout B student when I was in school. I was alright, but I hate mathematics. I like mathematics till you get to them . . . not divisions . . . but them decimals and all that ol' stuff, you know, x, y, and all of that. I got fed up with that right there. That's when I start cutting up. My best subject was reading. I hated science. It was reading, that and home economics was my best subject.

I skipped classes. When I came to the city I skipped a lot. I would do that like twice a month. Three times outta next month. Four times out of this month. Then I would slow down, then continue go to school for about two or three months. Start the same thing over and over again. That's how I would do that. My mother really didn't say nothing when I just stopped going to school.

She used to go to school every time they had teacher's meeting. They says parents invited. Yeah. And I ain't like that. So I would tear my paper up and say we ain't get none. I don't want her there 'cause then she be all in the business. I don't want her to know everything I might be doing in school. I just want her to know I'm doing alright in school. I got caught smoking reefer. I'd do things like put tacks on teacher's . . . underneath the teacher. When she sit down. Yeah. In the seat. Miss Ferguson's seat. That was her name. She was big and fat. She would sit down. . . . Stuff like that. That's what I would do.

I got in fights at school. Uh-huh. I got in fights at school 'bout me being gay. I learned how to swish. So I was like swishing, honey. Paying it no mind, you know. I was feeling free. And they didn't go for that in Jefferson. Oooh! That's one thing 'bout these boys up here. Didn't go for that! They said, "Uh-uh." Yeah. I was like just paying them no mind. Popping fingers, honey. "Oh, stand back, 'fore I beat you in the face." That's how I was with them. And they couldn't take it. And I would whoop they ass too. I would come for them. I would actually call up and come for them. They be like "faggot" or throwing a spitball at me and hit me or something. And I would be like this, "I'm a get you, pussy. Uh-huh. I'm a get you." That's how I would be like that with them. And they couldn't take it. Then after a while they got to know me, you know. They like, "Uh-uh. That motherfucker right there'll fight you, man." It's like a recognition, you know. Yeah. Yeah. And so they was like, "Yeah. What's up, such and such?" And then I got to know certain boys. Start having certain boys, you know. "Let's skip class. Come on, man. Swing out with me," you know. Yeah, they would. "I don't want my homey to see me," you know. Shit like that.

My mom wanted me to be a lawyer, and that lawyer bit got on my nerves. I told them, you know, they can take the lawyer stuff soon as I got a certain age. I always wanted to be a doctor, myself. I never wanted to be no lawyer. I don't like, you know, into law books and reading 'bout this and that and all that. That's too much school for me. I just didn't wanna be no high-class doctor and all that. A specialist. I just want to be a plain old doctor, you know. Just take the blood pressure, you know. Minor cold doctor. Like that.

But I got into the prostitution lane. The money started getting good in prostitution. And I just said, "Hell with doctors and all of that." See, the fast money was in the street on the hustling tip. Fast money was out there that was coming like that. So I just went where the money went. Then I start dressing real nice. Little fly . . . kept nice things, you know. And so when I started getting into them, I was like this, "Well, what I need school for when I got this?" So that's how I was.

I think I disappointed my mother behind the point that I ain't do nothing else with my life besides me wanting to be a woman. It's more to just wanting to be a woman and ain't doing nothing else with your life. So I think I hurted her that way. I feel kind of sad about it behind the point 'cause I got into the street life-wise, you know, I got out here. And I feel kinda bad about it. But there's nothing I can do now. I'm hooked on drugs and everything.

When I was growing up I wanted to get out of their house. I wanted to have my own. Yeah. I dreamt about it and stuff like that, but things didn't seem to go that way. I was just a child, you know. I felt like trapped. I couldn't do the things I wanted to do, you know. I couldn't feel free. I wanted to call the shots. Nobody else gonna call the shots over me. Just like my own roof over my head. I ranned away once at the age of sixteen. I went downtown at Jefferson Park, the Hangout. I ranned away just for couple hours, and my mom came down there. Somebody came by the house looking for me, and one of my so-called gay friends took her down there where I was at.

Well, when I was growing up, only person I looked up to . . . was women. I was going to be a woman, right. I looked in the mirror, in East Jefferson, and I said, "Ooh, I wanna be a woman." And I don't know if it's foolish or what, I just said, "I wanna be woman. I know God didn't make me no woman, but I wanna look like a woman." And bam! I start throwing makeup. Start looking like a woman. Arch my eyes. Hair started growing like a woman. Perm. My nails. Then I started taking female hormones. Taking pills. I started just taking them. Then I started getting more effeminate. Then people start mistaking me as a real woman in the world. See, I went in the world to test it, see. Just like I was walk into a store and they was like, "Excuse me, miss. You can go ahead." A gentleman would say that. Then I knew, right then and there, I'm on the right track, you know. Not acting. See, you gotta be yourself in order to be a woman also. You can't just act out "I'm gonna be a woman" and get and be all flaming. Yeah. You can't be all like this. 'Cause a woman is not like this. She's natural. She's unique. That's her, you know.

It's like how a man feel that he's a woman on the inside. He wanna bring that woman on the outside. The things the woman is . . . those things are more sensitive feelings, you know. I mean, it's all kinds of things you go through. You go emotions real easy, you know. Headaches. Very more disturbed. By mental disturbed, you know, because you can't really stay still. And I feel as though that the woman is in me and I'm, you know, trying to get that appearance. Trying to bring that woman more out. By stopping the man . . . by stopping the man that's in me, is stopping his hormones.

I started taking hormones at the age of eighteen. I took them until I was like twenty-four, then I stopped. I have been off hormones shots two years now. They gave me Hylutin and Delestrogen. Well, they, you know, bring the titties out. And the TACE pills help them bring them out more, help brang the breast out more. I never had implants. I would take them to a point where I just get a chest. A little, you know, titty. Little size for me. And then just stop. See, some . . . some men's chest will go down if they stop. Some of them don't. Mine are big enough to wear a bra.

I was gonna go to the sex change operation at the age of seventeen, but I was too young. I talked to this man in New York. I found out about him through other sex changes that I know of. And he told me I was too young. I had to be a certain age to get a sex change. And then I just started prostituting. I started being more out here, and then that just went one way and drugs came in another way.

I say by me getting hooked on heroin, that stopped a whole lot of emotions. A whole lot of things 'cause I got hooked with a bad crowd of people. Yeah. I got on heroin at the age of twenty-five . . . no, twenty-four. Over a couple years, you know. And by me got hooked on heroin, I just started going from one end to another end. I start going down and down. See, I was going with this man, right. I loveded him so much that whatever he did, I would do, see. And that's how I started off with it. Now the man is gone. He off of it and I'm still on it. And that brought me down a lot. A whole lot. It did.

I didn't really knew until I really got into the city what prostituting means. I just started thinking it was just like a sidekick thing. Something that I get into and then I just leave that outta my mind.

I would go out toward a girlfriend houses, and dress up over they house. Keep my clothes over they house. See, they had they own little apartment. They own little hotel room. Stuff like that. So I would go over there and get dressed up. I was like fifteen years old then. I was curious. I wanted to see how can a man dress up and look like a woman. And when I got into it, it was more than I thought it was to it. When I got into it I thought it was a fun thing. I thought it was just dress up, going out, meeting different guys, you know. Getting money from them and having a nice time. Which I didn't know 'cause I was all alone. I was out there prostituting. I was going along with the other drag queens. We going . . . like follow the leader. I was that type of person. And by me being that type of person, following the leader, I ended up in something that I didn't even know that I was getting myself into. What was dangerous to myself. But all along I was just having a good time.

So I got into drag and then I felt comfortable while I was there. Then I was getting money. I was like, taking care of myself, you know. I was like I don't have to ask Mom for this. I don't have to ask Dad for that. I can have money in my pocket. I don't have to worry 'bout allowance. I ain't got to go to school. I can pay my own rent wherever I'm living at. I mean, you know, then, by that money coming to me and I was so excited and everything, I mean, my eyes got big. I was like, "Oh. I'm having a good time." So, then, after I got into that, right, okay, I got into drugs.

But it was more to it than I thought. It was like, a hormone shot. Pills. Growing titties, you know. Having a husband. Being more independent, you know. And it was like, you get in a car with this man you don't know, see. And all that time that I didn't know, I thought it was just like a fun thing. Like mentally, okay. I went too far as thinking that I, you know, could fool a man. I was thinking like, "Yeah. I know I can fool a man thinking I'm a real woman," you know. I train my voice. I started sounding like one. Acting, you know. Making sure that each step I make that I would just try to fool him. And that really got me being into drag more, more strong.

It was all blending together. 'Cause by me dressing up as a woman that's when I went out to the street. I didn't just dress up as a woman everyday lifestyle thing. I went from in drag into the street. When I first started, okay, I got in full drag when I first started, and I didn't like it. No. I didn't like it because I was in heels, fish, you know, stockings. Wig and everything. But I didn't like that. It wasn't me because I felt like I was pretending. And so what I did was got in drag the way I feel as though I would be comfortable in, you know. As flat shoes, do my own hair, stuff like that. I was more like on the natural tip type of thing. I feel as though if I couldn't do it like with my own hair and everything, you know, it wasn't no need. I didn't wanna wear a wig. Nothing like false, phony, you know.

I was hanging downtown on Church Street, from Eleventh Street, when that used to be the whole strip. They tore all that down. And I used to hang up there all the time with high heels and everything. It was fast. Everything goes. It was like drugs. Like cocaine wasn't that popular. It was there, but it would took a lot of money to get it. It was mainly like heroin and meth. Crank. Speedballs. Black beauties. Christmas trees. Football. Acid. Marijuana. See those the type of things that was back then.

What I mean by anything goes is you got drag queen, female, like some of them sex change, and male hustlers, female impersonators, mens that like to be dominated, and mens that like for another female impersonator to dress them up in women clothes. It was so many other things, you know. And that's what I mean by being out there in the street like that. That's what I committed myself to. And all along I thought it was just fun. Fast money, you know. Just like some people say you live fast, you die fast.

The rhythm is going to the bar, okay. Leaving the bar and going to the stroll. They would hit the stroll like 'round 'bout nine, ten o'clock in the evening. Right on the corner of Eleventh and Beaumont, Eleventh and Mill, Church, see. They would just stand, walk, walk, you know. Might run into somebody they know. A trick or something. Talk to them, you know. Take them up in a little alley or something. Get them off. And come back on the stroll. See what I'm saying? That activity would go on all . . . well, it used to go all day long. It would never die down. It used to just come like a clockwork. When people going to work, the same thing was out there, prostitution, drug dealers and sellers and buyers, all twenty-four seven. It was like that. It was constantly like that. Somebody was out there working. Somebody was out there getting something.

Daytime was more slower than night behind the point you got people working in Metro Center and you don't know who's the narc and who's not the narc. You don't know who's who. Like say if you got drugs on you from the night, you might wanna sell it. I might wanna sell it. And by me might wanna sell it, I don't know who I'm a sell it to. You have white people come down there say, "Well, you got that meth? You got that coke? Do you know where we can get weed from?" You don't know if they a cop or what.

When I was younger, I couldn't get into the bars. So I would stand outside the bar. Work, you know, work. And then when the bars get real crowded I would go 'head up in there. And sit back in the crowd, you know. And as I got into the crowd like that, then I start painting my face more heavier. Make me look more older. I couldn't carry myself like I was a kid. Even though I knew I was a kid. But I had to act some type of mature, you know. I couldn't get too high, 'cause I couldn't handle that much liquor at that age.

When I left the Hewitt Center, they gave you a party, and then when

I turned my nineteenth birthday. And I was living over there by that hospital, Brennan Hospital. I was living over that way, by the college, East Jefferson around Twenty-ninth . . . Thirtieth . . . somewhere down around there. I lived there till I turned like twenty. I wasn't hooking any. See, I was like mainly into counseling. I was like seeing my therapist, then I would go see my counselor, you know. So mainly I stayed busy. Well, I would have like one friend come over, you know.

The two years I liveded over there at Thirtieth, over that way, when I had my own apartment, I didn't go out the street. I was working. I was working at that grocery store out there. I was a stockboy. That's the only way I, you know, could took care of myself. So I got tired of being a stockboy. It was just getting dull. I was an L7, a square. I wanted some excitement. I wanted to loosen up.

So when I left East Jefferson, I moved up to Sixth and Northway Streets. When I was at Northway Street, I'm out there. Yeah. I'm grown. I got my own little room. Bring my johns there. Turn my little date, you know. And so I was down there with this friend of mines, somebody I just turned dates with. I moved down there 'cause everybody in there was transvestites and they was out in the street prostituting. Those ladies of the night. See, these was people that he didn't even know really. He just knew they needed a room. So he just took them in and charged them rent. It was a house divided into different rooms. It wasn't like apartments. It was like rooms. There were 'bout eight or nine people living there. So I got back into prostitution 'cause I moved there, and by them being out there prostituting, that's makes me wanna go . . . I mean that made me wanna say, "Look, hey. I'm gonna go back out," you know. They bringing in money. Going shopping during the daytime. So that's what I wanted. I wanted money. I didn't have no job. So I had to make a living. Soon as I got situated, I say 'bout three days, I was back on the streets again. I lived there 'bout . . . not even that long. I say till I was 'bout twenty-three.

The stroll was still going on. I felt though I missed a whole lot. I felt though there was different people on the stroll, different dates, new . . . you know, new dates. You know what I mean? Getting more money. Price went up. Before it was nothing but fifteen dollars for a blow job and twenty dollars for a lay. That's how it was. So then it was like thirty dollars for a blow job. Sixty dollars for a lay. One hundred dollars all night, you know. So things was like jiggling, you know.

The place I am now, my girlfriend Shontae and Christie live with me. They use drugs. Well, they smoke cocaine. The place is decent. We got it cracked. We got it hooked up. For us to be out there working the street we got it real nice. We got our own room, our own little TV, own little component set, VCR, stuff like that. The place is small. It's a small two-story house, right. But it's comfortable. It's like, when you in your own room it's, you know, roomy. Then you got the dining room. You got the kitchen. And you got the living room. You know what I'm saying?

We all work on the street, and we bring our dates there. We watch each other's back all the time. We have to do that. You know, like one of the girls might answer the door and say, "Well, Sugar, got a date." And then we'll know who it is. I might say, "Well, Chrissy, you got a date." She'll say, "Who is it?" He'll tell me his name and I know who it is. Then we got a dog, a Doberman pinscher. We got Madam at the pet shop. We bought him. We all chipped in and bought the dog, one hundred dollars. Got him shots and everything. The dog 'bout twelve years old now.

It's fun living there, 'cause everything is comical. The way we talk, "Miss Thang. Don't try it honey." Stuff like that, you know. The way we be saying different things, you know. And we be for real with one another. When we got a problem we can come to one another and talk about it, you know. Not all that bullshit and everything. Put that on the side and we sit down and have a really serious talk, you know. Just like a family. See, that's our family outside our real family.

I had my first real relationship two years ago. That was the first time I really, really felt in love . . . what I really knew what love mean, you know. I met him downtown in a bar. I was going to the Academy of Beauty Arts. He was in the Downtown Pub. Right down there by the Municipal Building. Well, I just met him in there. I stopped in there after school and had me a drink and I met him in there. He kept looking at me. He likeded me. And I looked back at him. He asked what I was drinking, and I told him I was drinking—what was that?—Bacardi rum, Bacardi rum and Coke soda. He asked me could he . . . "Want me to buy you a rum and Coke?" I said, "Sure." And one thing led to another and then I took him home. We started talking. And he asked me what my name was and so on and so on, you know. And I asked him what he was doing out there. He say he was hustling. And he used to sell reefer. And so we went—where we go?—so we went over my house at Plainfield Street. He left his lizard shoes there and I sold them. He couldn't find his way back to Plainfield Street. I ran back into him, and when I ran back into him, he was just getting outta jail.

After that we just got back into where we left off. I took him to the house and everything. Then we get into . . . our little deep, you know, sexual intercourse thing. The little Miss Love Touch. And so, I mean, we was just like having a nice time and everything, you know. I loveded him. I really did. I still do have feelings for him.

He didn't move in that fast. It took him about a month to move in with me. And I was the first queen that he ever messed around with. He was a straight man and he was in a gay bar to hustle and selling reefer. And I was just the only one he ever really likeded. Yup. I likeded everything about him. I like the way he, you know, how he talk to a person. I likeded how he, you know, took care of real important things, you know. He know how to talk to a person, you know. He wasn't mainly just about street things. He was mainly about other things too. He was very creative, you know. He had a nice head on his shoulders.

He was twenty-seven when I met him, and I was like 'round twenty-four. He was black and he had a reputation. His name was Kane. So that was his reputation that he had to keep up. But it really didn't bother him because I was Sugar, see. And so we was like Kane and Sugar, you know. And so it didn't really make a difference, you know, I mean, to other people. So it was just mainly like just me and him going against the world. And it went for two years. And I likeded the brother. I really did likeded him.

It's a funny thing. When you in a relationship with a person and you just have a feeling that you just light this spark. Like something just hit your heart. And it's like, not a . . . a down thing, you know. It's something happy that lifts you up, you know. And then you got that glow on your face. You know, you so happy, you know what I mean? And he made me feel like that. He was very passionate, you know. He played that man role, and if I had to give him a grade for his performance I would give him a A. Yes. A plus! He was all that. Yes, he was too. All that and more.

I don't really . . . I couldn't even really tell the reason why it end myself, you know. All of a sudden he just went flying out the coop. Really I got mad because he went off with somebody else or something he said. Something about some . . . some other conservative child that had money. And he 'posed to took her under some old stuff and I went off. I went off.

He took her under. Took all her leather and sweatsuits and all that, you know. And I . . . I mean, he brought me the stuff, but I still felt, I ain't want that. That wasn't what I wanted. He coulda gave me anything in the world. He gave me nice watches. Diamonds. Watches with the diamond thing on top of it. It was real and everything 'cause I walked into the pawn shop and let them pawn it. I didn't want no money or nothing. I just was upset just thinking that he stayed over this child's all that time, all day long.

He left me Sunday morning. 'Round three o'clock Sunday morning. And went off with her somewhere and then come back home until Monday night. And then come back with a different pair of underwears on on top of it. And I was upset. He had never done anything like that before. I flew out the coop. I just did. I called him every damn name there was in the book. I did. And he respond to me start fighting like two grown men. I got my finger cut and I got my teeth broken out, you know. I stabbed him on the side right there. I stabbed him. See, it really still get me down by just talking about it, you know. It still do get me down, 'cause I'm still in love with the man, you know.

Before that we had a nice time, you know. We went on picnics together. Went bike riding. We went to the circus, you know. We went to New York together. Ocean City. We had a nice time. He just used meth. We help support each other habit, you know. But we wouldn't do it like constantly every day. It was just like weekend type of thing. He didn't know I was hooking in the beginning. He found out like three weeks, four weeks after we were together. He didn't like it, but like I explained to him I was doing it so long I was used to it. I earned the most money. I would earn like four hundred dollars, five hundred dollars a week. He didn't try to stop me or nothing. He just wouldn't take the money from me, you know. We would argue about it and stuff. Argument would be mainly about why I had to go out there all the time and do that, you know. Don't I know I can get myself killed. Don't I know I can get myself hurt. And stuff like that.

I was doing drugs when I was living with Kane. I was like 'round twenty-four. Before that I was just drinking. I was a alcoholic. And when I ran into Kane I smokeded weed off and on, but not like a habit. But when I met Kane I started doing heroin. I snuck behind his back and tried it 'cause they used to call it apple back then. And I wanna know what apple was. I wanted to see what apple was about, you know. That's my biggest problem. Curious. Curious George. Then when I got into it, I found out. I ended up prostituting more to support my habit and take care of business at home.

I snort a line of it first. When I snort a line of it, it was alright. But I wanted the full effect though. As soon as that high went down I snorted it again. After that first day, I went to banging 'cause they said it was more better. I was at Nina house. This child named Nina. She's a sex change and she was a seller. She was a girlfriend and I wanted apple from her. She wouldn't sell it to me. I got somebody else to buy it off of her to give to me. So I went in the basement. She was upstairs on the second floor. I was in the basement in a room down there. 'Cause she had her house remodeled, you know, real nice. And I was in a room down there doing it.

They showed me how to hit. They just say you hold the little point where the hole at. Make sure you pump your vein. And got it together and just go ahead in. And that's what I did. The first time I did it by myself 'cause I was scared of somebody else with another needle coming toward me. I told them, "Oh no. Wait a minute. Wait a minute. No. No. You wait one second right now." Talking, "Come on, come on, child. You crazy." I say, "Uh-uh. I ain't crazy. Just show me how to do it." That what I did. Blood came in the syringe. They say, "Push it on in." I pushed it on in and I got the thing.

In the beginning I was like doing two bags a day. I did one in the evenings. Then graduate from two to three. I would mix two dime bags together in the morning and one in evening. And then it graduate to four. And that's what I do now, four bags a day.

The first time I banged it was a rush and then there was a nod, you know. It was a mellow rush. Little slow mellow rush. It ain't no memorable . . . I just know it felt good. When I got that first hit, then I graduated, you know. I started going back for more, you know what I mean? And then by me keep going back for more I was wasting money. So I just mixed two bags together. That's how it was. It took me 'bout a month . . . 'bout two or three months before I was using two bags. I've sort of stabilized at four bags, that's the max right there.

I've never stopped using. I can't. 'Cause I get sick. I have to go in the hospital. 'Cause I'm scared to get sick. I'm scared to stop. It's a feeling that a person do not wanna go through. It feel like they whole stomach getting ready to drop. I've been through withdrawal and it's like your stomach's flipping. Like it just turning, turning. And you getting ready to vomit. Uh. Then your chest be pounding real hard from throwing up so much. Ooh! Uh-uh! So I continue because it's a habit now. Drugs mellows me out and keep me on smooth ground. Sometime is boost my ego, make me do other things I know I ain't got no business doing. It helps me to cope with life.

I don't even know what time I get up in the morning. I probably be up by nine. So I get up and I eat breakfast first. Then after I eat breakfast I have my shot that I saved from the night before. I nod out until about noon, one o'clock and then I look at the stories until about four o'clock. You know, when I come out of the nod, like I been asleep. I hear everything when I'm nodding. Like if you be talking I can hear you. Then I clean my room up. And after I do that, I'll sit down, listen to some music or keep the TV on, you know. Like that. Then I get my other shot out. No, I do my other shot as "227" go off at seven o'clock. When "Mama's Family" getting ready to come on, I go on take me a hit, 'cause I can't stand that loud mouth old white woman. I can't. After that I lay my clothes out and get ready whatever I'm a wear out to go out at night. That night. I leave the house around eleven and I work till six o'clock in the morning. During that time I would turn three good tricks at fifty dollars each. I head up to Twentieth and Hubbard to cop me some dope, but I get my works from this diabetic.

I always get high by myself. It's better 'cause you get high with somebody on heroin, you nodding out. They go in your wallet. They gonna rob you. They gonna take your TV out. They gonna do all those type of things to you. You won't even know. I'm a heroin user and see I nods and I don't know who I can trust. I don't even let my companion get high with me. I don't know what he might do or what he might take outta there. As for shooting galleries, I've been in shooting galleries, but I don't like shooting up in it. 'Cause you shoot up in a gallery, you get to nodding out there too. They take your money and stuff and rob you. I just go in the shooting gallery just to see, you know, like see who hanging out. See who 'round.

When I'm on the streets there aren't people I would never go home with. I just look over them. I'm strictly out there for business. You could look like anything. I'm just going with them for the money. It's not difficult to do, 'cause I'm used to it. Yeah, I know it hard sometimes. Long as that money look good I don't care. Long as that money look good, you know.

The most difficult thing is when they're crazy. You know how some people just got that look. They look crazy. You know how some white folks look, right? Some of them just look crazy, you know. Like that. But I've never been put in a dangerous situation. I thank God for that too. All the years I been out there doing that, I thank God that I haven't been through none of that. I really do. I really do thank God.

Now, the most unusual thing someone has asked me is to piss on him. That was a unusual thing. He paid me a hundred and fifty dollars. That's what they wanted to do. They were jerking off while I was peeing on them. We were in a hotel. People have asked me to beat them. They have asked me to shit on them. I got two hundred dollars for that. So I was squatting over them, and shit right on they chest. And they rub it down and jerking off. Yeah, rubbing the shit on they chest, all way down to they dick and start jerking they dick off. I'm telling you. Child! Child! I was so happy to get away from that motherfucker I ain't know what to do. Oh, people have asked to eat me out, rim me, suck my dick, you know. Stuff like, yeah, like that.

When I'm out there in drag, straight people ignore me. But see, that's the man I'll go out for is straights. These guys I be going out with they don't be knowing. See they don't be knowing. And then, you know what the funniest thing is? With some of them, they be like this, while I be putting the condom on they be like, "You sure ain't nothing wrong with you?" And I be like, "No." They go, "Never mind." No. Half of them don't, right. They be . . . I be like, "Well, come on." They be like, "You sure ain't nothing wrong with you?" They like, "Well, never mind, 'cause I think something wrong with you." I be like, "Huh-huh." Ain't that stupid though?

There are some who want more than a blow job. I tell them my period is on. If they say they don't care I sit on them. They don't know. They be so fast trying to stick it in any hole they can. I do it in the car, in the front seat. So they think they're going into a pussy, and they never know. I take my penis, and I hold it in front of my hand, with my hand. They may ask me why I got my hand down there and I'll just say that I wanna touch. I let them touch. They take they hand, they be feeling . . . they be feeling they dick on the side of my anus. They never feel my penis or anything because I got them in my hand. Only a pro know how to do something like that. Only a pro. I learned through experience. As you go on prostituting you learn different things. Different techniques.

No one said this is the way you do it. When they wanted to fuck I say, "What I gotta do?" I sit on it. And then I see what's up. When I sat on it, right, and I was riding and everything. Then they came like that. And then I took the rubber off and threw it away and had my money, seventy-five dollars. I thought, "That was cute. Let me try that again."

I've been arrested 'bout ten times for prostitution. One time I was in inside the car and the . . . and it was a undercover cop. And he locked me up. I met him at High and Radner. I got in the car and he asked me what was the price and I told him thirty dollars for a blow. He said, "Sure. Get in." And I gets in and I drives up Radner Avenue, up there where that factory be at? Where they put the cleaning stuff at? Right up that little street. And he told me you busted. You under arrest for prostitution. Put the handcuffs on me. And I was outdone. He ain't look like no cop. Young boy. He locked me up.

Now, I ask them if they're a cop. I go, "Are you a cop?" Some of them say, "Yeah. I'm a cop." Some of them say, "No." And the ones that say no real fast I just don't get in. I say, "Go on 'head. That's alright." I also touch them. I'm feeling in their penis. I reach my hand down and grab they penis. See if they cop or not. If they're a cop they be like, "Oh don't do that. Don't do that." I was like, "Uh-huh." Most men would sort of open, lay back and say, "Go 'head," you know.

Other times when I got arrested I was standing on the corner and they just drive up. Up and away. Everybody gets in. Yeah, locked me up for a couple hours, then let you go in the morning. Obstructing the highway ain't nothing. What, you do ten days in jail. They give you a fine. That's it. The fine is hundred and fifty dollars. It's been like four years ago that I was arrested.

Being in jail in drag is good to me 'cause I lookeded like a girl and they loved it. And I loveded them boys I seen. They treated me like a queen. You know, they just be talking. "What's your name?" And I tell them my name and "What you locked up for?" And I tell them what I'm locked up for and . . . that's it. And when they ask me do I want a husband I say, "Sure." They be, "You gonna act right?" I say, "Uh-huh. As long as you act right." And then they start coming down with these bag of goodies.

Longest time I spent in jail was a month. That was when the little white boy picked me up and got me arrested and busted me for prostitution. I got a month in jail and hundred fifty dollars fine. I was in Falk Corrections Center. And I had a husband know as Q.T. Gorgeous daddy. He was black, gorgeous, redbone, short, wavy hair, and all that. Sexy. I hated to leave him but I told him I like my freedom. Oh, honey, yeah. He was there for murder. They didn't have no room over Mount Alban so they just left him there. And I was like, "Uh-uh. I see you when I see you. I'm outta here."

Working on the street don't bother me. I'm not disturbed. No. I don't like doing it. I don't like being out there prostituting. But I just have a habit and that's the only way I can keep my habit up at this moment time till I can get me a regular job. I really don't like going out there and meeting strange mens, hop in a car and I don't even know them. Not knowing whether or not they might take me off and just kill me, you know. I do the prostitution to support my habit. I can't earn money in any other way 'cause I won't be able to be trusted. I mean, I can't even work. I mean, getting up in the morning like that? I couldn't keep no steady job.

I hope there's a time when I'll stop. I hope the Lord is just, you know

. . . nothing don't happen and things work out. Life ain't no joke, you know. It's hard. You gotta take the punches, you know. Sometime you even gotta kiss behind. Just don't make the mistake that I made. Of just getting out there so fast at a young age. It's me being hard-headed. Me not listening. I can't blame nobody but myself. Me being hard-headed, not listening, thinking I'm knowing it all, you know. My mother was trying to control the basic thing as far as me not going that way. And, you know, she was worried, you know, and I couldn't just let her keep worry and worry. It might mess around and give her a heart attack or something, you know. So I just went on my own, you know what I'm saying.

I ain't never sit down and thought about the future. I take it one day at a time. I can't deal with the future right now. I'm working on the street and I'm a drug user and I'm a prostitute and that's the life I chose. The fast life. I couldn't just . . . I couldn't . . . I couldn't just hop up outta the street life and go to school. I couldn't say, "Well, hell, you know, I'm gonna be a doctor" or "I'm gonna be a lawyer" or "I'm gonna be this or that." See I . . . it never crossed my mind. I wanted to be a prostitute. And that's what I am. I don't feel the curiosity and excitement I felt when I was fifteen. Now, it's a job. It's a job.

*"I cry today and take all them tears
and them thoughts and put them
in my back pocket and save
them for another rainy
day until the next time
I may cry again."*

Monique

I was born in a outhouse September twenty-third. I remember 'cause my mother told me this since I been older. She said that she knew she had to go to the bathroom, and when she went to strain to go the bathroom, I came out. My mother said I was underwater and that I would live a long time. She looked down, and she saw my navel cord attached to her and I was underwater. She took me out the water with the navel cord and she said she didn't lose any strength or anything. And she took me back inside and my grandmother clipped it and tied it up and pushed it in. She went to the doctor's to get the afterbirth tooken out. She said the afterbirth was the only hectic part. I wasn't a hard birth, and she said I was nine pounds, eight ounces when I was born.

I was her easiest birth. There was nine of us, but five of us died. It was . . . the five that died was Mark, Vincent, Walter, and two she didn't name. One died in her arms, the other ones died at birth, and one at sixteen months. They were all babies when they died. My mom was telling me that God didn't want her to have all these children knowing that it was so hard for her as it was with us. It's four of us now. She has one daughter and three sons or you can say one and a half daughters, two and a half sons.

I was really close to my little brother Mark when he died. He was sixteen months and I was about five. You know he suffocated himself. . . . He just suffocated. He was crippled, and the doctors said that he would never walk. And when he had died, I was a very young age at the time, I told my mother if they ever had anything for people that couldn't walk, I would join. The March of Dimes Walkathon came out and I walked it every year. I have a blood clot in my leg now, today, because I walk every year. My doctor tells me that I shouldn't, but I do anyway.

Me and my brothers are tight. My sister, that's the other half of me. She's my other half. Whatever she says goes, whatever I say goes. She works in a old folks home. My brother, he works in a auto mechanic shop. My little brother, he's trying to get his bachelor's degree somewhere out of town. I haven't seen my brother now for about a year. He got a four-year scholarship and he's using it, every bit of it. And I'm proud of him. They see me, I don't care if I got on a miniskirt and high heels, and my hair is what, snatch with a pony tail, they're gonna run with me and come find me. "That's my sister!" That what they say. They don't reveal me. They be like, "There go my sister right there, the sexy one 'cross the street." "I'll be back, wait for me."

Oh, they knew I was gay automatically. I mean, we was brothers and sisters. They knew everything about me. I say, "Child, I'm gonna go make me some money. Just go sit on the step. Don't lock me out!" And I'll say, "I'll be back, don't go to sleep." They say, "I'll put the key inside the mailbox." They used to sit on the step. I used to come back one o'clock in the morning. Give one them ten dollars. "Hey, go buy something to eat. Hurry up. Hurry up."

It was a party growing up with my brothers and sisters. It was fun. We were scared together, we were happy together, we cried together, and we laughed together. Oh, there was competition between me and my sister. She buys a new dress, I buy one, too. I'll buy new shoes, she buys some, too. I get my hair done, she get mad and get hers cut.

When I was growing up, I was closest to my mother and my sister. I'm close to my mother because she showed me the right direction. She was the one that told me what was right and what was wrong. What should I do and what shouldn't I do. I was close to my sister because she always say, "Don't worry about what Daddy say about you." When I got older, I would say, "Why did Daddy used to call me a faggot?" It used to always bug me. I started seeing a psychiatrist because of what he said to me, and my sister used to always say, "Don't worry about what Daddy said about you. You'll be okay."

My father would say it to my mother. He would turn around and say, "That boy's gonna be a faggot." He used to always say it and used to point at me. So I knew he was talking about me. So I mean, I mean, that's logic right there. He's pointing and apparently he was talking about me. "That boy's gonna be a faggot." The first time I heard him say that I think I was about six and I used to ask my mother, "Why did he ever say that to me?" It was a big strain on me because I used to go to school and people used to say "faggot" and . . . I didn't understand what it meant. I thought it was a nice word, that I was a nice person, and all the time was telling me in a sense that I was gay. Since I hear my father say it, I thought it was a nice word, so I used to hear that and say "thank you" to people.

Both my parents were in the household until I was twelve. My father was the kind of man that used to beat on my mother a lot and her children got together at very young ages and we found a way to make my father leave by attacking him. We used to take high-heeled shoes, while he was asleep, and hit him in his head and stuff like that for beating on my mother. Till the day he cut her. The day he cut her he ran. He never came back. I was twelve years old. But it wasn't like it was the last time we got to see him though. We would get to see him quite often 'cause he would want to come over and threaten her and what have you.

My mother is forty-five and was born in Randolph, South Carolina. My father is forty-eight and he was born in Virginia. I couldn't tell you where my father is now. I don't know where he is today. But I know he works across the street from a horse stable.

My father worked back then. I think he was a construction worker, but I'm not sure. He would steal everything from us. My mother would buy us Christmas toys and he would steal them to sell them so he could have money in his pocket to go drink. He was an alcoholic. His main goal, get drunk, hurt my mother. My father was drunk practically every day. High ain't the word, he was drunk every day. Loaded ain't the word. He'd get, pardon the expression, pissy drunk. He was an embarrassment. I used to let them know my father drink. I ain't never used to hide it. Other kids didn't come to our house. No! Oh, no! When he left, the kids used to come. Now, I feel that if someone drinks I don't want no bother. I tell them that quick, "If you drink, honey, leave me alone. You can go on 'bout your business, honey, 'cause I ain't having no wino try to attack me and I'm grown."

She bought us these big planes that the children could sit on. She said she was trying to make me this boy that I didn't want to be. So she would buy toys because she knew that would amaze the eye, that would amaze the child's eye. She bought me a airplane. It was maybe 'bout this big with big wings that I could sit on and pretend I was flying and be a airplane pilot. She said my father stole all these things from us. We got to see them, and that was as much as we did, is got to see them.

With my father being there, it was hell. It was hell. He threw a fan at my mother, he used to tie us up and beat us, and he used to make us sit in the closet all night long. It was complete hell. The day he lefted, that's the first day of being free. My mother used to say that, too. She used to always say it when we were young, that she was free. And it wasn't free of a marriage, it wasn't free 'cause she wanted another man. She was free 'cause we didn't have to worry 'bout her being hurt anymore. He used to tell her what she may cooked for dinner today, he didn't want that, and he would beat her up because he didn't want that for dinner. It was hell. It was like she had to actually sit there and concentrate while he's at work, what would he eat today or what kinda TV show we should watch that night. 'Cause if we watch "Sesame Street" in the daytime, he would slap her 'cause he didn't want us to watch "Sesame Street." And stuff like that. And it was like hell. It was all hell. There was nothing fun about being with my father.

If we stayed with my mother, he would hurt her. Let me get away from Mommy today because if Daddy walks in and see me hugging Mommy he gonna beat her up. Let me look at Mommy one time before Daddy gets here 'cause if he see me looking at Mommy with a smile he's gonna beat me up. Things like that. So it's like, who I got? I have no one.

I can't be with my mother 'cause I know she loves me and my father's gonna beat her up for her loving me, and that's how I felt. I had no friends to go talk to.

I was not allowed to tell my teacher no house problems. My mother was the one who used to say, "Tell the teacher." My father say, "If he tells I'm gonna beat you up," and I would never tell. 'Cause I knew what he was gonna do to my mother. So therefore I left well enough alone. I never told no one till I got old enough knowing he would not hurt my mother no longer.

I was very alone. I was a very sensitive kid. I'm very sensitive today, so I can imagine how sensitive I was when I was young. Today, if the man on the stage stumbles while he's performing, I know he's embarrassed. I feel his embarrassment. I'm not gonna laugh. I'm not gonna cry, but I'm gonna hold my head down as if I didn't see it happen, 'cause I know he's embarrassed. While everybody else laugh I hold my head down.

When my mother used to get beat up all the time, I used to cry as if this man was beating me up too. So I know I was very sensitive when I was young. We just sit there and just look. We were never allowed to say anything bad about what goes on in the house. We just go upstairs in our room and he used to tell us not to make no noise. We used to go up in the room and had the TV down low where you can barely hear it, but we sit there and watch the television, looking at pictures as if it was silent movies.

My parents never talked about sex. I realized that I was gay when I was in the sixth grade. I was in a school at Tenth and Draper, and a guy named Timothy Goods, he said that he's gonna show me what I am today and it wouldn't hurt me. He had sex with me in the bathroom of the school. It hurted. It bled. When we were done and we went back to our little classes and what have you, I felt as though that's what I wanted. I realized then 'cause I knew what "faggot" meant then. I realized that is exactly what I needed, right? It was my first time having anal sex. He was in junior high school. He was in the seventh grade and I was in . . . I was ready to graduate from the sixth grade to the seventh grade so he was, you could say he was about thirteen. I was twelve. I never seen him no more after that first time. I used to think about what he did. I thought, I thought that he was trying to show me something my mother couldn't show me. My mother can't have sex with me. He show me something my mother couldn't show me. He showed me and then I understood what was going on in life. I'm gay, I know from that. Since then, honey, I don't wanna get no sex in no bathrooms. Now, they stink. I can't take smelling nobody's pee. Oh, I go in the bathroom sometimes, I be dressed like a woman, I be like this, "I came in to take a pee, honey. Go back shopping."

I think they called me faggot when I went off to school because I had long hair, I didn't walk like a boy, I didn't want to play tag with the boys, I wanted to jump rope with the girls. I didn't want to sit up there and play with the blocks with the guys. I'd go over there and play with the dollhouse and the dolls with the girls. And they'd say "faggot." Boys used to throw paint on me, and they say that I was a fruitcake and stuff like that. They say I'll be glad when Christmas comes 'cause a fruitcake belongs during the Christmas holidays. I finally realizeded what I was. I was gay. And as time went on I said, there's nothing I can do about it. I tried everything in my means to try to see if I could come out. I tried to have a child, it didn't work. I wanted to be in love with a girl. It didn't work. I began to do boy things. I joined the Boy Scouts, it didn't work, 'cause then I was scared to be in the grass in the evening time with all the other boys. I used to cry and want to go home. They told me I wasn't equipped for it. Halloween they gave a Halloween party and they said that I won the first prize because I lookeded like a little girl.

It's painful sometimes being gay. From time to time, yes. Some things are meant to be seen and not heard. Some things are meant to be heard and not said. I hear things and I don't say nothing. See, it takes two to tangle. One cannot go into one, 'cause if one go into one, it's gonna make two. There's your tangle. And I'm not about to make a knot. At one time I was that kind of person to make a knot, to fight, and give back words. But today I'm like this: "Talk. Your words go right past me. It's not what you do, it how you do it that brings respect. It's not who you are, it's what you are. I am a person."

I think my father is responsible for me being gay. The first word he said to me is, "That boy's gonna be a faggot." I'll never forget it. I was watching "Gulliver" on TV, that cartoon "Gulliver" that used to swim with the giants and all this. So yeah, I think it's because he was so brutal. Yes, yes, I do, one hundred percent I do. He was very brutal to me. My father used to hit me saying, "I'm gonna break you outta this" and punch me in my face. I was a little kid. He scarred my face on the side here and he scarred my face on the side here, and my mother had to stop him. She said that's why he used to beat her up a lot because when he used to try to hurt me, she would get in the way for him not to hurt me.

But you see, if he would took me fishing or to baseball games. . . . I depended on my mother for everything. My mother used to buy our toys, my mother used to take us out to the movies. I never ever say my father took me anywhere. Before I went into school, I remember my dad put me inside a caboose, and the caboose was full of rats. And a rat bit me on my leg over here and he wouldn't let go and a Puerto Rican man shot him off. When my father left me there it was nighttime, but when I got out of the thing, it was the daytime. The Puerto Rican people got me out of there. When my father came to the hospital to get me, he told me that he would beat me if I say anything, so I didn't never say anything.

He put me in there in the caboose. He put me in the caboose, said, "When you come outta there you'll be a strong man." I don't think he knew that it was rats in there. When I laid down on the ground of the caboose, I fell asleep, and when I woke up there was a big rat laying next to my leg. When I went to get up, he jumped on me and just held onto my leg with his teeth inside my leg. As I was screaming, the caboose door opens. It was a Puerto Rican man, and I jumped out. I fell, and the rat still hunged on. I heard the Puerto Rican man trying to tell me to keep still and they grabbed me like this, from both sides like this, so the rat won't be able to bite one of them as well, and the Puerto Rican man shot him off my leg. And that was the last time that I ever trusted my father, 'cause I knew that he tried to hurt me.

Then we gave him a chance by letting me move in with him when I was seventeen. He tried to kill me. Gave me a overdose of sleeping pills while my aunt held me. She was his sister. She held me down while he did it. My best friend had pulled me, told me to come on. I kept saying, "My daddy gave me a lotta pills and I don't know what to do. I feel real, real sleepy." And I had the box that the pills came in in my pocket 'cause he sent me to the store to get them. And the girl looked at them and she said, "Do you know what these are? These are sleeping pills." She ran me to a phone booth and called the police and said, "He's going to sleep right here in the phone booth." They told her to keep me awake, and she kept me awake. All I had remembered is that the ambulance had came and then the next thing they were pumping me and I was throwing up all these pills and what have you. So I left that day. I stayed with my mom.

When I became twenty I was like this, "Daddy, if you lay your hands on me again I'll take you off this earth." And he did, he slapped me and told me that he's my father. I slapped him back and told him get his hands off of me. And he says, "Oh, your mother taught you how to hit me back." He grabbed me and he threw me against the wall where he works at today, and his friends was there—"Don't do that to your son"—and as he was throwing me against the wall I was saying, "Don't tell him nothing," and I leaped on him and that was that. I left him in the little street. I never bothered with him any more. Only time I see him now is when he's on the other side of the street when I'm walking past.

You know, I feel animosity but I have no anger. I just have animosity to my father. When I see him I just say, "Hi." I don't give him nothing. . . . I mean I may stop and I may say, "How you doing? How's your new family? I'll talk to you later." I have no more to say to him. Oh, he has a new family! And that woman's scared to death of him from what my mother says. Remarried and has kids and everything. I never met my half-brothers and sisters. Never want to. My family is here with me. My other family is up in heaven. I don't need no more brothers and sisters.

I think I was twelve when I went to see the psychiatrist. And his name was Dr. Lopez and he kept saying I held my feelings. I used to let people say things to me that hurt me, and I would never say anything. I would hold back on everything I say. If somebody would say something bad to me I wouldn't make a comment, I would just cry, you know, instead of just saying something back. My doctor said that it was best that I just say something back 'cause things would come out better for me.

From the time I was six to the time I was twelve, my life was hell. It was complete hell. Because there I was still seeing the psychiatrist and he never explained to me what was gonna come behind all of this. I guess he didn't know how people would start criticizing and nobody wanted to be around you and you lose a lot of friends and people will want to hurt you. I didn't know. I didn't expect any of that. And when I started getting things like that to happen to me, it would hurt me and I was back in the same predicament but it wasn't my father no more. It was my friends, my peers, and people that just walk by that stared, that would actually stare at you and say, "That's a faggot. Get away from him." And things of that nature. Then I used to say that I'm not worth nothing and it was no use for me to live. I used to say things of that nature, and my psychiatrist kept saying that he should have known that this would have happened and he shoulda had me prepared. He put me in a group therapy with gay people. . . .

I was thirteen when he put me into group therapy with other children that was gay, and they went through the same thing, but they were older. They were like sixteen, fifteen years old, and they went through the same exact thing. They said that they knew how to overcome it, overlook things, 'cause see people will only talk.

My mother got me to see the psychiatrist because I used to cry when people used to call me faggot in school and stuff when I was in the sixth grade. I was confused. I had a horse, a horse I called Pegasus from "Hercules," with the real big wings, and it was a white horse and it had real big glass wings. I would go home and I would cry to the horse, till one day my mother walked in and she didn't say anything. She was at the door, and I didn't see her and I was crying to my horse and it was as if this horse was answering me. It would try to solve my problems for me. Till I came home one day and the horse was shattered. My mother shattered the horse. She said that the horse was killing me. Believe it or not, today I agree with her. It was killing me because my horse was my only hope. I would come home from school and look for this horse. I'd come home and say, "I got homework, Pegasus. Sit here and watch me do my homework." Or "I'm gonna play with my toys, Pegasus. Sit here and play with the toys, I'll let you play with me, you'll be the horse. And these are the cowboys." I used to just be in another world. That was my own little world. I didn't want to go outside and play with the children, and I would just sit in my room all day. I would do my homework, and

I would study for my tests and what have you, but all in all the horse was my friend. When I was there seeing the psychiatrist, all I cried about was the horse. She killed the horse. He said at one time he thought I was talking about a real horse. But all the time I was talking about a toy, and he said that it was best that she did do that. When he said that, I stopped seeing him because I didn't agree with him at all. 'Cause I was young. As time went on I grew to realize that I noticed that my life was based on wanting a horse that wasn't real and I had no friends.

The horse was a Christmas gift. I got the horse when I was nine, and I kept the horse until I was fourteen, that's when my mother destroyed it, when I was fourteen. I had Hercules and the horse Pegasus. My little sister played with the Hercules and broke him up. I still had the horse and when she broke the Hercules, I said, "You can never play with my horse." My horse became a lot to me. I cut a hole in the top of him, stick my money inside of him, and my little secrets I didn't wanna tell I stick inside of him. Before I go to bed I make him stand on the floor while I'm on my knees saying my prayers, and I'll wake up in the morning and give it a hug. It was like another world.

When I went to school, I used to put it in my book bag. I would take a test and put my horse on the top of the books until my teacher took the horse one day. She checked the horse all around to make sure the horse didn't have the answers on the horse and what have you. She started complaining to my mother that I would always carry this horse to school. She began asking me about why do I carry the horse to school, and I never could answer that. Today I still couldn't answer. I don't know.

We used to liveded on South Lorraine Street, at Ninth and Crosby, and we liveded at Fifteenth and Winter, all in South Jefferson. All of them was fun. All of them was raunchy little raggedy little children that ran up and down the street, and we was raunchy little raggedy children that ran with them. When I was young, their mothers and my mother used to walk down the street with signs talking 'bout get the gang wars out the neighborhood and all that. Those are the kind of neighborhood I used to live in.

It was important to the neighbors that the children were secure 'cause there used to be a lotta kids, they had a lotta kids in the neighborhood. There wasn't a lot of crime in the neighborhood. There were just a lotta gang wars. The majority of the time it was on the weekend. The majority of the time the children didn't come out on the weekend. My mother, everybody's mothers and fathers and grandmothers would sit on the step and hold the children on the step and say, "Don't go off that step." You couldn't hang in this corner store, and when you go to the store you must let your family know you're going to the store, and have somebody with you when you go. There wasn't a lot of drugs either. I ain't even knew what drugs looked like when I was little. I used to see people walk by drunk and I used to say, "Oh, he looks like my daddy. Why he do it?" 'Cause he walking and stumbling. So they say he'd be drunk. I knew that, but never knew 'bout no drugs.

In my neighborhood, people wanted to make sure that no other child have nothing better than theirs. Johnny might have a scooter and your child don't have one. Johnny may be stubborn with his scooter. Don't let your child play with it. So you buy your child a scooter. Everyone valued their children. They valued their work, and they always kept clean little houses.

People never . . . people never really disciplined us when we were young. They would always come to my mother and tell her if we did something wrong. If someone called her and told her something, she'd ask me. She say, "The lady down the street called me and said you was doing it. Is that true?" And we were not allowed to lie to our parents, so it was either yes or no. If it was fatal, then I'd get a beating. But if it was something, if it wasn't fatal, she would say something like, "Don't do that again."

Sometimes when I did something wrong, she made me go into my room and stay there. You do not get no dessert. She knew I hated grits so she used to make me eat grits. . . . It was a way of disciplining us. The worst thing someone could do to punish me was make me eat grits. I hate grits, I hate it! Even today you couldn't get me to get a breakfast special with grits. I hate them. She'd say, "Eat it," and it would take me hours to eat grits. That's my worstest abuse. You could take the TV, you could put me in my room, please don't make me eat no grits.

Mama never really beated us when we were young. She was the kind of woman that disciplined you by taking things away from you, giving you things you don't like. You don't like grits, eat grits for breakfast. That's your beating. So I was never beaten by my mother. No. I've been popped for me saying things I shouldn't say to people. I called my brother a black dog and she popped me. That was just about it.

My father slapped me around a lot. He beat me twice. One time he beat me for asking him not to hit my mother no more. The second time he beat me because I peed the bed. It was just that night I snuck in the bathroom and drunk water outta my mind and then went to bed and forgot to go to the bathroom before I went to bed.

My mother was the mother and the father of our home. She's divorced now, and she has a friend that's taking care of her and she's taking care of him. My mother's happy now. I was twelve when she divorced my father. She was having her last child. My oldest brother was the one that went up to the hospital and gave her the papers. My mother was in so much pain, but she found enough strength to sign them divorce papers. She said when she was laying there, and we were all there, and she said, "I'm free." As we got older, we asked her why, and she said she was free of being in bondage. What would he eat today? Should we watch this show today? Should I sit the kids in this chair, 'cause he won't come and sit in that chair today?

So she loved him. She loved him, and she just couldn't leave him. She had to find a reason. When she started seeing him start to hurt her children I believe that's why she left him. She had to get rid of him before he destroyed us. That's how much she loved him. Now today, she is still scared to even go visit him. I told her where he worked at. She said, "Long as I know he working there, I'll never drive down that street."

This man would make money, but she said there wasn't a time that he didn't come home broke. So it was like my mother used to get everything. She would scuffle and buffle. She actually laid with other men to try to get us the things that we needed. My mother would do out of the way things to make sure we eat every night. If there's no more food in the house, she would go and lay with a man that would buy us something to eat so we would eat that next day.

She explained all this to us when we got older. Like we never understood these other men. I used to cry when she's in the bedroom with other men, and have sex with her. Me and my brothers and sister, we all cried, because we thought that he was gonna hurt my mother and we couldn't get in and she would lock the door. But all the time she was doing things to help us. She said that she would hear us out there crying, and she would be in there having sex crying at the same time. She said she knew she was doing something wrong but she knew she was doing something right, too. She knew that that man was gonna give us . . . give her some money to feed us. They were still married, but my father was probably at work or running the streets or something. He would never come home till like three, four o'clock in the morning, unless he was hungry when he got off of work.

He used to beat her to death. He used to actually have her crying. The next time we see her she would be in Epsom salt, in the water in the tub with Epsom salt to warm her body. And one time he hurted her he took me and he tied me to the bed and he beat my back with the ironing cord, and I have the marks today on my back. I will never forgive him for it. He put about one hundred, or something like that, marks, whips all over my back. When he did that to my back, my mother, I don't know what she did, but she made my back heal. She said, "Children heal very quick 'cause they young." But I don't care, my mother healed my back. It wasn't me, my mother healed it. Yes, my mother was a comforter.

He beat me as if I was a wild beast, and I never forgived him. I will never, ever, ever in my life forgive him. He would beat me because I asked him to stop hitting my mother. I asked him, I said, "Please stop hitting Mommy." "You got something to do with this?" and he grabbed me and he took me in the room by my hair and he tied me to the bed while my other brothers and sisters watched. He said, "Y'all stand there 'cause y'all better not ever do what he just did." He beat me and they stood there and they cried because they knew that he was hurting me. My mother would cry because she couldn't stop him. Then my uncle came in the picture and said that he would never hurt us again . . . and that's when she was divorced.

There were a lot of arguments. They were dumb arguments. "Why come am I eating beans today when I want cabbage?" That was one of the fights. One of her main fights was dinner. She baked me a birthday cake, and he smashed it in her face 'cause he said that he didn't want me to have a birthday cake. Another fight was about . . . she bought all of us shoes because it was getting cold and we couldn't wear sandals during the winter, and he said he wasn't ready to buy shoes. He beat her up for that. He would beat her up for silly things, things that didn't really mean anything. He would be drunk every time. Oh, yes. Every time. There wasn't a time he wasn't drunk. Today, I see him on his job, and he says, "There go my son." "Don't call me your son. Not the way you brutalized my family. Don't call me your son. Because that if you was my father you woulda showed what kinda father you were. But you showed that you didn't have a family, you had slaves."

The worst fight was when he threw the plate at her. We got to actually see a plate go glide across the air with pork n' beans in it while the beans was splattering on us, burning us. The plate fell on the table and cracked, and the piece popped up in her arm. That was the worstest thing we got . . . I got to see with my own eyes. But the worstest thing I know of is her swollen eye when she walked in my grandmother's house. We all cried. "Why'd Daddy do that to you? We hate him." And she always say, "Never say you hate nobody."

My mother drank, but my mother was a very light . . . she was the kind of woman that would drink and come home and tell us bedtime stories or. . . . Her drinking made her think of her children. This is what I see. She would come home and she'd say, "Y'all all sit around" 'cause a special show come on. . . . She would have cocktails and maybe a show may come on seven o'clock, a special. She would make sure she's home for us, to sit there on the floor with us and eat popcorn and look at the show. My father kicked the TV in because we were watching . . . the first "Gilligan's Island." He said that we didn't deserve to watch television and told her she didn't deserve it either. He didn't beat her up that night but she just sat on the floor and hugged us, had us all around her and was just hugging us to make sure he didn't kick none of us when he kicked the TV. 'Cause, see, in her heart she thought he was gonna stomp all of us because we were watching TV. We were all on the floor. She got us all and we all went in a little corner and she had us all around like this, just bundled up. She had my little sister and little brother behind her, and me and my oldest brother, she had us on the side of her . . . and she kept saying, "Patrick," which is my father's name, "Patrick, please don't hurt my children. Beat me up. Please don't hurt my children."

We all thought we were responsible for these fights. She sent us all to my grandmother's to live with her. And all the time she was having us live there, we thought it was because of us. But all the time she didn't want us to see her get beat up anymore. She'd come to my grandmother's house with swollen eyes and a broken jaw. One of her eyes she couldn't open, and she had a broken arm. I'd say the biggest bruise to me, when I was young, was when he destroyed her face and tried to take her eye out. When she came with a broken arm and my uncle looked at her one day and said he's fed up. He came and threw my father out the window. He came and my father didn't know he was staying with her. He kept saying, "Gail, I'm coming in to get you and the kids." We were scared, and she told us to all get under the bed. She ran and hid in the closet. My uncle was there, but she didn't think he was gonna do anything. He was cussing, he was using foul language at my father, saying, "He's not gonna do a damn thing to you guys. I'm not gonna see him hurt you" and all that. And my father came in the door, "Who's that? Your man?" He said, "No. I'm her brother and you hurt them like that . . ." and he pulled me from under the bed, said, "Look at my nephew's back, look at my sister's arm" and he . . . just seeing these things was making him madder and madder and madder and madder, till he said that "you will never hurt them again" and threw him out the window. We had a big bay window on the first floor, and he threw him out through of it. He fell on the ground and ran. We moved out of the house. Well, my mother moved out because of the fact she was afraid that he would come back to that house 'cause my uncle wasn't staying with us forever. He was only staying with us until my mother got her divorce and she was sure that my father would never come back.

My Uncle Monroe was my mother's protection. He's in jail now. He's been there since he was seventeen. He's thirty something now. They accused him of murder only he didn't do it. Think I was eleven when he was arrested. Anyway, the next time I see my father I was nineteen and he was hollering, "That's my son." "You're not my father. Don't tell nobody you're my father."

She was hospitalized for her arm, because he broke it in three places.

Her heart started getting bad and they said that my mother was gonna have a heart attack. So they kept her in a heart hospital. They told my mother to put us somewhere in a home or something, and she quickly took us all to my grandmother's and we stayed there while she was in the hospital. When we moved to my grandmother's, we laughed, we hugged, and everything. It was as if it was a dream come true. The only thing we were left out, the last link on the chain, my mother. She was the only one that wasn't there.

So my grandmother help my mother. My grandmother was just like my mother, my grandmother is the other half of my mother. Whatever my mother needed she was there. Whether it was from conversation to a pair of socks, my grandmother was there. Well, my grandfather was very supportive, too. Him and my grandmother used to give my mother everything she wanted. So whenever things got too hot at home, my grandmother was there to help to cool things off, her and my grandfather. She hated my father. But she's a religious woman, and she don't . . . she don't look at bad thing no more. She's the kinda woman that look at things and say, "Let bygones be bygones."

There was never any display of affection between them. He never showed her no kind of affection. Never. He may have showed her affection before we were born but he never showed us affection after we were born. I never got to see it. When he was there in the house, we were scared to sleep. My mother said that we were her only children that tossed and turned more than she did. Yes, he brutalized us. As long as we didn't have my mother's brothers there, he would brutalize us like dogs.

We jumped into these fights. Yes, we all did. When he was trying to hit her with the fan while it was on, my oldest brother jumped in the way of the fan. As it was coming down, it got unplugged and it hit him in the back. Thank God it was off, 'cause he woulda been dead. When it hit him in the back, it only scraped his back and that was it. But if it had been on, it woulda did a lotta damage.

He would be like, "What are you teaching the children? How to talk back to their father?" and stuff like that . . . and she would say, "No, they just tired of you hurting me," that's all she would say. Oh, my mother fought back every time, but we all knew just like she knew that with a man she has no winning. She never called the cops though 'cause she didn't wanna . . . she didn't want him in jail.

I left home to be on my own between thirteen and fourteen. Well, I was put in a home, 'cause I used to let so much bother me. I just didn't care about myself anymore, and she figured that if I went in a home they would help me. She wanted them to help me, that was it. So she put me there because I was a troubled child. Anything and everything hurted me. She figured that as I got older I might become suicidal, that's what she explained to me when I got older. But the home, I have to admit myself, it helped me a whole lot. It was the JJF, Juvenile Justice Facility, at Forty-eighth and Curry. I stayed there until I graduated out of high school. I was there till I was seventeen.

There were kids who were runaways and children their mothers put there. I was just someone there. My mother said she couldn't take it, 'cause she thought I was gonna kill myself and stuff, that's the only reason they took me. And it was true. I felt . . . I thought I was gonna kill myself. And it helped me. Being in the Juvenile Justice Facility I got to mingle with people. I got to be with people I didn't know. I got to eat with people I didn't know. I got to go on little trips with people I didn't know. I got to laugh, and I got to know people.

I was in a room with two other boys, and these two boys were the kind of boys that won at spelling bees, and they was encouragement. Boys, boys that would sit around and say, "I got homework, guys," and "Can you tell me what this mean right here?" They accepted me one hundred percent. They were like, it's not what you are, it's who you are. It's not what I do, it's how I do it. It's like . . . those words right there was the exact thing they say to me.

When I went to Juvenile Justice Facility, I didn't want to be bothered then. But about two months went by, I got to meet people and they would say, "Talk to the people. You don't have to sit there and eat and then say excuse me from the table. Sit and talk." They took us to a amusement park and the ice was broken. There it was. We laughed and giggled on the roller coaster, on the merry-go-round, and on our way back I was talking with everybody. The counselors was like, "Wow! We broke the ice." When I went to the graduation, they say did I have a speech. I said that I used to be one locked-in child, and I owed it all to my mother and to the Juvenile Justice Facility 'cause they broke the ice.

My mother used to come every Sunday morning 'cause she'd come get me every Sunday for church. So they were so immune to her coming and getting me for church that they would have me dressed for church every Sunday. She came to visit every weekend. There wasn't no weekend my mother was not there giving me a new toy, or giving . . . even if she didn't bring nothing she gave me a kiss and that's all I needed. My mommy was there to see me. That's all I needed.

My sister and brothers used to come with her every time she came. I used to run up and down the steps, that's the only time she see me mingle. The lady used to tell her that "the only ones he associate with is the children that you bring. Are they his brothers and sisters?" She said, "Yes." She said, "We have to make sure your son comes out of that. Do your other children play with kids?" She said, "Yes. That was my only child that refuse to play with anybody." And she said, "That's fine. We will do something about this." And that's what she did. They broke the ice. They did something about it. I am free. It's like she said she was free of my father, I am free of that locked door. My door is now open. I get to mingle.

I got a part-time job on my own. She was proud that I got a job. She didn't expect for me to get a job. Well, me and my oldest brother got jobs. He got his job like a week before I did. Well, I was in the home at the time, and I had a job. And she used to come visit me and give me a kiss and I would say, "Mommy, take some my money home with you." She say, "No, keep your money." "No, Mommy, take my money home." I used to cry till she wind up taking the money home and . . . when I got out the home she say, "Guess what? I saved every penny." I say, "Where?" and she show me, she got this big Pepsi soda jar . . . she say, "All this money in here is yours. Here, break it open." Ten dollars, and twenty dollars, I had like sixty dollars. Sixty dollars like a thousand dollars to me when I was young. "All this is mine? Come on everybody! Let's go outside and go and have some fun!" Mom said, "Here, you go out there, and I'll hold the money, and we'll go out there and buy pizza and stuff." All the time, she'd be buying it, and I just have her hold my money.

I went to Williams Junior High, Carpenter Junior High, and then I went to Joshua Bauer for my last years. I was still living in the home. They say that I shocked them, 'cause I was always ready for school the next day. I'd wake up, it'd be quarter to nine, I'm outta that house. "I'll see y'all. . . ." "Where you going? To school? You're late." "I know, I'll make it." I never missed school. They said, "Mr. Massey, your mother musta taught you how to love school." No, it wasn't that she taught me how to love school, it was that I loved school. I was the child that set next to the teacher's desk.

My mother would put us under punishment if I got bad grades and stuff 'cause she knew we were her good children. She always knew the teacher wouldn't lie on us. So every time the teacher told something on me, I used to always admit that she was telling the truth.

I just didn't have no friends. I got to hear them say faggot this and faggot that, and faggot this and faggot that, you're a faggot, you're a fruitcake, and it used to bother me. When I got into high school, I was like this, "You better leave me alone." They used to leave me be. They say, "Oh, that child grew up and that child ain't taking no stuff off of nobody." They broke the ice with me as far as me telling people to leave me alone. "Let me be."

I still got to see my brothers and sister every day 'cause they went to the same school. And even my brother say, "Leave my brother alone. 'Cause me and my brother'll eat you up out here." People started saying, "Oh, they're team. They'll come and jump you." My sister used to fight the girls. "You wanna say something to my brother? Say it to me." As time went on she stopped fighting, and they stopped calling me names and that was that. Yeah, I began to stand up for myself. I'd tell my sister, "Don't fight that girl, I'll punch her in the mouth." I'd tell my brother, "Don't say nothing to that boy right there, I'll kick him down the steps." And my brother used to say, "I don't know what that home doing, but it making you mean." I say, "I'm not mean. They just tell me to speak up for my rights." People began to respect what I was and how I was doing.

When my mother came the day that I graduated, and seen that I was hugging everybody, she sat there and cried. And she hugged the lady, my counselor, and said, "You did it. You broke the ice on my child. He mingles with people now." And she was happy. She said, "When can I take my child home?" And the psychiatrist lady that was there wanted her to give her at least a week more and then she come and get me. 'Cause she wanted to make sure that I didn't close back up. And ever since that day there I never close back up again. I'm . . . I'm . . . I'm . . . I'm the Monique, that lives the life of what? Her own. And I'm happy.

My mother told me I was gonna be a doctor. Said, "You gonna be a doctor when you get big." I say, "I am?" She say, "Yeah." She say, "'Cause you like playing with doctor toys." I had that thing that you put in the ears and stuff . . . she say, "You gonna be a doctor." And she bought my brother a fire truck, and she bought my sister a little nurse doll baby. She say, "You gonna be a nurse." And told my brother he gonna be a star on "Sesame Street," my baby brother. She used to tell us things. When I was young, I thought they was the truth, but when I got older, I say, none of these things are not gonna happen. But I knew for a fact my mother was trying like hell to make it happen. All she was doing was trying to make her childrens happy.

Yeah, I think my mother wanted me to be a doctor or something. Honey, I don't know what she want me to be but I knew what I wanted to be—a woman! I don't feel as if I disappointed her. I feel as though I just did my life as my life is s'posed to be. I can't make a life for my mother, and make it for me too.

My mother kept the house spotless. She was the kinda woman like she clean her house when she come home from work, but on the weekends, my mother would do a GI clean. One where the little corner, she'd say, "Okay, now, y'all, here are some mops and a little rag," she'd say, "and you get that corner over there, and run all the way, slide all the way down the wall 'bout four times." She say, "And you take this wall over here," and we would go, that's little minor things, we would run up and down the side of the wall, having fun. And she had the music up sky high so we can laugh, giggle with the music, and dance to the music. And when we done, she say, "My house is spotless." But she be done did all what we did over again, 'cause we don't do no perfect job. But she do it over again, she say, "Look how clean you left that," knowing good and well I didn't do that. But I sit up there and I'll smile and I say, "I know, Mommy, thank you, thank you."

The way it used to be it looked like my father wanted the house to stay a mess. When he used to beat her, seem like the next morning we had to step over glass, push the chair out the way. Every day it was like some kinda something we had to step over, glass, paper, her worksheets. She was a social worker.

My mother was a old-fashioned fabulous cook. My mother can cook her heart out. She used to make us these big cookies when we were little, right? Put little faces on them, right? And write our names on the cookie. She used to get icing, and put our name on the cookie, and put face. They used to be cookies 'bout this big, and she say, "Here go your face, and here go your face . . . y'all better not eat your faces up."

I learnt everything else from my mother. My discipline, how to respect people, to honor your elders, to make sure you get a good education . . . people wanna talk, let them talk. I learned so much from my mother, just so much, I can go right on down the line.

My values were, never say I hate a person, always say "I dislike," 'cause you hate no man. Another thing, to let life take you as far as you can. The next thing, whatever I'm going to be as far as gay, be the best. And these things are things of value to me. I learned that brutalizing people is not right. Those words was the main thing I learned from growing up in my family. I don't wanna see nobody hurt nobody. Today I see a person do something wrong it hurts me. I learned that hurting somebody you're not gonna accomplish anything. I had a guy the other day steal twenty dollars from me. It didn't hurt me. You know what hurt him the most? Me not being his friend no more.

I listened to my mother. Oh, yes, yes. That was a special rule. "Honor thy mother and thy father." That was part of the Bible. We honored my father until he left. We used to make sure what he said goes. We listened to what he said until the day he left our house. We used to cry, 'cause we have to honor the both of them. There's nothing we could do. So therefore my mother used to tell him 'bout things like that, honor the mother and father. He just send us in the room, just tell us to go. "Go in your room. I'm ready to beat your mother. Go in the room." Till the day we took the high heels and stuff and attacked him. And that's when he asked my mother what was she teaching us, she's teaching us how to attack their father and stuff. It wasn't her that taught us that. It was my uncle. He said if he hits your mother, you get him. And that was all we used to do. We get him.

I can't remember how old everyone was but I know that for a fact I was eleven and we used to give my father the business. Back in them days, women used to wear high heels with thin spike heels, the thin pencil heels. And we used to let my father see how each pencil heel felt. My little brother was the person for biting, he couldn't hold a shoe long enough to even hit nobody. He was one for holding on and putting his teeth in and never let go like a rat. Me and my brother and my sister, we used to be the high heel team. We used to call ourselves Pencil People, right? And we used to call my little brother Cookie Monster.

I was just ready to leave my family and I said, "I'm going to live on my own." My mother wished me the best of luck. I went to a place called Children's Services because I was still a child. And he put me in this little home, child care center. I depended on myself and no one else. I was seventeen then, and he put me on a thing called independent living and helped me get an apartment and I was just paying my bills. They paid ten percent of my bills and I paid the rest.

I just look in the papers for an apartment, but they wind up telling me that I couldn't have an apartment. I had to have an efficiency apartment, a very small apartment. I didn't mind. I finally found an apartment at Thirty-seventh and Somerset Street in College Park. I'll never forget the street. I wasn't living the life of luxury, but I was living a little peaceful life. But I was secluded from everyone. I didn't hang out with no one when I got my apartment. I was seventeen and I felt as though I was a college kid. I just do my laundry, come home. Go shopping, come home. Go to the movies, come home. Go see my mother, come home. Go with my brothers and sisters, come home.

I was working at the International House of Pancakes in Huntington. When I was working there, those were fun days to me because I was young. I was energetic. There was nothing in the world that could stop me then. I worked there for a long time, and when I quit that job there, I got on the corner. See the corners were an off-and-on thing at one time. If I got a job there were no corners. I was working at International House of Pancakes in Huntington and I was working at the House of Pancakes at Sixteenth and Oakland. My boss there was Faylene. I couldn't take her no more! I'm got 'bout sick of her. If I had one more day of her, I would've put her in the trash compactor or something.

When I quit the one in Huntington, they immediately said I was a good worker and they gave me good reference. And like two weeks later, I started working at Sixteenth and Oakland and that job didn't last no more than about a month. That one was a pain in my chewy.

I got fired, and I sat down next to the chair next to the door and I said, "What am I gonna do?" She said, "Child, there's other ways for you to make money. You got that woman face, you can make money untold." She say, "That's all you gotta' do is just meet me." I was wondering where she came from. She was eating. She say, "I'll give you the clothes to wear." I guess she said that to me because I had a girlish face. See, a drag queen would look at you different from a conservative queen. A conservative queen would look at you and say, "Oh, that child gotta find another job." A drag queen say, "There's always a job for another girl." I was a woman. I was walking down that aisle like this, "Oh, what am I going to do? Oh, God." She knew I was a woman. I wasn't trying to hide anything whatsoever. . . . I was like, "Oh, Lord, child, my goodness." She was like, "Oh, that's a woman. I have to help her."

I had already been doing that, but here's the thing, I was still what you call a amateur. When I got off the subway, I had to walk to Metro Center. Due to the fact that I had to walk to Metro Center I always tried to give it a little play while I was walking. "Hi, honey. Hi, baby. Hi, honey." With my uniform on. They say, "Oh, I got me a working girl that wants to work." Only reason I used to do stuff like that is because it was things that I wanted. Okay, they had a limit on eating. They give you like three dollars and seventy-five cents to eat with as far as your work. And whatever you buy that's over that, you got to pay that. I always like to buy things that I liked that costed more though. So I liked to have extra pennies in my pocket. And at that time, I was totally drug free. Only thing I wanted to do was eat and I was weighing like one hundred thirty-nine pounds and I was seventeen years old. I didn't know what the hell I was doing.

She gave me full ropes, see. Okay, when I was doing it before, I was doing my boy sneakers and throw on a pair boy jeans and a shirt and a jacket. I'm fine, 'cause everybody thought I looked like a girl anyway. But this girl that was there eating gave me wig, gave shoes, gave a dress. I was like, "Oh, this is a complete different look on me."

And she was a hooker. She showed me the ropes, and ever since that day I've been out there. And that's how I learned. I learned by somebody else's experience. I had to stick by her for at least two months. After two months I had to go out there on my own. And when I graduated I was like this, "I am grown! I shall do this! I can rebuild me better, stronger, faster!" And there I was.

I went to Eleventh and Beaumont. She told me to come there and she would be there. She gave me clothes to put on, she told me what to do and what street to take them on. If they didn't go to that street, get out the car. And everything worked out fine.

I wasn't a drag queen then. I was just wearing girl clothes and giving them back, and then go back home in boy clothes. She would give me everything I needed, earrings, wig, and all that. I was still living in the home and I had to be in the home by ten o'clock. And I used to go out and be out there like from six o'clock to quarter after nine and catch a taxi cab or something to the house. Tell the taxi cab to let me off at the corner, at the other corner of the house and then run down the street. I used to always used to make it there on time. If it wasn't five of ten, it was ten o'clock on the nose. I always made it.

I turned my first trick at sixteen. I waved at him and he waved back and told me to come here. When I went to the car, he said he had twenty dollars. He said did I wanna do something? I said, "Yes." He said, "Get in." And I remember what she said, take him to a certain street. I took him to a certain street. We have oral sex and that was that. He took me back.

The first time I was out there it was wild. It was wild. Man give me twenty dollars to have sex with me. I was like, I was like . . . kept looking at him . . . sure this man gonna bust me in my head? 'Cause I was thinking 'bout how they used to kidnap children, give them a lollipop and stuff. Man give me twenty dollars, then he's gonna kill me. But then it wasn't as bad as I thought. Then I used to just do it and get scared. Every time, every car I got in I was scared. But then it was just wild to me that I was with different faces, people I'd never known in my life.

It started feeling comfortable when I graduated out of school, and I got out there all night long. I was like this, "Oh, I'm a woman, honey! I'm a woman! The hell with this. I'm a woman! I'll buy my own clothes! I'll buy my own. Keep your wigs. I'll buy Naomi Simms tomorrow."

Nobody never knew I was a boy. They just like, "Hi, baby. Hey, slim, come here, sexy." And if they knew I was a boy they'd kill me. That's why he's always saying, "Just do not tell them you're a boy." And I never told them. I used to make money and not tell them nothing. They didn't know I was that young. I don't think too many dates would have chosen me if they knew I was sixteen. "Oh, my God. I don't want no date. Get out of my car." They's always asking how old I was and I used to say nineteen. I told one man I was eighteen. I told one man I was twenty-one. You see, I just lied. And as days went on I noticed I started getting better at it. I said, "Oh, Lord, I'm gonna make this a habit." I used to just do it, and then I noticed I didn't have to worry 'bout the age racket 'cause they never asked you how old you were anymore. Besides, if they saw me out on the street they're not gonna ask me how old I was. They just gonna say, "Oh, you wants to make . . . this child wants to make some money."

Yeah, when I graduated from high school, the day after I graduate from high school, I was like this, "Oh, wig, shoes, hat, dresses." I came back with the whole giddy-up. I had money. I had a nice little bit of money 'cause my mother had given me all that money back. While she was in the bed, I would dress up and then run out the door. Peeeunnnggg! I had my shoes in my hand. The people in the neighborhood would see me but they didn't know who I was. I just walk past and pay them no mind. They wouldn't recognize me. Then I'd come out the next day, next morning, and I say, "Child, I seen you last night talking to that girl. I'm telling your girlfriend on you." "Well, where you was at?" "Don't worry 'bout where I was at." Oh, I used to get them all. Then I slowed down with it and then I came back to it again. Like some days I say, "Well, I don't have to do it none this week. The hell with this. Go home and rest. I'm taking this next week off." And then next week I say, "Mama, I got to go. I'm gone."

Oh, honey, I was just a wingding of a wingdinger. It became like a new drug. I had to get out there practically every day, but then in the daytime I wouldn't be out. I'd be dressed in my little boy's clothes telling everybody who I seen last night. "Why, honey, you know I seen your boyfriend last night with that girl you can't stand." "How you seen him?" "Honey, I'll tell you what that girl look like. I'll tell you what she had on yesterday." "You ain't seen her yesterday." "Yes I did, honey, 'bout two o'clock in the morning. I did so. She had on a pair of green pants. Ask her did she had on a pair of green pants last night." And when the girl say yeah, I'd see her and her boyfriend fighting. I be like this, "Why y'all fighting?"

See, I was a good one. My mother told me that I should stop telling on people, but she never knew how I was telling them. But she knew I was running my mouth. She said, "Child, how you get in everybody's business?" "Child, don't worry 'bout that. I'm a woman! You know a woman see everything." "Yes, you is a woman." She said that all the time. "Yes, you are a woman. You see everything. Ain't nothing . . . things I don't see, you see." "You got that right. You be in the bed." I used to get her good. She loves it.

Oh, honey, I used to be one little hooked-out baby 'cause I was young. Men would give me twenty dollar here, fifty dollars there. I say within the night I'd bring home at least three hundred dollars. Within the week's time, oh, honey, I used to be one lulu of a lulu. I used to go home and say, "Mommy, guess what? I found somebody's wallet." And knowing good and well I made all this money myself. "Where the ID at?" "I threw it away." "Why you throw it away?" "Mommy, 'cause I didn't want no people running to me and saying I had they money." "How much is that?" "Thousand dollars." She say, "How much? How much? Come on, time for the store!" Me and my mother used to go shop off my little money. But then she found out I was a hooker. She say, "Don't put all that dirty money in my house."

Then she be like this, "Whatever you do be the best." I told her, "I hook, and I'm the best." She say, "You the best?" I say, "Mama, watch me when I come in. I'm gonna blow the horn. Just peek out your window." She say, "Child, you were in a Mercedes." "Yeah, I know, child! I know what I was in." She say, "Child, I don't want none of that dirty. . . ." She never accepted none of the money, though. She says, "I don't want none of your dirty money."

She found out because one day she was driving. Well, I told her one day. I guess she didn't kinda understood till one day she was driving and I went to walk over to her car. I thought she was a trick. And she said, "Get in!" And I said, "Oh, my God." She said, "Where these clothes come from?" I say, "Mom, I got a whole bedroom full of clothes." Mommy say, "You lying to me." She went in my room. She seen them. She said, "Child, you got a lot of nice things. . . . What the hell you doing with these damn clothes? You stole them?" I said, "Mommy, I bought everything I own." Then she say, whatever I be, be the best, just don't go to jail. Every time I went to jail I had money in my pocket to pay my bail. Ain't not one time I went to jail I didn't pay my bail. Till now. I get in jail now, honey, they let you go. So I don't pay no bail. I sit there and I wait. Keep my little money in my pocket.

Up until that time I met that girl I didn't have a lotta sexual involvements. When I started standing on the corner, it was practically every five minutes. You jump outta one car and you're back in another one. Sometimes I was out every night. Some weeks I may go out from Monday to Sunday. Some weeks I may go out just Sunday. See, it's just like that. Some days I'd be like, "Oh, child, I can't be going for these men having sex with me every day."

So after the first time, with the guy in school, I wasn't sexually active. That was my first time ever having sex. Maybe two months, three months, and I do it again. Five months, seven months, I'd do it again. And in time when my money was gone I'll be ready to do it again. Sometimes months go by and I wouldn't be doing it. Then it got so happy to me I just say, "Okay, let's do it once a month." And then I was doing it every day. I just became a plain ol' hooker.

These were black men, white men, Chinese men, Jamaican men, whoever. They were men. That's how I looked at them. It's as simple as that. I have no other way of saying it. I liked everybody. Population. I used to tell people, "I'm gonna have a baby and I'm gonna name him Population."

The most I ever got from turning a date was thirty-eight hundred dollars. At the end of the day, thirty-eight hundred dollars. The man took care of me quite well. He wanted me for a whole night, and I charged him one hundred dollars for two hours. He wanted me from that night to the next afternoon, and what it all boils down to I was with him that next afternoon to that evening. Every two hours that went by he gave me one hundred dollars. Till all of a sudden when it, it was time for him to take me back I was counting. . . . My mother was going, "Three thousand dollars, thirty-eight hundred dollars!"

I was seventeen. I never asked how old he was. Yeah, that's one thing you'll never worry 'bout. Oh, he looked like he was about thirty-seven, thirty-eight years old, in his early forties. He, he thought I was a woman. He kept me a long time before he even laid down with me. I slept in the guest room and everything. I didn't sleep with him. I said, "Honey, I used to sleeping by myself." Didn't want him to know I was a boy. Until that evening came. He say, "Let's do something." I say "Okay, fine." I got all this money in my pocket. I'm fine. So I say, "I meant to tell you something. You know my service, right? I mean, I've been with you all this damn long. . . ." I said, "I been with you all this time. Do you know my service?" He said, "What do you mean?" I said, "Do you know I'm a guy?" He said, "Huh!" He said, "Well, oh, what the hell. Come on, let's go back." And he just took me back. He said he's sorry to take up so much time. He said he didn't even realize he had a guy. He said I was pretty and . . . all guys should look like me, and all this other good stuff. He said don't go out there, somebody might hurt me. I took the thirty-eight hundred dollars and went to Las Vegas. That's right, I went straight to Las Vegas. "Honey, just drop me off at the airport!"

When I got on my own, my first real relationship was with this guy named Grant Harvey. It was my birthday, like the week before my birthday. It was at a party, and he was buying me cocktails and we were talking. He asked me if he could call me, and I said, "Yeah." He was a man. I was like this, "Oh, my God." He was so caring. He made me feel so good, but then came the drugs. He was younger than me, like two years younger. I was twenty and he was eighteen. He was a black. He was well known by people. People use to speak to him and what have you, but he didn't have any kind of reputation on the streets.

Anyway, he walked in and he said that he wanted me for himself. I kept saying you got to prove that to me. For my birthday he walked in with a thirty-five-hundred-dollar camera set with the stand and all these lenses. Later on, you know what, "You're gonna stay with me." "Spend money like that, you can stay with me." I was staying at the Schuyler Hotel at the time, and he paid the bills and he began to work there. We used to go to the beach. We would go to Six Flags-Great Adventure. We used to just do everything. It was like a dream come true. I run down the street, and he'll buy me a bundle of balloons and come and hand them to me and I walk down the street with a bundle of balloons. We just had little intimate times. He started acting crazy, getting strung out on dope.

The relationship lasted for five years! I ain't too long left Grant. But I have to stay away from him when he's strung out on dope. And he started stealing from me and stuff like that. He stole my mother's money. My mother gave me money to hold for her. She gave me money on Christmas day, and she said, "Hold this money." She was going to Philadelphia. When New Year's Eve came she told me to bring the money over. I went inside and looked around and it was gone. Right. Like with a note saying, "Monique, I really needed this." And my mother was saying, "Really need what? I know he didn't take my four hundred dollars and really need nothing." Me and her sat there and waited. He came in like nodding. And she said, "What the hell you did? What the fuck is wrong with you?" And it was drugs. Okay, he still had a little money left. But being on a nod like that you don't say but so much. You don't understand a word he said. A man knocked on the door. He was a drug guy. He said can he speak to Grant. Well, I said, "I'm Grant's wife. What's going on?" "Can you tell Grant that I have the dope for him. Will he give me the money?" I said, "The what! I don't go for all that. Get away from my door."

I thought he was using, but I wasn't sure. He used to always rest a lot. Lay across the bed, stretched out. I used to say he had a hard day. I would never admit it. When the guy said "dope," I say, "Okay, he's out of here." He got sober and my mother went home. I went to my little account, and I gave her a hundred dollars. That's all I could afford. She still got to go to Philadelphia, 'cause her friend gave her the rest of the money. When I seen my friend Grant, I said, "Grant, your friend gave me this for you." It was like three bags of dope. It costed twenty-five dollars apiece. He said, "He did? I'm sorry. Give them here." Good. Now they were all open. I never told him they were open. I said,

"Here," and handed them to him. And as he was grabbing them all the dope fell on the floor. I watched him act like a wild dog and try to get it up off the floor. I can't go through that. And then he hit me and asked me why did I do that and stuff like that. Started actually physically attacking me. So I said I don't need that in my life. I don't. I told him that I was going to leave him. He said that if I left he was going to kill me. I said you may as well kill me now 'cause I can't live with no drug addict. I can't live with no man that's strung out on no dope. They say them guys that do dope will steal your drawers off you, and I didn't want that. I wear mines.

I have a lot in my life that used to bother me. So for me the important points would be, you know, that period from the time I were born until the time I left home, not left home but the time my father left home, and perhaps another one would be when I had sex the first time because that confirmed in a sense that I was gay and what it meant to be gay . . . and . . . and then being sent to the home, that was another turning point. And then having . . . doing sex work for the first time because that took me into a whole different world.

It's called the world of chances. You're taking a chance on your life . . . okay? For instance, I have a scar on my face, a scar on my knee, almost died while turning a trick. A man paid me forty dollars. As he was putting the forty dollars in my hand his other hand was going across my neck splitting my throat. It's called the world of chances. You . . . you . . . you take a chance on living and dying. You take a chance on being hurt and not being hurt. You take a chance on finding a friend and finding an enemy. You see, the world of chances.

See, I never, I've never even looked at it like an illusion or some kind of wonderful thing with smoke and mirrors. I never go out there on the corner thinking like that. I go on the corner, before I go out my door, I say a prayer. I never go out there with no . . . with no fantasy on my mind. I always go out there by saying a prayer to help me, to make sure I don't get hurt. I'm going out into a flock of wolves when I am only one lonely sheep. To please guide me and give me the strength to maneuver around these wolves. I tell Him in my prayer that games are checkers and chess. Checkers and chess. I go out there by taking a chance. I am playing Russian roulette.

From being on the streets, I learned how to be conniving. You become conniving. You become very deceitful. You do not care about no one. If a man was on the ground and he needed a glass of water, you're so much, so much out of your heart, you'd walk past before you'd give him a drink. Because that's when you start running into a lot of problems. Run into your good and your bad. Like Clint Eastwood said, you go to the good, bad, and the ugly. I went through my goods, the people that want to just give me. . . . I went through my bads by a man cutting my face and my throat. And my uglies is when people just wanna holler at you and all this other crazy stuff, "Get out my car!" That's the ugly. That takes a lot from you. Takes all that kindness away from you. 'Specially if it's being done daily.

Okay, the main contents of being on the streets was survival, right. You lose a lot things as far as trust. You trust no one, and things of that nature, right. To live out on the streets today, you got to pick up and let go. You got to let go of all your past and grab on to your future as far as what's ahead of you. Okay, sometimes, right, I think about when I was young and I started off doing this. What was the purpose of me doing this? It was like a downfall for me.

My downfall, but it was a pick me up at the same time because I was closed in and it helped me open up. The streets helped me open up, but it made me change my attitude. See, like I used to be a real, real happy person. It wouldn't be a time that you couldn't catch me with a smile, at least. Right. Even though I was closed in, I did smile a lot. Just being on these corners it changes my whole disposition as far as my smile. Takes a lot of that from me. People ask me why don't I smile. It's because if you're seen there smiling they figure they got the advantage.

There isn't any relationship between sexual gratification and doing what I do. Okay. There is the image that you have to project. A image to make the man think that you're enjoying yourself when you're not. Okay? For instance, a man can give me a quantity of money and because of this quantity of money he expects a smile. Once he gives you the money, he expects a smile and cooperation and that's what I give them, a smile and cooperation, even though, quote, unquote, "I don't want to." So what you do is act like the man on the stage. Perform. Only thing's different, I'm not getting that Emmy Award for it. I'm just performing. So when I'm done this man and he's taking me back to my destination, he gets no more smiles. He might get conversation, but he will not get another smile. He may want a phone number. You lie to him and give him a phony phone number, give him a phony address even if it's two blocks away from where you live at, let him let you off two blocks away from where you live, and just make believe you live at this house. Your life becomes lies. Your life becomes as if you're on a stage. The only thing different is that it's real. You're lying to someone. I can't say that somebody wrote the script for me and I'm doing it this way. I'm doing it the way that he wants it done, the customer himself. If he wants smiles, he got smiles, and that's what I give him. I don't give them no more, no less.

It takes a while to develop a heart of ice. You can give or take about a good year, because you see like they say, "Man did not build Rome in a day." Even though you go out there with the position that you were brought up with, love thy neighbor—that's the main position I was brought up with, love thy neighbor—you won't make it to heaven saying you love God and don't love your neighbor because you'll go straight to hell. Now, today, those feelings still sit there, but my heart is surrounded by ice. Those feelings are always sitting on the top of the ice, they're not inside. When I'm on the corners, I'm a very nasty-hearted person. I mean, not as far as hurting anyone, but I'm a nasty-hearted person as far as I don't want to be bothered. My whole attitude changes. I don't go out there and say, "Hi! How are you? What are you doing?" I'd be like this, "Leave me alone. I'm out here to do one thing. Leave me be."

It's a heart of stone. Your heart becomes a heart of stone because of the work you do. First of all, in my heart, I don't want this profession, but I was brought up by "do what you do best." This is not what I do best, but I do it. I've been doing it for years. For a good fifteen years now. It's my profession. It's what I do. So now it's "get back happy world, hello dangerous world." I look out at it and I say I got a dangerous life. When I walk out my doors, I don't know whether I'll be killed today or tomorrow. Last night I got pushed and hurt my back. I thank God he didn't cut me or tried to throw me out a twenty-four-story building.

I don't have no gripes with no one and I carry no animosity. I have no conscience with the things I do no longer. When I get money from a man that's all I take home. No matter what I do with them, I just get money from them. I will leave him and that's that. I don't know him no more. After I walk out that door, if I walked back inside that door, if he's not standing at that door waiting for me, I would never remember his face.

You overlook what you're doing and just do it. Just like a man on a job. He may be a crook and at a desk. He don't like the job, but he do it. Just like me, I'm the same way. A man say, "Here's fifty dollars. I want you to beat me." You know I don't like hitting people. I'll overlook what he says and I do what he says, and pray to God that it doesn't take long because I don't like it. But I do it. When I leave out the door, it's like . . . in the elevator coming down I be like, "I'm so glad that is over," and when I walk out the door, pssh, all of that is out of my head.

I don't like requests to take pictures. To take pictures and to have sex with people I didn't know. I mean not one person, you be with them for about six hours and you be done had sex with about ten guys. In the same room and . . . and they're just taking pictures. I didn't enjoy it. It was a lot of money involved in that. It was a whole lot, that's why I didn't turn it down. It was like three hundred dollars. That's enough money to hold me and I did it. I didn't enjoy it, but I did it. I wind up getting VD in the process of all that. That's the price I paid, that disease was the price I paid. When you make money and you get a disease, the money means nothing no more.

I feel very unclean. I feel disgusted. There is times I walk out and cry. There were actually times I actually walked out and have the money and cry. Why I cry? Because it's disgusting the things that I have to do in life to make it today. I put it in my back pocket. I cry today, and take all them tears and them thoughts and put them in my back pocket and save them for another rainy day until the next time I may cry again. Yeah, some people go home and take baths, but that just don't work. I go home and I douche and I take baths. I just think about it and then I lay down and I go to sleep and wake up later on I feel better but before I go to bed I'm disgusted.

I've actually walked into my mother's house sometimes when I was doing this and I was disgusted. I was furious. I didn't want to be both-ered with no one until after I took this bath, this douche, and lay down. At the time when things like that happen I will go out and find me something to eat instead of eating out of my mother's refrigerator. Finding myself so disgusted, my hands has been on things that it shouldn't have been on and I'm in her refrigerator.

I usually sleep all day. I eat and I go out. That's my daily routine every day. I get up in the afternoon, about four o'clock, and go to Saint Paul's Refuge. Be there before four-thirty. Eat, come back and go to sleep, and then wake up and go outside. I go out about nine. I go to Eleventh and Beaumont. So I walk from Eleventh and Beaumont to Tenth and Southbourne, from Tenth and Southbourne to Tenth and Lawrence, from Tenth and Lawrence back to whichever one of my girlfriends that's out. When I'm done I go back to Tenth and Southbourne, put the pipe back, go back to Eleventh and Beaumont. I do that all night long. I cop at Tenth and Lawrence to cop. I've been copping there for about a year. And Lord, don't let me forget them matches. Matches are like diamond rings. Yes they are! People are selling books of matches for a dollar where you buy your drugs at. I buy a box of them.

So my typical days is running from the cops, trying not to get locked up. Running from corner to corner so this cops say, "Get off this cor-ner." You go from this corner and go to that corner. Get off of this corner and go to that corner. That is a regular course of a night. Running from a cop, jumping in and out of dates' cars, running from cops. That's a regular night. I would start like nine o'clock in the evening.

When I'm on the corner I call 'em. "Hey, honey." That's all I say. "Hey, honey." And they turn around, and then I say, "Come here." And they pull over. I just look sexy. I throw on a pair of high heels, one of them body dresses, them dresses that them video girls be wearing, them black, them real tight dresses, with the long sleeves. I wear a dress like that, high heels, seam stockings, and my hair done. And I have on makeup. I say, "Hey, honey, come here." And they think you're sexy. They stop their car, and they say, "What do you want to do?" And they be like, "How much you charging?" "Twenty-five." "For what?" "Head." "How much for round the world." I'll say, "A hundred." Round the world is having to get a blow job and have anal sex. I get a lot of people who want round the world, usually on the weekends. Those the ones I usually turn down. During the course of a week I'll make over a thousand dollars. Just about all of it is going back into drugs.

I've been arrested like thirty times for the same thing, prostitution. They give you a thing called Summary Release and let you go and you go to court. They give you probation, six months' probation. That's it. So if you get caught in that six months' time, you don't go to jail, you just go back to court again, and they give you six more months' probation. Sometimes it add all the way up to two years.

When you get picked up and taken to the Police Headquarters and you're in drag everybody hoots and hollers. "I know that ain't no man! That's not no man! Don't put that woman in here," and stuff like that. And before I walk out I take off my high heels every time, because I might have to clunk somebody in the head while I'm inside there. Because they want to touch and feel. They have to put us in a cell in the back with the girls, with the prostitutes. They hold you for no more than an hour, and then you're gone, you're out, you're out of there. There's no bail. They just let you go. Just to take you off the corner. They're called the lice. They come and take you off the corner and keep you in jail for an hour and give you a court date, and that's it.

If you want to be in good shape when you leave that police station, don't run. And I never run. They'll say, "Monique, you don't ever run from us. Why is that?" I say, "Because I want to walk out with my shoes on" or "I want to walk out walking straight" or "I want to walk to the jailhouse and not to the hospital." I tell them stuff like that, and they laugh. They say, "That's a cooperative child. She ain't no joke. She don't go for that." And they are right about that.

You know, you get in the car, they say, "Hi, you want a date?" "Yes." They say, "Get in." They say, "How much do you want?" You say, "Twenty-five." They say, "Good, you got it. You're under arrest." Oh, I've been in the car and said, "Oh, this guy can't be a cop." I look at him, and I'll say, "Honey, you can't be no cop. Show me some ID." They throw out a badge, and I say fine, no argument. I'm a hooker, you're a cop. Take me to jail. I don't never try to run. Never.

I try to find out if he's a cop by saying, "Hi, baby what are you doing." You're not allowed to touch a cop, especially an undercover cop. You're not allowed to rub all on them. And if you try to rub them at least on his leg, and he moves your hand, you know not to get in the car. "Okay, officer, bye."

As far as jail, I'm a queen. I go in there and mind my business. They leave me alone. I find a man to take care of me. He takes care of me until I go home. I was in jail once for three years and ten months. I was there for aggravated assault, simple assault, assault with a deadly weapon, and reckless endangering, and attempting to kill. A man punched me in my face and tried to take his money back. He asked for his money back. He said, "I want my money back. It's not as good as I thought it would be." I said, "No." And he punched me in my nose. It's as simple as that. And I said, "Who are you playing with? I'm a man." I stabbed him seven times, and then turned around and said, "See you later. I'm going to have cocktail." I got out of his car while he was bleeding. They just went to the bar and they arrested me.

You know, you don't meet your husband in jail. He claims you. He seen me and he said, "You're mines." And I said, "Fine." That's jail, you have no say-so in jail. I don't mess with them jail men. When they say, "You're mines." "Okay, I'm yours." I said I wanted a husband and then when I got there I didn't get the chance to pick a husband, but I got a husband. There was no arrangement. He wanted me and he had me. He takes care of me. He gives me everything I want. Whatever I want, he gives it to me. He'll walk with you and talk with you. Just like a buddy. He's your protector while you're there. When you're gone, you forget about him. I never remember them. I go back to jail, "Honey, what's your name again?"

How many of the dates are straight men? Zero percent. They act the role of a straight man, but you bet your bottom dollar they're not. You get in the car with a guy and they'll say, "This is my first time doing this." You look at them and say, "Okay!" Oh, I go along with the program. "Yeah, honey, this is your first time. Oh, fine, that's good, it's your first time."

Some of them don't know they've picked up a man. Don't get me wrong. I look tired today. Some of them don't. You get in the car, and they be like this, "Oh you're so pretty. Look at that faggot right over . . ."

and I look at him like, "Ummmmm," through the whole thing and then get back and say, "You can let me out on the corner with that faggot right over there. Oh, yes. There are no problems today. They're nice people." Get out of their cars, and say, "I'm just like them." And get out. And he'll be like this. And I'll say, "You better pull off or you'll hold up traffic." I get them with that one all the time. It could be dangerous.

But sometimes I don't tell them. Sometimes I'll go through the whole thing and don't tell them period. Instead of telling them to let me off in front of those faggot, I'll tell them let me off in front of Woolworth or something. Where there's nobody there that if I get out the car somebody say, "Monique!" and I don't want that to happen.

Sometimes I'll say, "Do you know what I am." They'll say, "What?" I say, "I'm a queen." He'll say, "Yes, you are a queen." And I'll say, "But you got me wrong, I'm a transvestite." And he'll say, "That's what I'm looking for anyway. A transvestite is fine." Good, now let's talk business. But then you tell some guys and they be "What? Get out of my car. Don't put your hands on me. Don't you put your hands on me!" Knowing your heart is beating twenty-five miles per hour. "Don't put your hands on me. Don't you touch me." "You can let me out right here in the middle of the street."

I did it many times. It's very dangerous. It is a very, very dangerous profession. Like I said before, games are checkers and chess. I live a life of chances. I play Russian roulette. Every time I walk out that door, I don't know if that barrel has that bullet in it. Is that the day that something may happen to me? Sometimes I think about stopping. I think about it a whole lot. I actually think about it extremely a whole lot, but then I tell myself things will get better. When things get better, I will stop.

A black gay man goes through so much hell. If they get the job, they have to go through so much to get it, and the white man doesn't. A white gay man can get a job in a snap. But I don't think there's much prejudice in the gay community. They're not prejudice. I have not yet seen a prejudice white queen towards a black queen. I have not seen a black queen prejudice towards a white queen either. I think if I went into a white club, a white gay bar, I could go into that bar and say, "I think I'll have some of that. You're coming with me." It's not that easy, but I'm quite sure I can pull it off. I don't think there's much prejudice in the community. I think it's a bunch of talk. People are always saying things they don't have no right to. That's like a rumor. You might have seen Joe and Harry fighting, and Joe and Harry had words. By the time Joe and Harry fight and their fight is over, Betty seen it and she told Sue about it. Sue tells somebody else about it and have it all messed up. Sue tells Jessie. Jessie done had the story so backed up that you think that it's a Tyson and Spinks fight. See, that's how it is, rumor. I look at it like that.

The only thing I ever had happen to me is if I went around with my white girlfriends and a white date pull up, they'll pick her before he'll pick me. That's the only thing. That doesn't bother me because I know that's going to happen. There it is right there, a white man and a white woman and he's riding in Metro Center. I have had a lot of customers who wanted black girls too. "I have always wanted a black woman."

When I was sixteen, I was a new face. I wasn't supposed to trust no one 'cause they can take advantage. They can make me do things I have never done before. Dates, and hookers on the corner, they have me do things I've never done before. And I learned to do things on my own. I did it by myself. Everything I did, I did it alone, but I took chances. It was a courageous thing. You had to be real courageous, but you went through a lot of compliments, a lot of happiness, a lot of sadness, you got scared, you got happy, you trusted people, and it was a different world. It was just a different world. It was a world of chances, that's all, you were in a world of chances. It's something hard to explain.

I would say "hi" to this one, "hi" to that one, and that would be it. 'Cause at that time I was still closed-minded. I didn't want to be bothered. I just wanted to make money and leave. So one day I met this girl named Sidney and Somora. They said, "We're your friends. We won't see nothing happen to you." And we became really good friends, but I never turned dates with them neither because I never put too much trust in them. That was fine. They watched my back, I watched their backs. It was as simple as that. It was a different world.

When I got cut that time I let my guard down. I felt as though I could trust this person, when I wasn't supposed to. Didn't know him, never seen him in my life. He was a Puerto Rican. And it happened so suddenly.

It happened so fast. I was in the hospital, on the operating table for six hours. He cut my jugular vein, and they saved me. They told me I almost died, you know. I was lucky.

Just after it happened, a little boy came out of his house and took his finger. . . . He went to run to get his mother and tell his mother that there was somebody outside with their neck cut open. His mother gave him some towels or he must of grabbed them. He ran back out there and he was holding the towels on my neck but his finger was inside my jugular vein. My neck was this big, but the doctor said the little boy saved my life. When he let it go, the blood gushed out. He said the little boy saved me because he clipped it closed. He was trying to hold my neck like this and his finger was stuck inside at the same time. I love him for it. See, if I would see this little boy today or tomorrow, it's nothing I would not do for him.

I did not know this little boy. I just turned around and looked at the little boy and he said, "You're bleeding" and I said, "Help me, please." He grabbed me and I fell to the ground. He got scared and ran. Well I don't know if he got scared. He ran and hollered, "Mommy, Mommy, Mommy, Mommy, Mommy, Mommy," and he opened up his door and he came running back out. When I looked up again, his mother was a nurse, and she pulled him away. And when she pulled him away he kept saying, "Mommy, my finger was inside the sore. Euh, euh." She said, "Put your finger back in the sore!" He put his finger back 'cause her fingers was too big to hold that jugular vein. He put his finger back. He was full of blood. She hugged him and she kissed him. She said, "You did the biggest, courageous thing ever."

The man wanted a date and he said he was going to give me forty dollars and he said, "Is that okay?" We got to the place and he said, "Okay, if you don't trust me, I gonna give you the forty dollars now." So he pulled the forty dollars out, and he put his hand out like this, and as I went to grab the forty dollars, he was cutting my throat. It happened so quickly. He was a lunatic. He said, "Are you bleeding? You're lying," and ran across my face with the knife. And that was that, it was over and done with. And I said, "Lord have mercy, Jesus." I just knew I was going to die that night. And I kept on saying, "I going to die. Help me, I'm dying, I'm dying." And people helped me, that little boy helped me the most. People in the bar came out to help, the lady, the little boy's mother, came out to help, and the little boy helped me. I'll never forget him. He's the one that helped me the most.

It happened right on the corner of my own block, that's the part that got me. We were going past the corner. "If you don't trust me, here's the money," that's when he cut my throat. And I figured I was in my own neighborhood he wouldn't have did none of this crazy stuff. I never seen him again. I never seen him again. I'm still out there taking my chances.

There was a time when it was fun, like in the beginning. I remember it was great when a man was giving me money and told me I was pretty and all this other crazy stuff like that. See, I used to go for it, but now they say that, and I'd be like this, "Okay. Big deal. Give me my money."

Do you remember the two girls, the two drag queens that was found, and one of them had their legs cut off and were in the park. They were my two best friends, Sidney and Somora. They got their legs cut off and their privates mutilated and put in their mouths. I was incarcerated that night. The next day I heard about it. And I was like, "Whoo!" God must of blessed me and pulled me away from them so I wouldn't be with them 'cause I'd probably had the same thing happen to me.

They were my best friends. We would hang out together twenty-four hours a day. We used to shop. We used to eat. We used to laugh. We used to giggle. We used to cry together, but they're gone now. I'm by myself. Now, that's why I have a lover. My lover is my support now. Whenever I need him, he's there. He wants me to stop standing on the corner. Then he says eventually he'll get me to stop, and probably so he will.

The only dream I had was being my mother's protector. I have to be honest with you. My basic dream was being my mother's protector and being my little brother's legs. I want people to know the good parts of my life. How my mother treated us.

As long as I had a profession I never had to stay on the street. To be honest I'm living in an abandominium now. I've been there for three years. I've almost fixed it as good as this room. It's owned by Jamaicans, and they are drug sellers. They've helped me. They've helped me buy sheet rock so I could make walls like these. They bought me plaster, and

I plaster the walls. I have a diploma in building maintenance when I went to the Skills Center. They bought me panels, so I could panel the building. The building looks very well. There is no garbage or nothing in the building. It just me and my boyfriend, and the people who live upstairs. It's a house with a store and then a house is on the top. You go through the door and go up the steps and you be on top of the store. That's the kind of building I live in. I live on the second floor back.

It was a coincidence how I found it. One day I was tired. I fell asleep in there and this Jamaican guy walked in and asked me what I was doing there. I told him I didn't have nowhere to go and this was the only place I could go. And he said that if I was to help him, then he would look out for me. I said like, "What?" He wanted me to sell drugs, and I told him I was afraid. "Well, you can't live in my building." When he said his building, the first thing that came in my mind was my diploma in building maintenance. Well, I said, I can help you fix this building up. He said show me something that tells me that you can fix this building up and I'll let you stay. So I went to my mother's and came back with my diploma. He gave me a week and a half to show him some kind of progress in at least one room. He said that he would buy the material and he said, "I don't want to see them just sitting there." Each day he brought materials that were used, and when he came he seen that I had not one, but three rooms done in seven days or a week and a half. He came, and he said, "This is great!" He said not to let nobody destroy it and all that. I said that I wouldn't because I did all that myself and I didn't want somebody to destroy something that I had done. I've been there ever since.

When I first moved into the abandominium, the place it was pathetic, from dog mess to trash, to broken toilets, stuff of that nature. I wanted to stay there, but I was scared because in the eveningtime, you know, rats come out and they see garbage like that. Something had to be done about it. Now, my floors are as clean as this one. There are mice there, but there are no rats. He said there were rats there. He did tell me that, but we knocked the rats out. I knocked the rats out.

It's like home to me now. It's like going home. Just like a person with a television and a radio and a refrigerator, like home. In the beginning it was hell. I thought Halloween was every day. I thought I was living with

Freddy Kruger. Every time I walked down . . . "Oh, my God! Somebody is gonna walk behind one of these doors and knock me in my head." And so what I do now that I have a flashlight, one of them flashlights that people carry if their car break down. The light blinks or you can turn it on so you can see inside your motor. I have one of them. It's like a big fluorescent light. I sit it in the corner and it brightens up the whole room. If my flashlight goes out, I buy candles. I'll sit a candle there and that generally is enough light that I can see.

I bought a Sealy Posturepedic, box springs, bed frame, and dresser. I went and did the whole thing, the kit and caboodle, because I said that if I'm gonna live there I'm gonna live there right. There isn't electricity in there, and I don't cook in there. I usually go out and eat at the cheapest place there is, the Chinese place. I eat so many chicken wing special till it's pathetic. Yes, every day. I'm so tired of chicken wing special. I think I'm going to grow feathers. There's a place on High Street where you go and take a shower every day, and they give you a set of clothes to wear. I would go there every day. In the wintertime, I usually try to have two kerosene heaters and they generates enough heat that I may not get cold.

I have a dog and he protects the place. My dog is trained. I have enough time and enough encouragement to put him in the police academy and they trained him for me. My dog goes by "Get them," "Get back," "Sit," "Come here." He's half pitbull, half German shepherd. His name is Pop. The only way he'll answer is you say, "Dadda." Like you hear a baby say, "Dadda dadda goo goo, dadda mama." I say "Dadda," and he comes. My back will be turned, and he'll walk right past me. He'll try to sense me out. Every time he try to walk around me and look, I would turn around. "I know you ain't going nowhere." He may decided to walk. Just to walk to sniff the ground, like all dogs do. I'll say, "Dadda," and there he is. Right next to me. I have a place where I go to called Saint Paul's Refuge. I go eat there every day. They close at four-thirty. Generally, by twenty-five after four my dog will be sitting there thinking that I'm inside there. Oh, yes, he will. He will walk there and sit on the steps. He will sniff me out and sit on the step and stay there.

We've been invaded, but my dog chase them out every time. He's my alarm clock when something goes on. If somebody walks through that door, the first thing he do is growl. And he inside the room with me. Then I may peek through the door to see what it is. He wants to see who it is first. He's my protection. As he's going out there, and I'll come down the steps and look out there. Whoever it is they done ran down the street.

I started to use marijuana first, then a glass of beer, then it was methamphetamines, and then crack. So crank was the first serious drug. It was IV. I was depressed and I didn't want to go out one day and my girlfriend said, "If you don't want to go out but you do want to go out 'cause you need the money, just use some of this." I let her shoot it in my arm and I felt like if I wanted to go tear the town down. It was as simple as that. I went on and did it. In other words, I was a people pleaser, because she did it, and she wanted me to do it. I never did get to use it regularly. I just used it like once a week. Sometimes once in a month. I only used it when I felt as though I didn't want to go out.

I used methamphetamines for about a year. I didn't like the point that I had to stick that needle in my arm. I told everybody that I was sick and tired of sticking needles in my arms. They said why don't I stop doing it and smoke. I said, "Well, reefer don't make me feel like meth-amphetamines do," and they said, "This is not reefer we're talking about." So I said, "What is it?" So they brought crack and I tried it. I said, "Fine and dandy. This will do just fine." I was in North Jefferson when this happened, at a girlfriend's house.

I've been using crack for about two years now. She showed me how to use the pipe. The next day I did it again. I went to her house and let her buy it because I didn't know the people. She had to hold the match for me, and it took me about three days to learn how to use the pipe and hold the match. I was like this, "Honey, I'm getting my own. Honey, I'm sick of you. You smoke more than me." Every time I went back home I didn't have nary penny in pocket. Not even carfare.

About a month I realized I was really addicted to crack, but I used to always say that I wasn't addicted. When I went home one day and seen myself looking at the TV and the commercial said, "This is drugs. This is what drugs do. This egg is drugs. This is what drugs do. This is your brain. Get the picture?" And when he said that right there and I was saying, "Okay, I'm an addict. I'm a drug addict." And that was that. I thought I could maintain control, up to that point I thought I could just do it and leave it be. So I could do it today and not do it the next day. Honey, that was a lie.

In the beginning my habit wasn't big. I was doing like maybe fifty a day, then it came up to one hundred dollars a day, and more, and more, and more. Sometimes I was seeing myself spending five hundred in a day. Now, it's about eight hundred a day! The way I feel right now my habit ain't two cent right about now. My habit right now is my Sealy Posturepedic. That's my habit about right now, because I'm tired. See, that something about some drug addicts, you can be tired and still do drugs even though you know your body is wore out. They won't feel it. My body is wore out.

I think drugs came with the deal. All that hustling and drugs came in the package. I believe it was the people I was hanging out with that got me into drugs. I believe so. I do believe so.

I stopped using drugs for five whole years. It's been a while back. My mother gave me a choice one day. She seen that I was smoking. She said, "You got a choice between me and them drugs." I was smoking pot then. I was a teenager then, and I just stopped. I just smoked cigarettes and drank a few beers. But I've never stopped for more than a month as an adult. I've been in treatment, but it didn't work. I was in treatment for one year, and I was using every day. I would go out and buy it. Make money on the corner and go back to the program and I'll be highed up. I was in Southeast Treatment Center. The only problem I had was that you can only go out when they say you can go out. I used to be like this, "Oh, honey, I'm going out anyway!"

It was horrible! The day that they found out that I was using drugs, they said, "You think you know so much." Then I rolled my eyes. "Oh, you're a big spoiled brat." Then they gave me a baby's bib and a diaper to put on and told me to sit in the window. And I was like this, "Well, tell your mother to go and sit in the window 'cause I'm not sitting there." And I up and left. I humiliated them. I went out and bought a cap and brought it back to them and sat it on the desk and left. I said, "Give this to the supervisor, please. He needs one of these," and sat it on his desk. And they were like horrified. I said, "You have a nice day." And walked out the door.

When I entered treatment, they asked me to come out of drag and wear boy clothes. I asked them was they drinking. That was a very big insult to them. They said, "We would like you to leave all your girl attire at home and we'll give you some boy clothes." I say, "Have you guys here been drinking?" He said, "Excuse me?" "Have you guys been drinking?" I said, "First of all, I don't change my clothes for nobody. Second of all, you got to be drunk and drugged up to think that I'm going to change my clothes for you."

I went into treatment because I figured they could help me. And they couldn't. I said they can go suck eggs! Eat baby poop. Leave me alone. I ain't putting on no baby's bib and that was that. I walked in there in drag. I was myself. I had on fire engine red high heels. Heels this high, and had on a red biker's suit. The ones the bikers be wearing, and a real, real thin red shirt. And I left, and told them to have a nice day. "See, you guys later. Find yourself another sucker." That's what I told them. When I left there I started working the corner. That's why I was dressed like that. I was living in hotels then, from hotel to hotel.

I don't know why I continue to use drugs. You know that another question I cannot answer. I do not know. I just use. I'm just an addict, see. An addict consist of a person that just uses. It doesn't do nothing for me. Nothing! Gets me high. When you're high you don't think about much. The only thing you think about is the drug. You don't think about no problems, no nothing. You just think about the drug. It makes it possible for me to cope.

I cannot stand to see myself around people that does drugs and I don't do them. And I'm around them every day. But today I'm going to shut my door and go to sleep. There is a day of rest sometimes. Sometimes there is a little will power in your heart sometimes and you can pull away from it. I try to control it sometimes. You tell yourself, "You can't be doing and spending all this money up like this. Before you leave, you are broke. I'm not going to spend all this money up. I'll put this money in my shoe so I won't spend it." Pooh, the money in your shoe is gone! There is no controlling it.

My schitz is checking my pockets. That's after I'm broke. I don't check my pockets when I'm not broke. I'm looking for another cap! Knowing ain't n'er cap there. I will look in them pocket ten hundred times until I get some milk. I drink milk sometimes to take the edge off. Milk brings it down. Milk brings it extremely down. I will feel just how I feel right now. You're able to go lay down somewhere. My doctor told me that once. I told him I was on drugs and I needed help. I said when I don't have no more money, I be like losing my mind. He said, "Have you ever tried drinking milk? It knock all that stuff out the way." Milk works as quick as anything else in the world in your body. See, just like an aspirin. An aspirin works in thirty minutes. Milk works in thirty minutes. So you're sitting there geeking, but that milk is going to take effect. "I'm tired." There it go, the milk is working.

My boyfriend's schitz is to get under the covers and go to sleep. He's the only one that I know who can do that so well. He will have not one penny and smoke his last cap. Sit there for about five minutes and you see him crawling in the bed like a little ant or something under the blankets. You don't hear two words out of him. I laugh at him all the time. "Look at you. Like a little daggone ant, you go crawling in the bed."

I wished I had never started using drugs or stood on corners. Those are the only two things in life I wish I never done. The two main things. If I didn't do neither one of them thing I wouldn't be in the predicament I'm in today. I wished I never let my mother know that I was using drugs. I don't care about my friends. Told you, I have no friend. Let somebody say, "Oh, child, you use drugs?" "Mind your business!" That's just how I am.

I've had only one intimate relationship, that's the one I'm with now. The other weren't relationships. I just didn't want to be by myself. My current husband is different. He's so caring. He make sure that I eat. If I was sick, he make sure that I have medicine. He does drugs and when I got, he got it. When I don't got it, he don't got it. He does the same for me. And if neither of us got, we do without it. I used to watch how everybody used to just misused him. He's really like a young guy and people used to just misused him. They used to just bother him. It used to just irk me to see it happen. So I was right there. "Leave him alone. Why do y'all pick on him like that?" Me being so protective I began to start seeing something else in him, which was that he had problem like I do. I was like this, "Do you want to come and spend the night at my house? You don't have to be out here on the street with them." 'Cause see he was sleeping in the park. I said, "You can come to my house. You don't have to be out here with them." And he said no for the first three times till one day I came home and he was sitting on my steps. I was shocked to see him. I said, "What's wrong?" He said that he can't take it no more, can he spend the night? I said, "Yes."

I let him spend the night, and he's been there ever since. First, we were friends, then we were lovers. At one time I used to say that he's my buddy. Now, I be saying that he's my husband! I like the fact that he's timid. He's not masculine, 'cause he's not. He's just timid. I have to set him straight sometimes. You know, like if one of my girlfriends come over and say that I'm gonna lay on your sofa. Okay. He says, "I guess Monique will say it's alright." "You're the man of the house. You tell her yes or no. If I'm not there you tell her yes or no. If you said yes, she's there. If you said no and she would have stayed there I would have drag her down the steps."

I've been with him about three months now. He has yet to get to know me quite well. But we'll know each other soon. He like understands a lot of things I be saying. He asks me every day to get off the street. "Why don't you get off the corner. Just go on DPA. Get off the corner." I would come out better. Then I'll say something smart like, "Honey, DPA can't pay as much as I make on the corner." I want to get off the corner because he wants me off the corner. He looks for a job every day, and that's the good part. As long as he looks for a job, I don't care. He can run the street all night long. I'll kill him if I found him with someone else. Case closed. I would put his brains at his feet.

He wasn't gay before he met me, and he isn't now. He's the man. He's the man of the house. He don't do things that I don't like. He don't make pancakes. He's not a Bisquick man. He not too much into Aunt Jemima.

There is two worlds. Your right world and your wrong world. Your right world is men and women. Your wrong world is women and women, men and men. You have a man and a woman. I don't care if they say that because he's with me that he's gay. But he's not gay. 'Cause he still can go and lay with a woman. I never looked at him as being gay. I can never explain that there. That's something that I will never be able to explain in life. As far as I'm concerned, he's not gay. Far as I'm concerned any man with a queer is not gay. He's just a man!

Gay means a man and a man, a dog and a dog, a cat and a cat of the same sex doing something. That's what gay mean. The same sex doing something. Two lovers, two men, two women, but my lover would never be a gay man.

I've been tested for HIV. It's something I don't want to talk about, because it's a lot behind that. That's why my mother wants me to come home. Now you understand. I don't want to go home so I hide. My pride, you know. That's what it is. That's all it is. My pride is in the way. Me and my friend we have sex, but we use condoms. He doesn't know. Just me and my doctor's secret, and my mother's.

Am I frightened? Very! I don't know if I'll be dead at the end of tomorrow. The doctor just tell me to keep my health up, to make sure I eat. I've known for two years. He said sooner or later I'm going to die and I'll be ready for it. Some people go blind, some people lose hair, some people's skin begins to decay. So out of the three of those things I will have one of those things. Either loss of hair or either I'll go blind.

They haven't put me on any medication yet. It's not bad yet. They say as far as they can tell, I'm doing quite well. They said that because I try to eat. I actually try to eat a lot. That's the best way to do it. Keep eating and keep your habits up.

That's what I was in Southeast for. Because everybody there had AIDS. My best friend Houston died in my arms a month and a half ago. He was at Southeast too, but he had left when I had left and he got real sick and he went blind on me. Me and him would talk and sit like we're talking now, and time would go on and the days were going by and he kept saying, "Things are blurry. Things are so. . . ." I said, "Oh, child, please." He was on DPA too, and one day we went to pick up our checks. I took him and put him on the bus. We weren't sitting together. He touched the chair and sat down. I said, "He can see." I thought he was playing. I got off the bus, and he was still on there. And what makes it so bad was, when I looked up, he wasn't looking at the window or looking at me or nothing. He was just driving past in the bus. I actually begged the lady in the car behind them, please let me in her car. "I left my blind friend in the bus. I feel so bad." The lady helped me. I said,

"Houston, you are blind. I'm sorry. I didn't know." It was like a shock to me. I threw him on my back. He had gotten real skinny. I carried him on my back and I carried him to the DPA office. I had to help him sign his check and I signed my check and we both left.

That was my first one. Oh, Lord, Lord, Lord, Lord. How long will this last now? Miss Houston was my friend. She was my only friend. She was my only friend. My only friend that went blind and died. And then when I went to the hospital the next day, they say, "Monique, you didn't hear." I say, "What?" He said, "Come here." They were trying to make me laugh. I said, "What's wrong?" Just trying to make me laugh, something's got be wrong. "Houston died last night at nine forty." I said, "How Houston died at nine-forty and I had Houston in my arms at nine-forty-one?" "No, you had him in your arms at nine-thirty-nine." I said, "Oh, my God." So I broke free from them and ran all the way up from the third floor to the nineteenth by the steps. Got to his room and he was gone, and I was all on the bed like losing my mind. They came and shot a sedative in me and I fell asleep and woke up and went off again and they shot another sedative in me. I was going crazy. His sister came and talked to me, and she said that he used to talk about me all the time to her.

It's very hard, and it's scary. Believe me. I am scared a whole hell of a lot. When this man cut my throat and I looked down and seen all my blood, you know what I said? "AIDS blood all on the ground." I didn't say, "My blood is on the ground." I said, "Look at all this AIDS blood." I came out the hospital, so nobody would catch it, I went out there with disinfected water, Pine, and scrubbed all that blood off the ground. They said, "Why you scrubbing it off the ground? It's only blood." And in my mind, "It's not the kind of blood you use." That's why I just cleaned it up. That's another reason why I'm a loner.

The thing that frightens me most is to die. My worst fear is death, and it's the stuff leading up to it too. All I have to do is see my skin begin to break out, I'm going to fall. All I gots to do is my eyes getting blurry, I running to the eye doctor. All I got to do is see my hair getting thin, I'm going off and get some hair research or something. See, I don't know what to do. We have to go some kind of way. That's all I say now. I have to realize that much. I'm going to tell my boyfriend. I've been trying.

"There is something that I want to tell you." And he keeps say, "What, what, what?"

In a sense I feel cheated. Like I was cheated on life. I guess that's the way it goes. That the way life is. You're only promised two things, life and death. So you leave it at that. I need to bear with it. All that support group this and that support group that, that's not help to me. The only thing that you're around all people with HIV, and you hear the different stories. But it's making things worser. It makes things much worser. You think about it too much. Every morning you wake up, "I got AIDS. Oh, my God. What am I going to do today? I'm going to this thing. I'm going to the group." And you go through the same procedure. It just make you worry about it. They make you think about it more. I don't think about it too much. I don't know. I know what I have. I leave it be. Let bygones be bygones. I'm not going to walk around every time I go somewhere, "Lord, have me mercy. . . . Excuse me, sir, can I sit here, I have AIDS." I don't advertise myself. I know what I got. I leave it at that. I think the same exact way some other people feel. . . . Oh, you know, AIDS! It's like the black plague and the kiss of death. If you've got AIDS, nobody's gonna want to be around you. Nobody is gonna want to love you. You're gonna be thrown to the wolves. So I leave bygones alone. Leave well enough alone while you're ahead. That's what I do. I leave it alone.

My mother wants me to come home so I can tell the world. I know that. She wants me to tell the whole family. And I'm not ready for that. I am not! But I'm gonna shock them. That their Christmas gift this year. I'm gonna let them all know. I really don't never get nothing for Christmas. Everybody else get new things. I always spend a lot of money, but never get nothing. "Why I spend my money on y'all 'cause I'm dying. I have AIDS. I am dying and I spend my money up on y'all. Y'all don't think about me." And make them all feel the way I feel. Guilty! I feel guilty for spending so much. Last Christmas I spent almost nine hundred dollars and I got a Christmas card and ten dollars. That's was it, and that was from my mother. I spent the majority on her. I bought her a five-hundred-dollar fur coat. I got ten dollars from her and a Christmas card. My brother got, my oldest brother got a coat, a sweater, socks, and. . . . So where do I come in at? See, that's another thing I say too. She knows what's wrong with me, and she just gave me money. 'Cause she know that I'm an addict and you're gonna hand me money for Christmas. I want a gift. I want to open up things like everybody else. If I wanted money I could have stood on the corner. Give me a gift. Give me something in a box. Give me something that's wrapped up. Make me smile. Let everybody look at me while I open my gift. See. That's how I look at thing. So my Christmas gift this year is to let each and every family member knows what's going on with me.

I'm gonna show them how it feels. And I'm not going to stay and eat anything. I'm going to say, "Can everybody sit at the table. I would like to say something. My Christmas gift this year is very small, but very big. My Christmas gift this year is for each and every individual, except the children. It's for every grown-up in here. I'm dying. I'm HIV positive. I have AIDS."

I'm angry with them. You mean to tell me that I almost have to be dead for them to love me. Do I have to be out on my hands and knees, frostbitten from head to toe, in the hospital with IV's all through my body for you to come and see my face. No. I want to be walking the streets like you're walking the streets. Come ask me if I'm alright. Ask me if I'm hungry. Don't let me ask you if I can eat. Ask me if I'm hungry. Ask me do I have a pair shoes on my feet. Ask me if the shoes I'm wearing mine.

I'm human and they can always look at me and I won't turn them to stone and they won't turn into a pillar of salt. I am only one sheep. Life give us all the same thing, one chance, and that's to live. To let me live my life with my HIV, just let me live. Just let me be happy. I just want to be happy. Just be settled and be happy. No problems, no worries. Just be happy.

Epilogue: Several Weeks Later

I went to the doctor, and I asked them why my skin is beginning to break out. They told me that things are starting to progress, and they wanted me to see a skin person. I have started night sweats now. This has been for three days, I mean cold, cold, cold sweats. I'll be freezing. They tell me that I have to watch the things that I do, right. They say my leg, the right leg's is quite bigger than the other. Well, it's not swollen. This is what they told me. It's that . . . like, okay, when a person dies they body blows up. It's beginning to happen in this leg. They went through the whole leg. They found that nothing was wrong. Right. It gets bigger than this. Sometimes it gets so big I can't put a shoe on it. It gets so big sometimes it will run into the feet. My feet be like about this big. It's like all the fluid that's in my body, medication and all that . . . they don't know why it does it, but it's settling in this leg here. Actually that leg is dead. It just swells up on me. It get feverish real, real bad. Sometimes now . . . they told me that I may get a fever in my leg that may make me limp . . . to come to the doctor immediately.

He was talking about putting me on AZT at my next appointment. Most likely they would because things are beginning to progress. I told her I'm beginning to bite my nails a lot. She said, "That's only worry." I beginning to catch a ulcer. They had told me at the other hospital that I was catching an ulcer. And I told them about the ulcer and they said that comes along with it as well. "All your sicknesses is gonna try to combine into one." Well, you know there won't be nothing you can do about it. How long will it take before this starts hurting me, hurting me? And they told me that they can't say. They said, they took my T-cell count when I went. When I go back for my next appointment . . . I don't know what T-cell counts are, right, but they say it's like my blood level or something like that. I'm not sure.

I'm just not sure about nothing. I'm getting scared and all this other crazy stuff now. I'm in the dark right now. I don't know nothing now. Only thing I know now . . . I know I tend to forget things. Like last night for instance we had went to a thing that feeds you, and I brought the food home and forgot what I had. When I asked the lady specifically what I wanted and she gave it to me. When I got home I kept saying, "What did I get?" I couldn't remember until I seen it, right. They said a lot is going to happen to me. Loss of memory. They said that they not sure if I may get blind. They're not sure. They told me that they want to take the CAT scan of my brain because I catching these constant headaches.

It's kind of scary. Kind of leaving me in the dark, and I don't know what to do. Like my friend . . . I just don't know what to say to him now.

I don't know what to say to him. I find everything to be an argument now. I argue about everything. Just so I can keep myself, keep myself uptight. I don't want to find no reason to think about what's going on with me. I'm trying to find everything wrong with him. Okay, like he got fifteen dollars today, and I only got forty cents out of his fifteen dollars. Which is kind of . . . I really didn't care, but I have to find something to argue about just so I can. Keep me from thinking about it, period. That's what I've been doing. Since I've been going to the doctor, the doctors make you think about it. They give you a reason to think about it. That's what I do. Sooner or later the doctor said I'm going to get tired. I ain't gonna never want to go nowhere, I'll want to go to sleep, and I'm praying that doesn't happen soon. Because I'm just too young for this.

I have a good appetite. Matter of fact I'm hungry right now. I keep a good appetite, but it vanish quickly. So I try to catch my appetite when it's there. When I'm sitting home seem like everything I push away. I'm just getting scared. Should I put myself in some kind of program or just stay at home, or go home to my mother?

I got into Southeast because I did the AIDS test, and told them that I didn't want to be around nobody. If I was going to be around anybody, be around people with AIDS, and they told me about Southeast. And I signed up for Southeast, and they gave me an appointment. I wasn't full blown at that point when I was at Southeast. It's just bugging me. It's scaring me. It's actually, actually really scaring me. I haven't thought about it, but I've been thinking about it lately. I've been thinking about it a little bit more than before, and it's actually scaring the life out of me.

They said that you could fight as long as you possibly can. They say as long as you keep yourself occupied, you can always fight it too. Working gives you exercise. I don't want people to be too much concerned about me. I ain't looking for no sympathy. I'm just looking for someone to help me because I'm getting scared. I'm scared now because things are starting to change. I haven't caught no fevers or nothing, virus or flu or nothing. They say that was good.

I don't need to be out in the weather, because it really will bring me down. And then when I left here I was going to pick up some pamphlets from "We the People." They have some pamphlets on that. I'm just not sure anymore, but . . . I'm not sure anymore of how things worked but they say just read up on it and you'll understand more.

I'm scared. I'm always scared. I gonna always be scared. The bottom line is Monique Delores Johnson is afraid. I'll always be afraid. Just like when I leave here, I'm praying it's not dark outside because I'm so far away from home. That man cut me once, and I was looking from corner to corner before I turned. I will walk until the trolley comes before I'll sit there and wait. That's how nervous I am. My life now is just scared. I'm just scared. Every time I get into a date's car, I be like this, "Honey, what's in your hands? Can you put both hands on the steering wheel while you drive?" I do crazy things now. It's like a big bother with me now. I got to go out here and see all this costume. You know everybody's in costumes out there. You know, I'm like this, don't know which way to look now. Monique Delores Johnson is scared. Her life is wild! She's taking a very big chance at life.

need diff. from the ethnography of Mal. in that
the racial stereotypes
gender
come from the subject.